W9-AQG-827

TEQUILA JUNCTION

OTHER TACTICS MANUAL SUPPLEMENTS FROM POSTERITY PRESS:

THE LAST HUNDRED YARDS: THE NCO'S CONTRIBUTION TO WARFARE
ONE MORE BRIDGE TO CROSS: LOWERING THE COST OF WAR
PHANTOM SOLDIER: THE ENEMY'S ANSWER TO U.S. FIREPOWER
THE TIGER'S WAY: A U.S. PRIVATE'S BEST CHANCE FOR SURVIVAL
TACTICS OF THE CRESCENT MOON: MILITANT MUSLIM COMBAT METHODS
MILITANT TRICKS: BATTLEFIELD RUSES OF THE ISLAMIC MILITANT
TERRORIST TRAIL: BACKTRACKING THE FOREIGN FIGHTER
DRAGON DAYS: TIME FOR "UNCONVENTIONAL" TACTICS

TEQUILA JUNCTION

4TH-GENERATION COUNTERINSURGENCY

ILLUSTRATED

H. JOHN POOLE

FOREWORD BY
MAJ.GEN. RAY L. SMITH USMC (RET.)

**POSTERITY
PRESS**

Copyright © 2008 by H. John Poole

Published by Posterity Press
P.O. Box 5360, Emerald Isle, NC 28594
(www.posteritypress.org)

Protected under the Berne Convention. All rights reserved. No part of this book may be reproduced or utilized in any form or by any means, electronic or mechanical, including photocopying or recording by any information storage-and-retrieval system without full permission in writing from the publisher. All inquiries should be addressed to Posterity Press, P.O. Box 5360, Emerald Isle, NC 28594.

Cataloging-in-Publication Data
Poole, H. John, 1943-
Tequila Junction.
    Includes bibliography and index.
    1. Infantry drill and tactics.
    2. Military art and science.
    3. Counterinsurgency.
I. Title.   ISBN: 978-0-9638695-1-7   2008   355'.0218
Library of Congress Control Number: 2008927221

This work contains a compilation of copyrighted material from other sources. The permission to use that material is recorded in the "source notes" at the end of the book. It may not be further reproduced without the consent of the original owner. Every effort has been made to contact all copyright holders. Any who were missed can identify themselves now to negotiate the appropriate permission agreements.

Cover art © 2008 by Michael Leahy
Edited by Dr. Mary Beth Poole
Proofread by William E. Harris
First printing, United States of America, September 2008

To all U.S. security establishment personnel worldwide.
Your continuing sacrifice is appreciated by all Americans.

Disclaimer:

Herein lies constructive criticism of the U.S. Department of Defense, as well as an easy (though nontraditional) way for it to fix its most pressing problem. America's five service branches are not perfect, though most maintain large legal and public-relations contingents to prove otherwise. Their's is a moving target. As the battlefield continues to evolve, so too must their strategies, tactics, and small-unit training. Unfortunately, Western "bureaucracies" tend to resist change, however useful. As a result, both infantry branches still practice a "high-tech" version of 2nd-Generation Warfare (2GW). To win what has become a global 4th-Generation War (4GW), they must now bypass echelons and amend procedures. The first step in their sacred obligation to America is to embrace (as opposed to refute) valid objection.

Current and past members of the U.S. Army and U.S. Marine Corps should not confuse organizational criticism with personal faultfinding. What they have accomplished on the field of honor transcends all discussion of how better to support them. Their bloodletting, hard work, and years of separation from loved ones have been every bit as heroic as that of their forefathers. But those sacrifices in no way absolves their respective organizations of the responsibility to minimize bureaucratic impediment. In an increasingly complicated and dangerous world, America can no longer enjoy the luxury of large, overloaded, clearly visible, and totally predictable infantry contingents.

Contents

Illustrations

Maps

Foreword

The author has long been recognized as a student of small-unit tactics, but his ability at open-source intelligence gathering has just recently been discovered. This latter gift seems to spring from three concurrent areas of interest: (1) the Eastern thought process; (2) military history; and (3) worldwide current events. In *Tequila Junction,* Poole first calls on this unique perspective to warn Americans about the possibility of a politically oriented and drug-funded attack from a non-Muslim source. Then, he describes how such an attack might be thwarted through advanced counterinsurgency techniques.

That makes *Tequila Junction* a two-part counterinsurgency manual with obvious applicability to the wars in Iraq and Afghanistan. While the book's main focus is on Latin America, its lessons are so universal that they could easily form the basis of America's future counterinsurgency model. *Tequila Junction* further satisfies the need to finally address the least-talked-about of America's ongoing struggles.

The first part of Poole's book has been dedicated to the intelligence situation in the Central and South America as of July 2008. It shows how the various cartels, maras, guerrilla movements, and terrorist factions have been strangely cooperating. It also points to their most likely coordinator. A constant traveler of the world, Poole has postulated that the main attack against America is now coming up through Central America and not from embedded Moslem extremists. While the attack's ultimate goal appears to be political, it has been fully supported through commodity trading (namely, drugs). This could make it a well-camouflaged variant of 4th-Generation Warfare (4GW)—that which is fought in more than just the martial arena. According to Poole, stopping it will take deploying lone U.S. infantry squads to isolated Combined Action Platoons (CAPs) and patrol bases in Colombia, Panama, and possibly even Mexico.

The second part of the book has the unconventional warfare (UW) techniques that these U.S. squads will need. They have been derived from the counterinsurgency methods of the Vietnamese, Chinese, Japanese, and Iranians (those whose armies have the most cultural predisposition toward 4GW). Like the FARC of Colombia, Afghanistan's Taliban is largely funded by drugs. Thus, the book's later chapters of "Deep-Interdiction," "Buffer Zones," and "Working a Heavily Populated Area" would be equally applicable to either place. Their many illustrations and vignettes make very enjoyable reading.

Throughout the work, Poole refers continually to widely dispersing U.S. forces to help more foreign communities to reestablish security. Recalling my exploits as a PFC and then alone as Vietnam was falling, I can see that Poole is right. Only through the initiative and good will of hundreds of tiny and well-dispersed U.S. enlisted contingents will we be able to stabilize a worldwide insurgency. We have long known that the Americans with sufficient leeway contribute most. Young Marines and soldiers are no exception. Like Poole, I have seen their potential. With a little UW training, they could easily elude any serious attempt on their lives.

At the end of *Tequila Junction* is an Appendix entitled "Bottom-Up Training." It contains a much better way to train infantry squads than the one currently in use. Poole has personally shown it to 39 battalions, eight schools, and six special operations units over the last ten years. While only three of those battalions subsequently adopted the method, all three later said that it works. Without more skilled and self-sufficient squads, the U.S. military will have little chance of stabilizing the world situation. Even if Poole's Western Hemisphere intelligence analysis does not specifically apply to all U.S. forces, his new training method should still be seriously considered by all U.S. commanders. The similarities in enemy method between South Asia and Latin America are shocking. I highly recommend this book to all U.S. military professionals.

M.GEN. RAY L. SMITH USMC (RET.)

Preface

Since 9/11, the U.S. government has become increasingly obsessed with Sunni-led *al-Qaeda*. Having chased its leadership through the back-alleys of Iraq, Afghanistan, and the southern Philippines for seven years, Washington has yet to explain why Muslim extremism continues to thrive.[1] All the while, its official news releases only occasionally mention any other Islamist movement (like that of revolutionary Shiite Iran). Either America's administrators have been using the term *"al-Qaeda"* to describe an umbrella over all Sunni and Shiite radicals, or they have been oversimplifying the situation for the American public. Both would make the "War on Terror" harder to win. To blame all that happens on a structureless "bottom-up" entity like *al-Qaeda* is to allow it to function as a dummy headquarters, and hidden affiliates to escape retribution. Focusing too heavily on *al-Qaeda* further diverts attention from any non-Muslim nation that might be concurrently trying to expand its global influence.

Latin America provides a perfect example of what can happen from too narrow a focus. Because of so little *al-Qaeda* activity there, U.S. leaders have all but ignored a potential catastrophe at their doorstep. In a place where the two biggest threats to personal freedom combine (i.e., drugs and revolution), they have settled for another of their patented "top-down" solutions. Such a solution will have little chance where the source of the problem has yet to be determined.

In its April 2006 report on global terrorism, the State Department highlighted threats in Colombia, Peru, and the tri-border area of Argentina, Brazil, and Paraguay, but noted that there were *no known operational cells of Islamic terrorists in the hemisphere* (italics added).[2]
— Congress. Research Service Rpt., January 2007

Correctly identifying the instigator is only part of the answer in this part of the world. Here, one must also deal with chronic discrimination, pervasive crime, friendly government excesses, and any number of other factors. By far the most controversial of these factors is the U.S. military's ability to assist. In such a bucolic setting, the "shock and awe" of bombardment would clearly not be appropriate. But, could tiny U.S. ground detachments survive without it?

The centralized control over training and operations that has come to symbolize Western bureaucracy has its limitations. With regard to the U.S. military, it creates the initial impression of mission accomplishment despite a constant flow of new people into every job. But, it also permits the many headquarters throughout the system to overestimate the extent to which they have accomplished their missions. To stand the best chance at budget time, all U.S. service branches now dedicate large numbers of legal and public relations personnel to keeping their images pristine. Some of those personnel may have done their jobs a little too well over the years. Most U.S. infantrymen are still unaware that German squads had more surprise-oriented (safer) assault and defense maneuvers in 1918 than American squads do today.[3] While forced to endure standardized training and ever-changing equipment, U.S. soldiers and Marines have been unable to keep pace with their Eastern counterparts on a wide assortment of tactical techniques.[4]

That little establishment oversight has limited the number of options open to U.S. commanders who might want to reverse the downward spiral in Latin America. It also makes that region's cash-glutted opposition capable of a tactical victory. In no way constrained by doctrinal parameters, procedural habit, or misplaced loyalty, that opposition can not only hire the world's best tactical trainers, but also follow their advice in combat. Any reader not yet alarmed by this kind of talk, should be.

That's not the extent of the bad news. If there is no Islamist operational presence in Central and South America, then who has been stirring up the trouble? All groups designated by the U.S. government as Foreign Terrorist Organizations (FTOs) are either Maoist, Marxist, or deeply involved in the drug trade.[5] So, the most likely candidate for hidden instigator is Communist. However, the Soviet Union dissolved in 1990, and Cuba lacks the wherewithal to accomplish all that has happened on its own. That leaves the

People's Republic of China (PRC). As in southern Africa, the PRC probably inherited most of the Soviet Union's Latin American initiatives. After a conventional attempt at expansion was thwarted by North Vietnamese irregulars in 1979,[6] China may have decided upon a more subliminal way to project its global influence. Wherever trade and politics cannot be swayed its favor, it may try a 21st-Century sequel to the same Maoist method that worked so well in the 1970's and 1980's.[7] To handle the first challenge, America appears to be forming as many free-trade agreements as it can muster. Such a strategy has its merits. For one thing, it puts the young men of volatile areas to work. But considering all the drug-related activity in Latin America's free-trade zones, it can also have a downside. That downside is more drugs reaching the American public. To save Latin Americans from the Maoist choice between leftist candidate and open rebellion, Washington probably plans to bolster incumbent rulers.

Any contemporary PRC power grab would necessarily include thousands of tiny ground contingents swimming independently and unseen through scores of target populations. While their main mission would be to influence elections, they might alternatively foment rebellion. That's probably why the PRC has recently increased its number of special operators. There are now 320,000 of them (a full 20% of China's 1.6 million-man ground force).[8] The Light Infantry Training Guidance Bureau of its hermit neighbor has another 100,000. Those 100,000 are good at more than just *ninja*-like reconnaissance. They also know enough world-class squad assault and defense technique to instruct others on the subject.[9] That means they could help any number of Communist soldiers or indigenous guerrillas to hold their own against a much larger and better-equipped Westernized force.

The U.S. military currently has about 50,000 special operators who have traditionally performed mostly reconnaissance-type missions.[10] Unless it is now willing to create eight times that number of "more-assault-oriented" special operators, it must rely on its infantry forces to respond to the new Communist challenge. That means spreading lone rifle squads across the most volatile regions of several foreign countries. Besides advanced light-infantry training, those squads will need instruction on criminal investigative procedure. Then, instead of filling the unpopular role of occupier, they can help local policemen and soldiers [through Combined Action Platoons

(CAPs)] to maintain order.[11] With enough of these joint platoons in each hot-spot, there will be much less chance of host-nation atrocity. A Marine expeditionary brigade commander has strongly endorsed such an approach to the problem.

> "A fight against . . . insurgents is not won by soldiers; it is won by local police who know who should be in a particular neighborhood . . . ," [Maj.Gen.] Allen said.[12]
> —Associated Press, 16 September 2007

Of course, any form of violence begets more violence. Breaking this age-old cycle will take one more change to the U.S. style of fighting. To survive without supporting arms or dedicated rescue force, those lone American squads will also need training in unconventional warfare (UW). Then, if beset by a murderous mob, each could revert to escape-and-evasion (E&E) or guerrilla tactics. Though not adequately covered by any U.S. manual, such methods are now available through *Dragon Days* and Part Three of *Tequila Junction*.[13]

Finally, each U.S. squad will need an engineer and medic attached to assist with the rebuilding of local infrastructure. To succeed over the long term, a counterinsurgency effort must do more than just provide local security. It must score commensurate gains in all 4th-Generation Warfare (4GW) arenas: (1) martial/combat; (2) political/media; (3) economic/infrastructure; and (4) psychological/religion.[14] Two of the easiest to achieve are better sewage and inoculations.

By calling the current affair a "War on Terror," U.S. leaders may have saddled their constituents with a never-ending conflict. They have also unwittingly provided the world's dictators with another way to suppress dissent. Though 9/11 came as a terrible shock to all Americans, what has happened around the world since is not a particularly virulent outbreak of man's inhumanity to man. It is instead a global insurgency in which the perpetrator or perpetrators are more than willing to resort to electoral intimidation, drug trafficking, and mass murder. As drug routes are impeded and surrounding regions pacified, the number of heinous crimes will diminish.

If America does not now choose to counter narco-insurgency worldwide, its next generation will almost certainly inherit an embattled island in a sea of Maoist, Marxist, and Islamist nations. In essence, its traditional foes have—over the last 60 years—perfected a type of low-intensity invasion that the Pentagon cannot counter without decentralizing control and applying less force. To accomplish something that paradoxical, the leaders of its Army and Marine components can no longer focus on launching and stopping armored phalanxes in open terrain. For their willingness to adapt to the narco-insurgency threat, they will be rewarded with a better understanding of what loosely controlled infantry squads can contribute to conventional battle.

First must come a rapid counter to the downward spiral in Latin America. Unlike the "top-down" approach with which U.S. forces initially had so little success in Iraq, this counter must be "bottom-up" (one village at a time) from its inception. It must be less violent and more tactically sophisticated than the one previously tried in this region. "Operational" Spanish is easy to learn on the job, so Latin America provides the perfect place to develop 4GW counterinsurgency procedures that would work anywhere in the world. Whether or not most of that world continues to be free may well depend on this experiment.

Those now tasked with the stabilization of Latin America must keep one thing in mind. This is a region in which a rural majority of indigenous lineage has long been dominated by an urban minority of European descent. While the area has been subjected to Communist influences since the end of WWI, not all of its peasant discord has been Communist inspired. Much of the ongoing turmoil is due to the governing faction's inability (or unwillingness) to distinguish legitimate complaint from Communist agitation. And not just the Indians have suffered. During Mexico's "Persecution" of the 1920's, at least 70 Roman Catholic priests and Knights of Columbus (men's club members) were killed by "anti-Catholic" authorities. Their only crime was association with those who ministered to mixed populations in violation of "anti-religious" laws. There exists photographic evidence of a priest's execution by Mexican Army firing squad in 1927.[15] As late as 1934, one Mexican state governor was still condoning the killing of Catholic clergymen.[16]

Thus, it is more important to concentrate on the underlying reasons for revolution in Latin America than that revolution's battlefield signature or degree of foreign endorsement. Once the dissatisfaction is eliminated, so too will the rebellion. Then, only necessary will be enough local security to permit free elections. Unfortunately, the extent of that security will often depend on whether some organized-crime element has established a smuggling conduit nearby. The challenge then becomes how to combine military and police procedure with Christian ethics.

H. JOHN POOLE

Introduction

The Muslims in Latin America Today

Over the years, hundreds of thousands of Muslims have immigrated to the Caribbean and Latin America. Jamaica, Trinidad/Tobago, Guyana, Suriname,[1] Brazil, Argentina, and Paraguay all have sizeable Islamic populations. The largest of these are in Brazil (almost a million), Argentina (700,000),[2] Guyana (88,000), and Trinidad/Tobago (80,000).[3] There are tens of thousands of Muslims in the Tri-Border Area (TBA) of Argentina, Brazil, and Paraguay alone. Additionally, sizable Muslim communities have sprung up in Merida (Mexico),[4] Chuy (Uruguay), Guayaquil (Ecuador), Maracaibo (Venezuela), and any number of other towns.[5] Thus, the region has not totally escaped the attention of Islamic extremists. While their most recent activity has been illicit fund raising from the free-trade zones between countries, that of the early 1990's was far more threatening. *Tehran's Wars of Terror* is a good source of its detail.

In 1990, a faction calling itself *Jamaat al Muslimeen,* staged an abortive coup against the government of Trinidad/Tobago. In this good-sized island nation just north of Venezuela, a full sixth of the population is Islamic.[6] [Many years later, a Guyanese affiliate of *Jamaat al Muslimeen* would be arrested for plotting to blow up the jet fuel lines that feed New York's John F. Kennedy (J.F.K.) airport.[7]]

Also early in the 1990's, *Hezbollah* conducted two suicide attacks on Israeli targets in Buenos Aires, Argentina. The first on 17 March 1992 was against the Israeli embassy, and the second on 17 July 1994 was against a Jewish community center.[8] Then discovered after six years were "*Hezbollah* and *al-Qaeda* plots" to bomb American embassies in Asuncion (Paraguay), Montivideo (Uruguay), and Quito (Ecuador).[9] Shortly after 9/11, *Hezbollah* operatives—allegedly wanting to attack President Vincente Fox and the Mexican

Senate—were detained in Mexico City.[10] All the while, regional authorities had pictures of *Hezbollah's* "al-Mukawama" training camp on a farm outside of Foz do Iguazu, Brazil.[11] As these activities all appeared to originate from the TBA, that area was thought for a while to be a coordination center for Islamist attacks against Western interests. But, as the 2007 U.S. Congressional Report now attests, most intelligence agencies no longer perceive such a threat from any place in Latin America.[12]

Over the years, the TBA has been visited by both Shiite and Sunni radicals. Shiite *Hezbollah* has been the most visible, but the following Sunni groups have also appeared: (1) Islamic Group of Egypt; (2) *al-Qaeda;* (3) Egyptian Islamic Jihad; and (4) *Hamas.*[13] At one time, 30,000 Muslims lived in the twin-cities of Foz do Iguazu (Brazil) and Ciudad del Este (Paraguay). However, since 9/11, as many as 11,000 may have moved to less closely watched parts of Latin America.[14] Both *Hezbollah* and the Taliban are known to depend on drug trafficking for income.[15] So, the presence of *Hezbollah* and *al-Qaeda* in the TBA would logically pertain more to fund raising than exporting *sharia* law, extending the caliphate, or attacking Western facilities.

In several Latin American free-trade zones with large Middle Eastern populations, terrorist groups and organized-crime syndicates enjoy a mutually beneficial relationship with corrupt officials. Those areas include the towns of Colon (Panama), Iquique (Chile), and Maicao (Columbia); the islands of San Andres (Colombia) and Isla de Margarita (Venezuela); and the TBA.[16] In 2002, there was a summit of sorts between the various drug syndicates, *Hezbollah,* and *al-Qaeda* affiliates at Ciudad del Este.[17] Again, most of the region's intelligence agencies considered the meeting to be strictly economic in nature.

> For nearly a decade, the presence of *Hezbollah, Hamas,* [and] Islamic Group of Egypt . . . have converged with organized crime groups in the triple-border area. . . . Although al-Qaeda's regional network is supposed to be based in the triple border, no . . . intelligence agency has yet presented concrete proof of an al-Qaeda presence.
> . . . The Islamic Group of Egypt has merged with al-Qaeda. . . . Argentinian *(sic)* intelligence submitted a report in 1999 confirming that "agents of the al-Qaeda organization . . . had been identified in the triple border area" (Montoya,

"War on Terrorism Reaches Paraguay's Triple Border," *Jane's Intelligence Review*, December 2001, 12). An official Argentine report added . . . Muslims politicised and radicalised by Hezbollah were providing finance to al-Qaeda (ibid., 12). . . .
. . . Islamist groups active in Latin America are also establishing [unspecified] links with organized crime groups in East Asia. . . . [Members of] the Chinese mafia (14-K Triad, Pak Lung Fu) have . . . been detected in the triple border area (ibid., 14).[18]
— *Inside al-Qaeda,* by Rohan Gunaratna

Venezuela is now closely allied with Iran. As a result, Lebanese *Hezbollah* operatives frequent not only the TBA (some 460 in 2000),[19] but also Venezuela's Isla de Margarita.[20] Both are free-trade zones in which narcotics proceeds can be easily laundered.[21]

Because of increased security measures in the TBA, a "second tri-border area" has now sprung up in the region between Brazil, Bolivia, and Peru.[22] Regional authorities are also closely monitoring the twin cities of Chui (Brazil) and Chuy (Uruguay). Chui has a Muslim population of 1,500.[23]

The Communists in Latin America Today

Communist gains across the Caribbean, Central America, and South America have far outdistanced any by Islamists in recent years. This can be partially attributed to the pressure that the U.S. and local governments have placed on Muslim radicals. However, it is also due to their relative indifference toward Chinese expansionism. Fully to appreciate the contemporary Communist threat, one must first acknowledge two things: (1) that China has any number of ways to deceive its foes (the many facets of its famous 36 Stratagems); and (2) that Chinese subversion may have substantially evolved since the heady days of the Red Guards in southern Africa. If much of that subversion now occurs in the nonmartial arenas of 4GW, then who in election-and-trade-oriented America would notice? It would only be apparent to regional historians who just happened to be tracking the applicable details.

By 2001, the city of Ciudad del Este was home to almost half of the 25,000 Lebanese who inhabited the TBA. But it also had 30,000

Chinese residents (of whom only 9,000 were registered) and many Koreans.[24] Several Chinese organized-crime families operated from Ciudad del Este as well.[25] Thus, while much of the continent's illicit activity was undoubtedly being coordinated from the TBA, it was no longer clear who was doing the coordinating.

China—like its hermit neighbor[26]—has often been implicated in the international trafficking of narcotics. The CIA's (Central Intelligence Agency's) *World Factbook* describes the PRC as a "major trans-shipment point for heroin produced in the Golden Triangle."[27] In a virtual police state, such things don't normally occur without government endorsement. Thus, there is a good chance that the PRC was somehow represented at the Ciudad del Este summit of 2002. Its agenda could have been pushed by a friendly Triad, People's Liberation Army (PLA) front company, or liaison person. The PRC has openly supported *al-Qaeda* in Afghanistan,[28] and *al-Qaeda's* ties are known to be with the Hong Kong Triads.[29] There were no fewer than 7,000 Chinese companies in Ciudad del Este at the time.[30] And, Aajkumar Naraindas Sabnani is known to have been the middleman between a Hong Kong syndicate and *Hezbollah's* TBA front companies.[31] Or, China may have more discreetly influenced the summit "negotiations" through a representative from its hermit neighbor. Heavily relying on drug trafficking to bolster its sputtering Marxist economy, that neighbor deals openly with the Hong Kong syndicates.[32]

To promote revolution throughout Latin America, the PRC's ruling party need not personally decide all that gets directed from the TBA. It has only to encourage enough mayhem to destabilize the countries targeted. In a predominantly Christian place, there would never be enough Muslim unrest to obscure its expansionism. So, within Latin America, it would need the additional diversion of a drug war. Without any traceable support from Beijing, drug-funded proxies could openly operate in the political and economic arenas of 4GW.

Within the Caribbean basin, most of the trouble can be traced to Venezuela and Cuba. Their growing affiliations with China will be discussed in Chapter 2. "Chavez has ideological affinity with" and "Cuba provides safe haven to" the members of two Colombian insurgent groups, the Fuerzas Armadas Revolucionarias de Colombia (FARC) and the Ejercito de Liberacion Nacional (ELN).[33] FARC operatives have been spotted not only in Venezuela, but also in Mexico, Honduras, Nicaragua, Panama, Ecuador, Peru, Bolivia, Paraguay, and Brazil.[34] FARC has gone so far as to donate money to Brazil's national elections. Representatives from both FARC and the ELN have also been promoting "the revolutionary movement" in Brazil's schools and labor unions.[35] Thus, throughout the region, one or both of these Colombian factions may be recruiting/training revolutionaries or otherwise implementing a 4GW variant to the Maoist method.

To have any chance of containing so widespread and deceptive a Communist takeover attempt, U.S. leaders must now look beyond that which is too obvious or comforting. To sense the Chinese dragon in Latin America, they must review the long history of Communist subversion in the region. They must also remember that most of the Soviet programs were there for the taking in 1989.

The Region's Initial Exposure to Communist Subversion

Latin America's first serious scrape with the Communist version of "progress" came with Che Guevara. Though born and raised in Argentina, he moved to Guatemala and Mexico in the early 1950's to preach Marxist revolution. In 1956, he joined Fidel Castro's 26th of July Movement. During the three years it took to depose Cuba's dictator, Che became known as a skilled and ruthless guerrilla commander. With his "suicide squad" concept, he accomplished some of the most dangerous and important missions of the conflict. He also ran a guerrilla-warfare school in the Sierra Maestra. Two years after Castro's forces won (April 1961), Che helped to repel the ill-fated "Bay of Pigs" invasion by U.S.-supported exiles. Then, after serving in various government jobs and writing extensively on guerrilla warfare, he left Cuba in 1965 to foment revolution in the Congo and Bolivia. He was subsequently captured and executed in the latter location.[36] Still, his legacy lived on, and over the next 15 years, many a Latin American country would experience trouble with Marxist rebels.

There have been Marxist/Leninist factions in several South American countries for years—some legal and some not. Though their degree of foreign sponsorship is not clear, some did quite well in the political arena. In 1970, Salvador Allende of Chile became the world's first democratically elected Marxist president. He soon embarked on a program of nationalization and radical social reform.[37] When he was ousted from power three years later, the whole area descended into an uncertain competition between military dictatorship and armed rebellion.

Of course, the region's oldest, most-capable, and best-equipped insurgency is that of the Colombian FARC. It began as an outgrowth of peasant self-defense leagues in the early 1960's and soon acquired a Marxist identity. A military offensive against the FARC's home turf has recently enjoyed some success in southern Colombia, but the faction still has over 15,000 rural combatants and is far from being contained. Its units regularly find safe haven on Venezuelan and Ecuadorian soil, but the extent to which the Ecuadorian government condones this relationship is not clear.[38] Though the FARC regularly targets rural outposts, local infrastructure, and political adversaries,[39] it is now so heavily involved in drug trafficking that it only nominally appears to fight for Marxist goals.[40] Cuba and Venezuela both provide it with medical care, safe haven, and—most notably—political consultation.[41]

The ELN appeared in Colombia in 1965. Marxist from its inception, it was formed by urban intellectuals (Fabio Vasquez Castano and a few relatives) who had been inspired by Fidel Castro and Che Guevara and then trained in Cuba.[42] Over the years, the ELN has targeted not only government infrastructure, but also petroleum companies. While it has derived much of its revenue from taxing the narcotics trade, it appears more interested in overthrowing the Colombian government than does the FARC. Like the FARC, it gets medical care and political consultation from Cuba. The ELN has been recently talking with Colombian emissaries in Cuba, but it has yet to agree to a formal peace process.[43]

From 1976 to 1981, the military junta that replaced the final Peronista regime in Argentina waged a "Dirty War." As the "People's Revolutionary Army" was thought to be the opposition, the effort was anti-Communist and probably condoned by the U.S. During that five-year period, some 30,000 young Argentineans were arrested, drugged, and dumped into the ocean (or otherwise killed) by Argentine authorities.[44]

In 1980 (during the Chinese-and-Soviet-sponsored revolts in southern Africa), another guerrilla movement emerged in Peru. It was called the Communist Party of Peru (Partido Communista del Peru [PCP]) or Shining Path (Sendero Luminoso [SL]). Espousing a rural Maoist (vice urban Soviet) style of guerrilla war,[45] the SL has operated from one of the biggest coca-growing areas of Peru. Though now greatly weakened and with no known foreign means of support, it still has about 200 armed members who live off the trafficking of narcotics.[46]

Then, during October 1983, U.S. and Organization of American States (OAS) forces invaded Grenada to evict its Cuba-backed Communist regime. The runway and oil storage facilities at that tiny island's airport were far too big for its commercial aviation needs. They were therefore thought to be the start of a Soviet-Cuban airbase.[47]

Shortly thereafter, the previously unknown "M-19" guerrilla group made a dramatic debut in Colombia. In 1985, it brazenly attacked the Colombian Supreme Court at its Palace of Justice in Bogota. Though its political affiliation was decidedly Cuban,[48] it was also supported by drug traffickers.[49]

Within Central America, even bigger things had been happening. After Nicaragua's last Somoza regime had been toppled by a Marxist revolution in 1979, the Junta of National Reconstruction was to run the country. But, the real power lay in the hands of the Sandinista National Liberation Front (Frente Sandinista de Liberacion Nacional or FSLN). The U.S. government soon accused the Sandinistas of importing Cuban-style Socialism and aiding leftist guerrillas in El Salvador. On 23 November 1981, the CIA got the authority and funding to recruit/support "Contras" (Spanish for counterrevolutionaries). Aiding the Contras was, in effect, part of the Reagan Doctrine. That Doctrine called for the military support of movements opposed to Soviet-supported Communist governments. In 1985, the FSLN won the elections in Nicaragua. A year later, an International Court of Justice ruled against U.S. involvement there. When this ruling was upheld by the U.N.'s General Assembly, America was forced to cease all aid to the Contras. After the Iran-Contra scandal of 1986-1987 (funding Contras through the sale of U.S. arms to Iran), the American Congress shut off all funds to the controversial endeavor.[50]

Throughout the 1980's, the U.S. had also provided economic and military assistance to El Salvador's struggle against a leftist insurgency. It had further supported the Guatemalan regime's counterguerrilla effort. That regime was later implicated in "more than 600 massacres" of guerrilla sympathizers.[51]

Then, in December 1989, American forces invaded Panama. Though their mission was ostensibly drug related, there is more than enough evidence to suggest a more anti-Communist agenda. The daughter of a Panamanian college professor confirms that Noriega had been installing Cubans into his government (just as Chavez is doing today).[52] Marines who took part in the invasion also remember seeing Cuban casualties on two separate occasions. One Marine Sergeant reported shooting a Cuban infiltrator who had been using night vision goggles to stalk his position. A Marine Gunnery Sergeant found people wearing Cuban insignia among the dead after his unit fought off an assault against its ammunition dump.[53] Panama had become a center for money laundering and drug shipments to the U.S. and Europe, and its president was deeply implicated.[54] But Manuel Noriega was also trying to create another Socialist state, and the U.S. didn't like it.

Some semblance of peace came to El Salvador in 1991, when its government signed a U.N.-brokered peace accord with the Farabundo Marti National Liberation Front (FMLN). As part of the deal, the FMLN was given political-party status and allowed to participate in national elections. Not until 1996, did Guatemala sign a peace accord with its rebels.[55]

In April 1997, a vigilante organization—Autodefensas Unidas de Colombia (AUC)—appeared in Colombia. It was to function as an umbrella over the paramilitary groups that had been fighting leftist guerrillas in the northwestern part of the country. However the AUC's members soon turned to drug trafficking and have since been mostly demobilized.[56]

Other problems were brewing to the north. Jean-Bertrand Aristide had been elected president of Haiti in 1990, but was soon deposed by a coup. After three years of rule by a military junta, U.S. forces returned Aristide to power in 1994. Widely suspected of violence and corruption, he was then ousted as president of Haiti under the threat of further U.S. intervention in February 2004. Shortly thereafter, China's "special police contingent" arrived in a country that still diplomatically recognizes Taiwan.[57]

It was also during the 1990's that various *maras* (Spanish slang for a type of gang) appeared in El Salvador, Honduras, and Guatemala. At their respective cores were young men who had fled civil war in their homelands to join Los Angeles street gangs. Upon being deported from the U.S., most continued with their gang-related activities in Central America. They would soon help to establish sophisticated drug routes that led up to the U.S. border.[58]

In late 1996, members of the Tupac Amaru Revolutionary Movement (Movimiento Revolucionario Tupac Amaru or MRTA) seized hundreds of hostages at the house of Japan's ambassador to Peru. Their principal demand was the release of 400 of their own people from Peruvian prisons, but a secondary demand had to do with a "revision to the government's free-market reforms." Peru had a prime minister of Nipponese descent at the time, so the attack may have been simply to intimidate him. Originally formed from remnants of the Movement of the Revolutionary Left in Peru, MRTA identified with the Castroite factions throughout Latin America. It had been fighting its own limited guerrilla war against the Peruvian government since 1982, with the ultimate goal of establishing a Communist state.[59]

America's Traditional "Protectionism" of the Region

Since the days of Teddy Roosevelt, America has dealt swiftly with any perceived threat to the Caribbean nations or Central America. The extent of its anti-Communist intrigue in those areas would fill many volumes and dismay many readers. As a result, the U.S. is not universally liked in this part of the world. Now that most Latin American nations are being inexorably drawn toward the political left, America's policies have had to change. Of late, it has taken more of a hands-off approach in most places (possibly because it still thinks it has the invasion option). In truth, only the smallest of Caribbean islands would still be easy for America to "liberate." Even its traditional protectorates of Haiti and Panama might now constitute a 4GW quagmire.

Thus, America needs a way to deal with the region's unique problems at the grass-roots level without having to invade any of its nations. That way must accomplish two very difficult things at once: (1) provide a tactical alternative to U.S. bombardment; and (2) preclude host-nation atrocities. This book provides such a way. It differs in many respects from ongoing U.S. special-operations initiatives in the region. Instead of indoctrinating local forces in the U.S. way of war, it helps them to develop their own guerrilla-and-crime-fighting techniques. Only with an experimental format can such techniques be tailored to a highly fluid situation. Wherever a 4GW upgrade to Maoist insurrection is at work, only the most innovative and flexible of approaches will now suffice. Just as in Vietnam, technology and firepower will no longer accomplish the mission.

The Communists' Most Recent Accomplishments

Colombia, Peru, Ecuador, and Bolivia have clearly become Communist targets in South America.[60] Leftist candidates have already won the elections in the last two. Bolivia soon nationalized part of its energy sector. And, in April 2006, Ecuador imposed rules that increased the State's share of windfall oil profits.[61] By January 2007, Venezuela had promised to nationalize all Western oil company holdings.[62]

Of course, these are not the only leftist political victories in South America in recent years.[63] Luiz Inacio Lula da Silva, a founding member of the Workers' Party of Brazil, was elected that country's president in October 2002 and then reelected four years later.[64] Argentina's President Nestor Kirschner came from a more obscure leftist background but has often sided with leftist contemporaries. In 2002, he won by default when former President Carlos Menem mysteriously withdrew from the race. In a speech to the Venezuelan National Assembly, Kirschner proclaimed that "Venezuela represented a true democracy fighting for the dignity of its people."[65] Whether his newly elected spouse will follow suit has yet to be determined.

Then, there is the little matter of a recognized extension of the PLA having control over both ends of the Panama Canal. The PRC wants either to import oil from the Caribbean or export something else into the Caribbean. For a nation so little concerned with human rights, that something could be drugs or revolution. When the Soviet Union dissolved in 1989, Cuba had to look elsewhere for support. Much of that support has subsequently come from China.[66]

Throughout the 1990's, Cuba lacked the wherewithal to export much rebellion. But now it has new friends who are more than willing to support that agenda. They are China, North Korea, Iran, and Sudan. Of the four, the most capable of providing UW training is North Korea. It has embassies or consulates in Cuba, Guyana, Belize, Mexico, Venezuela, Peru, and Brazil.[67] With Venezuela as a go-between, Cuba will have little trouble spreading the military and political advice of its new partners.

There are disturbing indications that Venezuela is about to become the world's fourth truly revolutionary government.[68] While its president has befriended the leaders of Iran and Sudan, its governmental structure more closely resembles that of the PRC. Chavez's military reserve lacks the ideological supervision of an Iranian-Revolutionary-Guard or Sudanese-Popular-Defense-Force equivalent. Instead, Cuban advisers currently provide that service.[69]

Distant Mentors

In May 2001, officials from Russia and China promised to coordinate their policies toward Colombia and Cuba. Both Eastern powers have military—as well as political—relations with Cuba. Their joint policy may therefore involve support through Cuba for anti-U.S. forces in Colombia and elsewhere. Or, it may simply make provision for the advice and funding necessary to get more leftists elected throughout the region.[70]

The PRC has joined OAS as an observer,[71] but enjoys little direct influence over that organization. In mid-September 2006, the Non-Aligned Movement (NAM) held its conference in Havana. This is more likely to be the forum through which China will influence the action. After all, China was once a member.[72] In attendance at that NAM conference were Chinese "observers,"[73] delegates from China's hermit neighbor,[74] and the presidents of Iran, Venezuela, and Chinese-bolstered Zimbabwe.[75] Just two weeks earlier, the supreme leaders of Venezuela and that neighbor were both in Beijing on the same day (28 August 2007).[76] One doesn't need much imagination to smell PRC orchestration at the Havana meeting. Cuba was awarded NAM's rotating presidency, and Iran was chosen to chair the G15 (though never previously a member).[77] Both terms of office are for three years.

In late 2006, America's leaders learned that their long-time Socialist nemesis—Daniel Ortega—had won the election in Nicaragua, and that his Mexican and Peruvian counterparts had just barely lost. What happened next was sadly predictable. With Chinese funding and expertise, Ortega was planning to build an alternate canal across his part of the Central American isthmus.[78] Such a move clearly had more to do with military strategy than free trade. After all, the Chinese already had economic access to middle

America from the Pacific. Besides a new seaport at Lazaro Cardenas, Mexico (where the Rio Balsas drains into the ocean west of Mexico City),[79] they enjoyed a legitimate trade corridor to the north. That corridor was defined by the following: (1) the North American Free Trade Agreement (NAFTA); (2) the Central American Free Trade Agreement (CAFTA); (3) a north-south Texas turnpike;[80] and (4) cross-border leeway for Mexican trucks.[81]

That the Chinese are coming should now be readily apparent to almost everyone. Why senior U.S. officials have done so little to stop them, is still a mystery.

The Research Method

The research was twofold—to uncover the PRC's strategy in Latin America, and then to develop appropriate infantry tactics. For the first, regional news media sources were searched for proof of PRC involvement in the following: (1) military support for guerrillas or leftist regimes; (2) manipulation of election politics; (3) oil company sabotage; and (4) drug trafficking. With enough of a drug war, Communist China might screen guerrilla activity. Then, with enough guerrilla activity, it might discourage Western oil companies or steal elections. Or, flooding America with the corrupting influence of drugs may be its main attack, and the other things only subsidiary. Either way, the proof will largely depend on how well the attempt has been hidden. For the world's master of deception, much of the evidence must necessarily be circumstantial. Such things will occasionally suffice in a court of law, so they should also lend credibility to a warning.

Then, the tactical methods with which America might counter this new threat will be largely derived from how East Asian armies deal with guerrillas. Those armies are considered expert at unconventional warfare (UW) and political "stabilization," so they should know the most about 4GW counterinsurgency. Any hint of their chronic brutality will, of course, be removed from the tactical suggestions for U.S. troops.

Limitations to the Research Method

Removing a single thread from a broad carpet of evidence can be misleading. So doing could cause an emerging superpower to look more culpable than it deserves. Yet, the instability in Central and South America has now metastasized to the point where "Militant Islam," "Organized Crime," or "Residual Evil" can no longer be blamed for the problem. So much unrest must have a more substantive architect.

As for the tactics, they must be somewhat visionary in nature. There are prerequisites to their use. Without concurrent training in E&E and guerrilla warfare, those who would try them may not succeed.

The Book's Utility

The extent of Chinese meddling in the Americas is explored only as a reminder of the tactical sophistication required to bring peace to the region. If the Communists have now applied their Maoist method to all 4GW arenas, the problems of Latin America can no longer be addressed as they were in the past. Only a nearly invisible, yet widely dispersed, local-security effort will be strong enough to combat it. Thus, the real utility of this book lies not in Part One's warning, but in the tactical content of Parts Two and Three. It is there that "bottom-up" counterinsurgency methods will be described in detail. These methods substantially differ from the philosophical gymnastics with which the responsible U.S. agencies have thus far filled their plans, briefings, and minds. It is hoped that this detail will help those agencies to turn everyone's prayer of peace into reality.

Acknowledgments

This book has been made possible by three factors: (1) scores of fellow researchers; (2) a full-blown information age; and (3) God. To the first, a heartfelt thanks is offered [and in particular to Col. G.I. Wilson USMC (Ret.)]. Because of the second, there are fewer secrets to undermine the democratic process. And with help of the Third, no problem—however immense or chronic—must go unsolved forever.

Part One

A Dire Emergency in the Americas

"To be a successful soldier, you must know history."
— Gen. George S. Patton

(Source: Attributed to Gen. George S. Patton)

1 Dope Dealers, Gangs, Islamists, or Maoists?

- Which groups want funding from Latin America?
- How many are trying to overthrow the regimes?

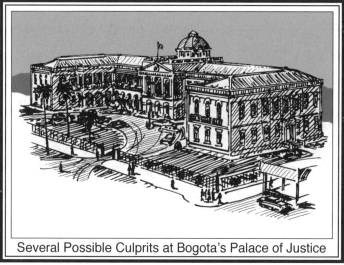

Several Possible Culprits at Bogota's Palace of Justice

(Source: DA Pamphlet 550-82 [1993], p. 107)

The Most Confusing Threat to America

There are drug traders in the U.S., crime families in Europe, Islamic militants in Africa, and Maoist guerrillas in Asia. But, only within Latin America, are all four active at once. (See Map 1.1.) With so many suspects from which to choose, America's regional advisers have been hesitant to attribute the resultant mayhem to a foreign takeover attempt. Still, "chaos" is known to be an integral part of an Asian style of war. So, one is tempted to look for links among the four categories of illicit activity. If too many links can be found, America's leaders may have more trouble brewing on their southern doorstep than anywhere else in the world. This multi-faceted trouble, and how best to control it, are the objectives of this study. For those Americans who consider the most simplistic of conspiracy theories to be bunk, any Sun-Tzu-like strategy will take some real effort to consider. As most of the world's cocaine comes from Latin America (for the U.S. market), all other categories of regional unrest must somehow be linked to drug production and trafficking. The military defense of the Americas cannot therefore be accomplished as a separate issue. And only through drug flow reduction will any battlefield action make much long-term difference to the overall situation. On 11 November 2007, cocaine remained the biggest drug (and possibly strategic) threat to the United States. Despite recent intelligence gathering and hostage rescue forays by the Colombian government, the emergency remains dire. As of 4 July 2008, Colombia's cocaine production had increased 27% over the previous year.[1]

The Latest Trend in South American Drug Trading

Most of the cocaine gets grown and processed in remote areas of southwestern Colombia. From there, it is sent to market over three main routes. One takes it through Central America to the U.S. Another takes it to Africa and then on to Europe. And the third takes it to various Caribbean stopovers (most notably the Dominican Republic and Haiti) and then on to the U.S. East Coast. Some of those drugs almost certainly pass through Venezuela. The many rivers and roads that intersect Columbia's 1,300-mile border with that nation are poorly monitored by Venezuelan authorities. Hundreds of trucks cross that border daily. While some checkpoint personnel have probably been bribed or threatened, others may simply be following policy. The Chavez regime does not allow cooperation with U.S. anti-narcotics agencies and may—along with its Communist and Islamist allies—be helping to destabilize Western society. At least one of those allies (Iran) is known to have militia proxies (Shiite *Hezbollah* and Sunni *Hamas)* that depend for much of their income on drug trafficking. As such, Venezuela's porous frontier may be an integral part of its foreign policy. Like China and its hermit neighbor,[2] Venezuela is now a linchpin in the global narcotics network.[3]

4

Map 1.1: Strategically Vital Parts of the Western Hemisphere
(Source: Courtesy of General Libraries, University of Texas at Austin, from their website for map designator "world_pol02.pdf")

What's with the Gangs?

Wherever there is drug trafficking, there are gangs trying to share in its profits. Two of the world's most notorious narco-trade hubs are no exception. Like *Hezbollah*-controlled Beirut, Caracas is now rife with gang activity.[4]

The infamous *"maras"* of Central America are also deeply involved in the dope trade. They have established and actively defend drug routes that lead right up to the U.S. border. Theirs is no slipshod effort. The *maras* have been doing so well in Mexico that one suspects tactical advice from somewhere.

> Mexico's President . . . Calderon has put an unprecedented number of soldiers and federal police on the streets to battle drug gangs. But the war isn't going well. Violence is soaring, the army is being accused of human rights abuses, and drugs shipments across the border continue unabated.[5]
> — National Public Radio, 16 May 2007

> Vowing to topple drug cartels in Mexico, President Felipe Calderon has deployed thousands of troops to fight deadly drug gangs. The bloodiest gunfight recently occurred along the border with Arizona when armed assailants killed 22 people, including five policemen, in a five-hour gun battle. More than 900 people were killed in drug-related incidents in Mexico this year.[6]
> — National Public Radio, 18 May 2007

The most widely known of the *maras* are Mara Salvatrucha (MS-13), Mara 18, and the former Salvadorian death squad Sombra Negra.[7] Their roots may help to explain their *modus operandi*.

> The maras have been present in Central America for a relatively short time. In 1989, the Mara Salvatrucha, or MS-13, appeared in Honduras, and in the early 1990's, the Mara 18, or M-18, surfaced. Both gangs were the result of the migration of refugees fleeing increasingly deadly engagements between rebel groups and government forces and the heavy-handed actions of state security apparatuses. Most of these Central American war refugees sought shelter in the United States especially in Los Angeles in areas already

infested by gangs. To assimilate into their communities in the United States and just to be able to survive, the children of these refugees either joined or formed street gangs, and many members of these gangs eventually returned to their home countries to victimize the region's societies.[8]

— *Military Review,* July/August 2007

That the two biggest *maras* have been named "MS-13" and "M-18" may be a coincidence or somber clue to their sponsorship. The brutal M-19 faction that hit the Colombian Supreme Court in 1985 was the creation of Cuban Communists.[9]

The Explanation for *Hezbollah's* 1990's Attacks

As already shown, most intelligence agencies now believe the Islamists' only goal in Latin America is fund raising. *Hezbollah* is closely allied with *al-Qaeda,* and the two have been cooperating in the money drive.[10]

One could expect a certain amount of strong-arm activity during a fund-raising endeavor in a violent region. Former insurgents would also hire out as "enforcers" for other factions. Without a chain of command, they would never realize how so doing might adversely affect their cause. With this in mind, one must reassess all "terrorist acts" by militant Muslims in the Western Hemisphere.

Hezbollah's two suicide attacks against Israeli targets in Buenos Aires, Argentina, were in retaliation for the killing of its secretary-general.[11] The "*Hezbollah* and *al-Qaeda*" plots to bomb America's embassies in Asuncion (Paraguay), Montevideo (Uruguay), and Quito (Ecuador) were indirectly aimed at Israel.

In 2000-01, TBA-based *[Hezbollah* and] al-Qaeda operatives expanded their targeting to include the U.S. and Israeli embassies in Asuncion . . . . (Israel closed its embassy in Asuncion in early 2002).[12]

— Fed. Research Div., Lib. of Congress, July 2003

The "*Hezbollah* operatives" arrested on their way to attack the Mexican senate and president were—in all probability—paid assassins. "In 1997, [the] U.S. Drug Enforcement Administration [DEA] reported . . . intelligence showing mercenaries from a number of countries training the Mexican cartels in the art of killing."[13] The DEA then identified Lebanon as being the most common country of origin.

> Over the past several years, there have been several different Lebanese criminals who have come in and worked with the Arellano-Felix group [a Mexican drug family]—actually teaching them in paramilitary-type operations, the use of weapons, and the use of counter-surveillance.[14]
> — Past Deputy Administrator of the DEA, 1997

"The Lebanese mercenaries are described as former guerrilla fighters. They had traveled up from the Triple Frontier Area (TBA). Using that as an entry point and a base of operations to work from, they have branched out offering their services to the various drug cartels. The money earned from these activities, was believed to be funneled into various *Hezbollah* groups."[15]

The Extent of Muslim Caliphate Building in the Region

While Venezuela may be friends with Iran and Sudan, it is not being actively courted or involuntarily exploited by any Islamist nation. The goal of the Islamic revolution is to create more countries governed by *sharia* law. Venezuela is 96% Roman Catholic,[16] and its chances of becoming an Islamic state are virtually nonexistent. So in Venezuela, as in the rest of Latin America, the most active of the Islamist sects—i.e., *Hezbollah* and *Hamas*—are only interested in fund raising. While part of their haul is alms from Muslim immigrants, the vast majority is proceeds from the illicit trade in narcotics.

China's More Ominous Presence

China already has all the money it needs, and its interest in Latin America is therefore more strategic in nature. Its relationship with Cuba has become much more than economic. In fact, Cuba is now well on its way to becoming a Chinese satellite, and Venezuela its regional proxy (both points will be further proven later).

Thanks to the development in bilateral relations, the relations between the armies of the two countries [China and Cuba] have also been fairly rapid.[17]
— China's Defense Minister after 1999 Cuba visit

Just as the TBA has been the center of Chinese subversion for South America, Panama may now fill that role for Central America. While Hutchison Whampoa controls the port facilities at both ends of the Canal, Chinese intelligence officials work nonchalantly out of a Panama City bank building.[18] They could be from the PRC's Ministry of State Security (MSS), but they are more probably from the PLA's own intelligence agency. According to a U.S. Customs report, "intelligence sources [have] indicated that Chinese and Russian organized crime factions are active in narcotics, arms, and illegal alien smuggling utilizing Panama as a base of operations." That report goes on to say that "the Chinese population in Panama has grown dramatically in the past five years, and the Chinese government maintains an embassy in Panama City."[19]

In addition to Hutchison Whampoa, the PLA has COSCO (China Ocean Shipping Company) as a civilian extension.[20] COSCO's ships are suspected of the massive smuggling of weapons, drugs, and illegal aliens.[21] Now that increment sections of China's new missiles may fit into shipping containers,[22] COSCO's many trips to the Caribbean should be of more concern to Americans. Yet, there are those who still have trouble seeing how a country so far away could pose any threat to this Hemisphere. For them, something other than "worldwide revolution" or "anti-Americanism" must be shown to be the motive.

The Most Obvious Reasons for Chinese Expansion

While China has openly purchased only one of Venezuela's oil fields, it has been allowed to develop 15.[23] In April 2008, Venezuela may have agreed to a joint venture with China on all oil exploration and production. State-run Petroleos de Venezuela (PDVSA) would handle 30 percent of each activity in return for China's receipt of a million barrels per day by 2010.[24] China already has a $10-billion energy deal with Brazil,[25] which produces 1.1 million barrels of oil per day (mbpd). That makes the PRC's interest in Colombia (0.8

mbpd), Ecuador (0.35 mbpd), and Mexico (3.0 mbpd, with 48 billion barrels in reserve) more understandable.[26] Trinidad/Tobago is the region's other oil-and-natural-gas-rich nation.[27] That Islamists tried to take over its government does not necessarily mean that only Islamists want it. The PRC would love to have a Sudan-like partner in the area.

Throughout Africa, China has worked hard to acquire oil, gas, and other natural resources. There are large petroleum reserves all around the Caribbean Basin. Because Venezuela has allowed China National Petroleum Corporation to operate its oil fields, it and Sudan are often compared. Like Sudan, Venezuela now has a government that views insurrection as an inherent part of regional progress. But unlike Sudan, Venezuela has few ties to militant Islam. That puts it squarely into the Chinese camp. Venezuela's president has gone so far as to refer to the PRC as "the great Chinese fatherland."[28]

The PRC has additionally made, or is exploring, energy deals in Brazil, Ecuador, Bolivia, Peru, Colombia, and Argentina.[29] Argentina and Brazil have already received Chinese road/rail construction assistance. To qualify as stopgaps to U.S. intervention (like Iraq and Afghanistan once did), they need only telecommunications help. Thus, China's sharing with Brazil of satellite technology with military applications came as no real surprise.[30] But Mexico has so far resisted all but the most trade oriented of Chinese enticements. Perhaps that's why it has experienced so much internal discord. Since NAFTA of 1994, China has viewed Mexico as a key point of access to the U.S. market.[31] As such, it already has permission to expand several of Mexico's ports on the Pacific and one in the Gulf of Mexico.[32]

Of course, China also wants Taiwan back. As such, it can be expected to economically woo the eleven remaining Western Hemisphere nations that still recognize Taiwan: (1) Paraguay; (2) El Salvador; (3) Belize; (4) Guatemala; (5) Nicaragua; (6) Honduras; (7) Panama; (8) the Dominican Republic; (9) Haiti; (10) St. Vincent and the Grenadines; and (11) St. Kitts and Nevis.[33] Of the eleven, Nicaragua will almost certainly abandon Taiwan now that Ortega is in charge. The others bear watching. Not only has China been accepted as a formal observer to the OAS, but it now has a military presence in Haiti. As part of U.N.-mandated peacekeeping force in 2004, 125 Chinese military policemen now serve there.[34] If they were to install a few local commissars, they could have a considerable influence over the next election. Of course, there is no concrete proof of such a thing.

The extent of the PRC's other activity in the region is yet to be determined. Any evidence of pushing revolution through national proxies (Cuba and Venezuela) is mostly circumstantial. Yet, one still suspects this because of China's flagrant expansionism elsewhere. For petroleum rights and shipping lanes alone, the PRC may have supported rebellions in Southeast Asia.[35] The only thing certain in Latin America is that leftist candidates are now winning all the elections. That would not be occurring without a central source of subversion. To believe otherwise is to refute the inherent strength of democracy.

According to a reputable intelligence source, "China has identified its ties to Mexico as one of [its] four 'strategic partnerships' . . . in Latin America.[36] Those partnerships may be based on strategic commodities like oil or strategic ambitions like revolution. They may involve the biggest oil producers in the region (world ranking in parentheses)—Mexico (6th), Venezuela (9th), Brazil (13th), Argentina (23rd), and Colombia (29th).[37] They may coincide with Hutchison Whampoa's port facility locations: Mexico, Argentina, Panama, Bahamas, and Ecuador.[38] They could pertain to countries that already have leftist regimes—Bolivia, Venezuela, Ecuador, Nicaragua, and (to a lesser extent) Brazil, Argentina, Chile, Uruguay, and Paraguay. They may include places reported to be Communist targets—Colombia, Ecuador, Bolivia, and Peru.[39] Or they may be some combination of those or other variables. Only one thing is clear to those who are willing (and able) to do objective research. Now that the Soviet Union is gone, it is China that has strategic designs on the Western Hemisphere, not *al-Qaeda*.

Latin America's Newest Exporter of Revolution

Whereas Cuba once distributed Communist zeal and support to the countries that bordered the Caribbean, Venezuela has now expanded that role to all of South America. Cuba's backer was the Soviet Union. When the Soviet Union collapsed in 1989, Communist China took over most of its revolutionary initiatives in southern Africa. PRC-backed factions have since won the elections in Angola,

Namibia, Zimbabwe, and South Africa.[40] Of the four, Angola and Zimbabwe are now most obviously being turned into Chinese satellites. For cooperation on oil and internal-security matters, Angola was recently awarded a $2-billion line of credit from China.[41] More discreetly to handle Western-Hemisphere interests, the PRC may have chosen a satellite/proxy combination—Cuba and Venezuela. Unlike Cuba, Venezuela is land locked and oil rich. Chavez's interest in the "democratic processes" of neighboring countries smells much like the "politicization" stage of a Maoist takeover.

Chavez doesn't just use oil as a foil against enemies like the U.S. He also uses the windfall profits to help friends, including other regional leftist politicians running for election, especially high office. For example, he unabashedly bankrolled successful presidential candidates in Bolivia (Evo Morales), Nicaragua (Daniel Ortega) and Ecuador (Rafael Correa). To Chavez's disappointment, his candidates fell short in Peru and Mexico.[42]

— *Armed Forces Journal*, July 2007

The Possibility of Communist Proxy Militias

To maintain adequate deniability, Eastern nations will often fight for foreign lands through proxy militias. Did not Iran vie for Afghanistan through the Northern Alliance while Pakistan did so through the Taliban? Thus, one can reasonably conclude that PRC-affiliated militias may exist in Colombia or other targeted nations. Those proxy militias would most likely occur in places where they could rest, re-outfit, and retrain in Venezuela, and take more permanent refuge in Cuba. Three out of the four Colombian factions fit that description. The only exception is the rightist AUC.

All three Colombian FTOs (FARC, ELN, and AUC) reportedly exploit the Venezuelan side of the border with Colombia as a safe area to trans-ship arms and drugs, rest, secure logistical supplies, and commit kidnappings.[43]

— Congress. Research Service Rpt., January 2007

Cuba also was reported "to provide advice, safe haven,

communications, training, and some financial support to several violent South American organizations." This included training Colombian M-19 guerrillas, with the objective of establishing a "people's army" ("Cuba's Renewed Support for Violence in Latin America," Dept. of State Bulletin, Feb. 1982, 77). . . .

. . . In January 1982, State Department officials asserted that Cuba was involved in providing arms to the M-19 in exchange for facilitating U.S.-bound drug smuggling (Gedda, "U.S. Claims Cuba Linked . . . ," AP, 27 Jan. 1982).[44]
— Congress. Research Service Rpt., 13 May 2005

The PRC May Be Using Organized Crime As a Tool

It is "chaos" that diverts attention from the main attack in one style of Asian warfare. As the level of chaos rises, strategic initiatives become less apparent and therefore less likely to be countered. Anyone interested in pursuing this style of warfare in Latin America would want as much criminal activity as possible to screen its other activities.

Many organized crime families are active in the TBA and other parts of Latin America. Some are indigenous to their areas of operation, and some are not. The foreign families that crop up most often in the research are from China or Russia. That Russia and China have now formed an anti-Western alliance of sorts may help to explain the "dual presence." Factions backed by the Chinese and Soviets also vied for the same prizes in southern Africa in the late 1970's.

Within Latin America, just as in Afghanistan, one cannot hope to quell the insurgency without first slowing the drugs that fund it. According to the U.S. State Department, "Brazil, Ecuador, Peru, and Panama have adopted an unstated policy mix of containment and non-confrontation with Colombian narco-terrorist groups. . . [while] Venezuelan President Chavez has an ideological affinity with . . . the FARC . . . and ELN."[45] Thus, one suspects that drugs (and the political favors they can buy) are linked to an ideological takeover of the region. Such a takeover would require the cooperation of certain organized-crime elements.

13

The biggest of the 50 Hong Kong triads are Sun Yee On, Wo Shing Wo, and 14-K. Their members are often quasi-legitimate businessmen, so many of their deals appear legal.[46] First detected in the TBA were 14-K and something called Pak Lung Fu, but then Sun Yee On appeared.[47] Elsewhere active in South America (primarily in people trafficking) is Fu Ching—one of the many triad-affiliated gangs.[48] Both 14-K and Sun Yee On engage in overseas crime, but a Congressional Research Report claims the latter to be more active in Latin America. 14-K has long specialized in heroin, so it probably has Mexican channels. But, Pak Lung Fu is nowhere to be found on the lists of Chinese triads and gangs from the Federal Bureau of Investigation (FBI) and *Wikipedia Encyclopedia*.[49] One reputable news article refers to it as a "crime syndicate." And the same article mentions the presence of the "Cantonese mafia Tai Chen" and "Chinese intelligence service" in the TBA.[50] Americans might like to know what Red Chinese operatives are doing in one of the most isolated parts of the Western Hemisphere. They would also be shocked to learn how easy it has been for Chinese criminal elements to penetrate their own national security screen.

> By utilizing their worldwide web of criminal contacts, members of Chinese criminal enterprises are able to orchestrate [the following:] 1) the smuggling of, wholesale quantities of Southeast Asian heroin from the Golden Triangle to North America for distribution, 2) the smuggling of hundreds and thousands of Chinese aliens from China into the United States. . . .
> . . . The Chinese "Snake Heads" [anyone who trafficks in human beings] have used a variety of methods and routes to smuggle aliens from China into the United States.[51]
> — recent FBI study for the U.S. State Department

Snake Heads are sometimes, but not always, associated with 14-K. Both 14-K and Sun Yee On have greatly contributed to the flow of illegal aliens and drugs into the U.S. While only Sun Yee On has been directly alleged to be a PRC instrument, both may be.[52]

Arms Deals and Military Training

If there is a Communist takeover attempt in the works for South

America, then there would be further proof of it in the form of arms deals and military training. When the U.S. discontinued military financing and training to nations that would not agree to bar the extradition of U.S. citizens to the International Criminal Court, it opened that door to China. The list includes 11 nations, the most critical of which are Peru, Ecuador, Brazil, and Bolivia.[53] Everyone knows which weapon finally gave the edge to the *mujahideen* in the Soviet-Afghan War. So when China offered to sell new shoulder-fired anti-aircraft missiles to the leftist government in Bolivia, the U.S. Southern Command undoubtedly took notice. Unfortunately, that particular offer is not the extent of Chinese arms initiatives in the region. China has already supplied military equipment to Cuba and is currently cooperating with Brazil on a joint satellite project thought to have a military application. It has further offered its new FC-1 jet fighter to Venezuela, after last year's sale of three JYL-1 mobile air-defense radar units.[54]

Larry Wortzel, a former Pentagon intelligence official, has said that China recently dispatched a delegation of Second Artillery [Corps] officers to Cuba.[55] That particular "artillery unit" just happens to be the branch of the PLA that controls the PRC's nuclear and conventional strategic missiles.[56] Why the U.S. news media has failed to elaborate speaks volumes about somebody's expertise at information management.

In addition, there has been a joint Beijing/Caracas effort to develop telecommunications capabilities in Venezuela that include the launch of a satellite. Finally, the PRC is reportedly "developing" the former Rodman U.S. Naval Base so that it can better control maritime traffic at both ends of the Panama Canal.[57] That can only mean one thing—ships of the PLA navy will soon be docked there.

How Arms Are Sent to the Communist Factions

Not all of the arms flowing into the region have come from the PRC directly. Any of its national allies or business affiliates can also fill that role. There have been drug deals in which guerrilla groups are paid off in assault rifles. In 2001, the commander of the Colombian Armed Forces reported that Russian criminal organizations had sent 10,000 AK-47 rifles to the FARC through Brazilian narcotics dealer Fernando Da Costa. In return, the FARC helped Da Costa to move large shipments of cocaine from Colombia to Brazil.[58]

15

It's not hard to prove that the Chinese triads deal not only in drugs, but also in arms. By tossing in a few Muslim clients, they easily draw attention away from their homeland.

> Although the Chinese Mafia in the TBA is characterized by internecine [deadly] rivalries, it is known to collaborate with the Islamic terrorist groups in the region. At least two organizations—the Sung-I and Ming families—have engaged in illegal operations with the Egyptian al-Gama'a al-Islamiyya. (Bartolome, "The Tri-Border," *Military Review*, July-August 2002). The Sung-I family, which is based in the Paraguayan town of Hernandarias, used three photography and electronic businesses located in Ciudad del Este as fronts for its activities. In December 2000, Sung-I sold a shipment of munitions to the Islamic Group, sending it to Egypt by ship as "medical equipment." The Cameroon-flagged vessel was intercepted in the Cypriot port of Limasol. The Ming family managed Islamic Group funds from Ciudad del Este in the financial circuit that includes Guyana and the Cayman Islands (Ibid., citing Godoy, "Triplice Fronteira . . . ," *O Estado de Sao Paulo,* 11 November 2001).[59]
> — Fed. Research Div. Rpt., July 2003

Again, neither Sung-I nor Ming are on the FBI's nor *Wikipedia Encyclopedia's* list of Chinese criminal enterprises.[60] That means they are either local gangs or something more sinister—like manufactured affiliates of the PLA or MSS.

Too Much Deception to Be Anyone But the PRC

Over the last 15 years, there has been an actual assault on a national supreme court (in Colombia) and an aborted attack against a national senate (in Mexico). In the first incident, a Marxist/Communist organization conducted the operation and then destroyed all extradition records, thereby seeming to care more about drugs than ideology. In the second, *Hezbollah* was paid by someone to intimidate the Mexican government. That someone may have wanted more leeway for drug traffickers and populists, or simply to get *Hezbollah's* name into the headlines.

Over the same period, there has been one actual assault on a U.S. ally's embassy compound (in Peru) and a foiled plot against American embassies (in Paraguay, Uruguay, and Ecuador). In the first incident, a Marxist/Communist organization conducted an operation that had as its secondary purpose some kind of free-trade provision. In the second, *Hezbollah* was implicated. Thus, it is not unreasonable to conclude that a coordinated effort (with clever diversions) had been in progress. The only actual attacks had been by Communist factions, while all unfulfilled plots were by Muslim extremists. Might the Muslim plots of 2000 and 2001 have been purposely engineered to divert attention from an ongoing Communist strategy? To obscure some particularly heinous act, American organized-crime figures will sometimes work for years to create an elaborate trail of false evidence. Why then, couldn't an atheistic regime bent on world domination?

In Panama, where government corruption is rampant, there is a dangerous convergence of well-financed Chinese and Russian mobs with Cuban government operatives and Latin American drug lords, leftists and narco-terrorist militants. This dark partnership is a threat to democracy in Panama and in neighboring countries, and is a direct long-term threat to Mexico and the United States.[61]
    — American Foreign Policy Council Report

The Maoist guerrilla's way of first consolidating all rural areas fits in well with Latin America's history. Its big land owners have always gravitated toward the cities, thereby leaving the rural peasantry to fend for themselves. Coca and poppies grow best where those peasants live, so Mao's concept of decentralized industry also meshes well with drug production. The specifics of how Latin America's drug traders, gangs, Islamists, and Maoists interact can best be determined by studying the recent histories of its various nations.

17

2 Cuba, the Caribbean, and Venezuela

- ● Who became Cuba's mentor after the Soviet collapse?
- ● What is Venezuela's role in the new Communist plan?

Vestiges of Colonialism

(Source: DA Pamphlet 550-36 [1991], p. 127)

Cuba's Angolan Adventure

Most of what happens in the world has occurred somewhere else before. To gain a better understanding of current events in the Caribbean, one can look at the recent history of West Africa. In the mid-1980's, the Soviet Union arranged for 3,000 of its military advisers and 45,000 Cuban ground troops to fight a U.S.-backed South African expeditionary force for Angola.[1] The South Africans were eventually disenfranchised by the West, and Angola ended up with a Marxist/Leninist form of government.[2] That government has since evolved into a "multiparty presidential

19

regime,"[3] the noncommittal term for one-man rule. Dos Santos has been both chief of state and head of government since 1979.[4] That Angola is now being heavily courted by the PRC should come as no surprise.

> Angola finds itself equally in the good graces of the Chinese, who take 25% of that country's oil production. As with Zimbabwe, the regime in Luanda is widely viewed as particularly corrupt. The PRC offered the Angolans a $2 billion soft loan to be used for reconstruction. . . . It was reported by human rights groups that some of that money was channeled into the ruling party's campaign coffers.[5]
> ─Ctr. for Internat. Develop. & Conflict Mgt., 2005

China has always been friendly with Angola because of their mutual roots in Marxism/Leninism. But during the last five years, the PRC's influence over Angola has markedly grown. Today, Angola is China's most important partner on the African continent. This is due in large part to that country's huge supply of oil and diamonds. In 2004, Angola became Africa's largest supplier of crude oil to China. Two years later, its state-owned oil company Sonangol and China's Sinopec launched a U.S. $2.2 billion joint bid for blocks 17 and 18. These new blocks have estimated reserves of 3 billion barrels and 1.5 billion barrels, respectively, and will make Angola the world's second-biggest supplier of oil to the PRC. In addition, Chinese companies have begun work on a good-sized oil refinery at Lobito. Between 10,000 and 80,000 Chinese nationals are already living in Angola. Through additional entrenchment in that nation's economy, China will have much more influence on Luanda's policies.[6]

Unfortunately, the two countries' relationship goes far beyond economic. As was the case in Iraq and Afghanistan, China has been preparing Angola to resist any further Western intervention. In 2005, Chinese Vice Premier Zeng Peiyan pledged $400 million to Angola's telecommunications sector, and $100 million to upgrade its military communication network. Chinese companies have also been building roads and bridges. Early in 2006, the same companies began to rehabilitate Angola's famous Benguela railroad [linking the port of Lobito with mineral-rich Zambia and the Congo].[7] The PRC's attempt to turn Angola into a Sudan-like surrogate has been so subtle that it has largely escaped the West's attention. The PRC has influenced that country through "temporary immigrants," "foreign aid" (estimates run as high as $9 billion [8]), and "commodity bartering." So far, that bartering has been limited to arms for oil.

China has been promoting arms-for-oil deals with Africa as the continent is becoming one of its major sources of oil. Since last year, top Chinese leaders and military officers have made frequent visits to Africa. . . .

In 2005, Angola exported to China nearly 17.5 million tons of crude oil, becoming China's second largest oil supplier after Saudi Arabia. . . .

. . . In June last year, China Petrochemical Corp. . . . signed a $1.4 billion deal with the Angolan Sonangol Co. to develop new oil fields. China also offered Angola a loan of $3 billion to help rebuild its economic infrastructure, destroyed by years of civil war.

At the Zhuhai Air Show, which opened last Thursday, military delegations from Angola and Sudan were allowed to make very careful examinations of FC-1 fighters and K-8 trainer aircraft. Angola and Ethiopia were the first African countries to receive Su-27 SK fighters. . . .

. . . [T]hrough an arms-for-oil deal, it is possible that Angola may resume importing weapons systems from China, particularly light weapons. . . .

With China's demand for oil from Africa increasing, more Chinese weapons are expected to enter this region in the years to come.[9]

— United Press International, 5 November 2007

So, the obvious question arises. Why would a small African nation with every intention of minding its own business need an ever-bigger supply of light-infantry weapons? Is not the eastern Congo now being heavily contested? It does, after all, contain one of the world's largest supplies of uranium. The Angolan example is offered here because of a quickly developing parallel in Latin America. More ominously, its Latin American equivalent (Venezuela), is being assisted with its Socialistic transformation by a nearby Chinese ally. Most Americans have never been told by their news media or government who that ally might be.

Cuba May Now Be a Full-Fledged Chinese Surrogate

Havana's Marxist system is too fragile to survive without financial and ideological support from elsewhere. It may be getting much of the money it needs from other members of the Bolivarian Alternative for the People of Our America (ALBA). Purportedly the invention of Hugo Chavez, ALBA is an organization that strives for the social, political, and economic integration of all the countries of Latin America and the Caribbean. The following nations have already entered into an ALBA-related "people's" trade agreement: Cuba, Venezuela, Bolivia, Nicaragua, and several tiny Caribbean island-nations. The latter include St. Vincent and the Grenadines, Antigua and Barbuda, and Dominica.[10] (See Map 2.1.)

With the demise of the Soviet Union, only one country could provide the ideological support (and U.N. protection) that Cuba requires. That country is the People's Republic of China. Like the Soviet Union, the PRC equates regional progress with revolution. It takes arms and training to pursue revolution. Some of the more controversial types of arms may have already reached Cuban shores.

"China is stepping up military training in Latin America," the general in charge of the U.S. Southern Command told Congress yesterday. . . . "[W]e are seeing those who formerly would come to the United States going to China."

The growing Chinese role comes amid numerous high-level visits by its leaders and other activities aimed at building military and economic ties to leftist governments and other states in a strategic region long-considered within the U.S. sphere of influence. . . .

Sen. James M. Inhofe, Oklahoma Republican, said China is seeking deals with the leftist government of Hugo Chavez in Venezuela and with Argentina on civilian-use nuclear goods. . . .

Less is known about arms sales, however, China recently offered to sell new shoulder-fired anti-aircraft missiles to the leftist government in Bolivia. The Chinese have supplied military equipment to Cuba and are cooperating with Brazil on a joint satellite project thought to have military applications. . . .

Map 2.1: Countries in and around the Caribbean
(Source: Courtesy of General Libraries, University of Texas at Austin, from their website for map designator "central_america_ref02.pdf")

An eight-member military delegation to Cuba earlier this month was led by Lt. Gen. Peng Xiaofeng, political commissar of the Second Artillery forces [the PLA's long-range missile branch].

"We know almost nothing" about Chinese military and intelligence activities in the region, a Pentagon official said.

Mexico is also being courted. Last year, three of the nine members of the ruling Communist Party of China Politburo Standing Committee, the collective dictatorship that rules China, visited Mexico.

... [The same] Pentagon official said ... the activities in the hemisphere are part of a "counter-encirclement" strategy by Beijing, aimed at neutralizing what China views as a U.S. policy of building up bases and alliances in nations around China.[11]

— *Washington Times,* 15 March 2006

Further Clues to China's Caribbean Strategy

The same PLA extension (Hutchison Whampoa) that controls both ends of the Panama Canal also runs a port in the Bahamas. And the PLA now has a "police contingent" in Haiti. One wonders how these seemingly unrelated facts might help to define China's Caribbean strategy. A Hutchison Whampoa port could provide many of the services of a PLA base without limiting access to the host country. A tiny Chinese contingent of continually traveling police advisers could create a far-reaching political-commissar network. Only for Mexico, might both initiatives be happening at once. Hutchison Whampoa will soon have its own seaport on Mexico's Pacific coast, and Chinese soldiers have been seen with Mexican army units that assist with the drug smuggling.[12]

A full-blown Maoist rebellion in America's backyard would be far too obvious. There must be some other reason for the Chinese military presence that the Bahamas, Haiti, and Mexico all share.

When Viewed from an Economic Perspective

Haiti, the Dominican Republic, Jamaica, and the Bahamas all

qualify as trans-shipment points for the narcotics that cross the Caribbean and enter the U.S. Similarly, Mexico is a trans-shipment point for drugs that cross the Pacific or come overland from South America. Thus, PLA affiliates may be profiting financially from both routes, while concurrently undermining the nation that poses the only serious opposition to Chinese domination. Of course, the PRC's most useful arrangement exists on the north coast of South America—an area rich in petroleum. And this arrangement just happens to occur where most of the narcotics destined for the U.S. East Coast depart that continent.[13]

While a conspiracy that complicated may be hard for a straightforward Westerner to embrace, it's not for any follower of Sun Tzu. A closer look at the Caribbean points of transit and South American point of debarkation should help to define the problem.

Jamaica and the Bahamas

There is little information readily available on how drugs are shipped through the Bahamas and Jamaica. The southernmost island in the Bahama chain lies only 60 miles north of Haiti, so the drug runners most likely "island hop" by fast boat. The Bahaman government has been cooperating extensively with U.S. counter-narcotics agencies, but the 2,000 cays and 700 islands that make up the Bahaman archipelago pose an almost endless combination of routes.[14] Jamaica also cooperates with those agencies but remains the largest producer and exporter of marijuana in the Caribbean.[15]

Hutchison Whampoa operates the sprawling Freeport Container Port on Grand Bahama Island. In 2006, the Bush administration acknowledged a no-bid contract with Hutchison to run a sophisticated U.S. radiation detector at Freeport without any U.S. Customs agents present. The CIA had no problem with the arrangement, but other defense agencies might. In 1999, a U.S. military intelligence report cited Hutchison as a potential risk for smuggling prohibited materials into the U.S. It said that Hutchison's port operations in the Bahamas and Panama "could provide a conduit for illegal shipments of technology or prohibited items from the West to the PRC, or facilitate the movement of arms and other prohibited items into the Americas."[16]

Haiti and the Dominican Republic

The number of drug smuggling flights from Venezuela to Haiti and the Dominican Republic increased by 167% from 2005 to 2006, with one third of those flights landing in Haiti. According to a U.S. State Department report of March 2004, "serious allegations persisted that high-level government and police officials [were] involved in drug trafficking." There were even allegations that former President Aristide was involved directly.[17]

In September of 2004, 2005, and 2006, President Bush reaffirmed that Haiti remained a major drug transit country. At a regional summit on drug trafficking in the Dominican Republic in March 2007, Admiral James Stravidis (head of the U.S. Southern Command) pledged to help shore up the porous Haiti/Dominican Republic border. Since that time, drug shipments from Venezuela have reportedly declined, and the counter-narcotics cooperation between Haiti and the Dominican Republic has improved. In early June of 2007, the Haitian government recorded a major drug bust.[18]

Sadly, the Dominican Republic qualifies as a major trans-shipment point for both cocaine and heroin.[19] In September 2004, President Bush designated it as one of four major drug transit countries in the Caribbean, with 8% of all the cocaine entering the U.S. flowing through it.[20] Many of those cocaine shipments had come from Venezuela.

Venezuela

Venezuela is more than just a point of exit for drugs leaving South America. (See Map 2.2.) Chavez and his international backers have been trying to turn that country into a totalitarian state with a "revolutionary" government. He is not following the Islamic model, but that of Communism. Both require ideological monitoring at every level of governance and endeavor. In Iran, there are Revolutionary Guard detachments in every agency and neighborhood to fill that role. In Sudan, "Popular Defense Forces" keep an eye on things for the ruling Muslim Brotherhood. However, the heads of Communist countries generally accomplish such supervision through the vested members of their ruling political parties. Their twisted equivalent of ward bosses have colloquially been called "commissars." Either Venezuela's president didn't have enough Bolivarian followers to perform such a mission, or he was encouraged by foreign backers to borrow some.

Cuba is the Chavez government's closest ally. . . . As of February 2005, Cuba reportedly had 20,000 doctors, dentists, teachers, and sports trainers in Venezuela, mainly working in poor pro-Chavez neighborhoods of Caracas. Fidel Castro pledged in early 2005 that the number of Cubans would increase to 30,000 by the end of the year. In 2004 President Chavez reportedly posted dozens of Cuban "advisers" to the internal security and immigration agencies of the Ministry of Interior and Justice, other key ministries, and the Central Bank. . . .

. . . Chavez government has sought to develop military relations with China, Cuba, Russia, and Ukraine. China's defense minister visited Venezuela for the first time in September 2001. Venezuela signed a military cooperation agreement with Russia in 2001. The arrangement facilitates the acquisition by Venezuela of Russian military aircraft or helicopters and other weapons. Some Cuban advisers reportedly have been posted in [Venezuelan] . . . Military Intelligence (Direccion de Inteligencia Militar—DIM), and some Cuban military advisers reportedly are engaged in training the military. In early 2005, Venezuela's National Assembly ratified a 1999 security agreement with Cuba that is intended to facilitate cooperation between security personnel in Venezuela and Cuba. . . .

. . . The Chavez government apparently now sees the United States as its principal adversary. Now closely allied with Fidel Castro Ruz of Cuba, President Chavez reportedly has ordered Venezuela's armed forces to implement a new Cuban-style strategy in which the top priority is preparing to fight a war of resistance against an invasion by the United States. In addition, Chavez has ordered a doubling of the army's reserve, to more than 100,000 [estimates range up to a million] troops under his personal command. "Popular defense units" of 50 to 500 civilians are to be established in workplaces and on farms. . . .

. . . In April 2004, Venezuela's Ministry of Defense embarked on a US $2-billion arms-acquisition program

and subsequently signed an agreement . . . with Russia for various armaments for the army. In February 2005, Venezuela also was evaluating Russian MIG-29 fighters as replacements for its U.S.-made F-16's. . . .
. . . Venezuela . . . has contributed to the U.N. peacekeeping force in Haiti. . . .
. . . In addition to the official security forces, Chavez has distributed weapons to the estimated 10,000 members of the Bolivarian Circles, independently organized groups of Chavez supporters at the grassroots [sic] level of Venezuelan society. These groups are modeled on Cuba's Committees for the Defense of the Revolution and operate in groups of between seven and 11 people.[21]
— Lib. of Congress Country Profile, March 2005

Cuba is . . . providing intelligence and security officers to Venezuela. They've helped Chavez develop an improved intelligence capability—and undermine the political opposition in true Cuban style.
Cuban military advisers are also present, making Venezuelan officers increasingly anxious about the creeping influence of Havana in military matters. Caracas is also sending officers to Cuba for training—and, undoubtedly, political indoctrination.[22]
— *Armed Forces Journal,* July 2007

Of particular note in the above excerpt is the reference to Chavez's "Popular Defense Units." Sudan's watchdog element is called "Popular Defense Forces." That much coincidence in such vastly different cultures could mean a shared mentor.

Venezuela Now Spreading the "Revolutionary" Fervor

Hugo Chavez fancies himself as the reincarnation of Simon Bolivar—the Venezuelan hero whose revolutionary armies rid much of South America of European colonialism. As such, he wants to replace Fidel Castro as the vanguard of Socialist revolution in all of Latin America. Since 2005, he has bought more than $4-billion worth of foreign weapons (mostly from Russia).[23] He has also made several personal trips to China and North Korea.[24] One to the latter location in July 2006 was expected to involve an oil-for-arms deal. Hopefully, that deal didn't include UW trainers from that country's Light-Infantry Training Guidance Bureau. North Korea has had an embassy in Caracas since April of 2006.[25]

Map 2.2: Venezuela
(Source: Courtesy of General Libraries, University of Texas at Austin, from their website for map designator "venezuela_rel93.pdf")

Venezuelan and North Korean military delegations have traipsed back and forth on numerous occasions between Caracas and Pyongyang. . . . North Korean ballistic missiles could be on Venezuela's shopping list. Pyongyang is [a Chinese proxy and] the world's most prodigious proliferator of missiles.[26]

— *Armed Forces Journal,* July 2007

Unfortunately, Venezuela's interest in weapons extends well beyond any possible self-defense needs. Chavez has already transacted a deal to build Kalashnikov small arms (AK-47's) in Venezuela under a Russian license. He has promised to export guns and ammunition to Bolivia and other allies once the Kalashnikov plant is finished. He has further been providing small arms and ammunition to two of Colombia's rebel militias—the FARC and ELN.[27] The fear is that Chavez may next create guerrilla warfare schools for regional revolutionaries or send "volunteers" to fight in other countries. There have already been reports of Venezuelans training rebels in both Colombia and Ecuador.[28]

Yet, Chavez is obviously up to more than just a Vietnam-like Maoist offensive. He has been dabbling in the politics of other nations and "supporting" their leftist candidates. That support has no doubt included both funding and advice. While his proteges in Bolivia, Ecuador, and Nicaragua managed to win their elections, those in Mexico and Peru just barely lost. Additionally, Chavez has reached out to four incumbents who are not generally known to be leftist. They are from Argentina, Uruguay, Chile, and Brazil.[29] Thus, his Bolivarian dream has already advanced far beyond the drawing-board stage. He is now trying to form a fully modern military coalition throughout South America. Having left the Venezuelan paratroopers in 1992, he displays far too good an understanding of telecommunications technology. Like Nepal's Pranchanda, he must be getting advice from a foreign expert.

Venezuela's domestic satellite system has three earth stations, including one Intelsat (Atlantic Ocean) and one PanAmSat, and is participating with Colombia, Ecuador, Peru, and Bolivia in the construction of an international fiber-optic network.[30]

— Lib. of Congress Country Profile, March 2005

A Temporary Reprieve

On 2 December 2007, the government of Venezuela held a referendum to reform its constitution. Among the 69 changes proposed were the following: (1) an end to presidential term limits; (2) presidential ability to detain citizens without charge during "states of emergency"; (3) more governmental authority to nationalize private property; (4) aid to left-leaning regimes in the region;[31] and (5) control over all news media.[32] In essence, the referendum would have turned Venezuela into a Socialist state.[33] There were large protests on the streets of Caracas before the vote, so Chavez mounted a massive advertising campaign. His ads, posters, and statements equated a vote of "yes" with help for the poor and revolution, and a vote of "no" with being a traitor (and its implied consequences).

Just prior to the balloting, Chavez threatened to shut off all oil to the U.S. if fraud accusations after a successful referendum led to violence.[34] When that referendum was narrowly defeated by a vote of 51% to 49%, Chavez calmly announced that the "democratic process was maturing in Venezuela" and that his proposals were not dead.[35] As his current term of office lasts until 2012, he undoubtedly meant that he still has enough time to achieve all Socialist goals through the democratic process.

All the while (according to NPR News), "his allies dominated the National Assembly, courts, and armed forces."[36] The *Christian Science Monitor* confirms the first two and says Chavez also controls "most of the media and almost all of the local and state governments."[37] One might have expected the normally boisterous Chavez to nullify the referendum's result based on the closeness of the vote, but that's not what happened. Earlier in 2007, his National Assembly had already given him sufficient powers to reshape Venezuela's government. In effect until mid-2008, those powers include the following: (1) to enact laws by decree on everything from the economic model to justice system; (2) restructure state institutions; and (3) redistribute Venezuela's wealth "more equitably."[38] Yet, Chavez still gratuitously accepted the referendum's outcome. He most probably did so after Sun-Tzu-like political advice from Cuba.

By unfortunate coincidence, Russia had held a parliamentary election on the same day. The United Russia Party won 65% of the vote, thus making it possible for career KGB (Komityet Gosudarstvyennoy Bezopasnosti) officer, Vladimir Putin to stay on indefinitely as the *de facto* leader of Russia. Claiming other candidates had been arrested and ballot-boxes stuffed, international observers asserted that one-party rule had returned to Russia.[39] As in southern Africa after Communist-backed rebels won hastily organized elections at the end of the last century, one-party rule must be the next best thing to a Socialist state. After massive arms sales to Venezuela,[40] Russia appears now ready to support Chavez's vision of regional revolution. So provocative a stance is most likely the result of Russia's new friendship with China.

Venezuela shares long borders with Guyana and the largest country in South America. More than just drugs are now passing across those borders.

3   The Guianas, Brazil, and Paraguay

- How strong are the Muslim extremists in Guyana?
- To what extent has China been courting Brazil?

Peasants Attached to the Land

(Source: DA Pamphlet 550-36 [1991], p. 75)

More Than One Influence on Guyana and Suriname

At South America's northeastern end is one of the few places in the Western Hemisphere where Muslim extremism has had much chance of gaining a foothold. Guyana boasts the highest Muslim percentage of its total population (12% of 800,000) of any nation in the entire region. Both it and Suriname are members of the Organization of the Islamic Conference (OIC)—the Saudi equivalent of the Egyptian-dominated Arab League.[1] But, other than loose ties to the people who attempted the Trinidad and Tobago coup in 1990 and J.F.K. fuel line bombing in 2007, the Islamists of Guyana and Suriname have been relatively inactive. They have never fomented insurgency, nor have they pushed all that hard for a Muslim state. Still, Guyana has not been totally devoid of trouble. On 17 February 2008 in the southern part of the country, attackers killed 12 people in the second such incident in two weeks. Some of those killed were policemen, and their weapons and vehicles were stolen. If the episode had not happened near the Brazilian border, it might have looked like the sparks of a fledgling insurgency. But, local officials blamed it on criminal gangs.[2] So, it probably had more to do with human-being smuggling or drug trafficking.

Brazil

There are close to a million Muslims in Brazil, but they are not to blame for that country's troubles. Those troubles have more to do with world economics. According to the BBC, "Brazil's natural resources, particularly iron ore, are highly prized by major manufacturing nations, including China."[3] (See Map 3.1.) Now the world's thirteenth largest producer of oil, Brazil also has vast untapped petroleum reserves (12.22 billion barrels of oil and 312.7 billion cubic meters of natural gas.)[4]

Luiz Inacio Lula da Silva (popularly known as Lula) is Brazil's left-leaning president. He is popular among the poor and had little difficulty winning a second term in 2006. Promising to boost economic growth and to narrow the gap between rich and poor, Lula marked the start of his second term in office by announcing an ambitious investment program. With a weakened presence in congress, his left-wing Workers' Party may have to rely on political alliances to pursue its goals.[5] Lula's past affiliations may help to define those alliances. His increased trade with China has already bolstered the Brazilian economy.[6]

The Communist Party of Brazil (Partido Comunista do Brasil or "PC do B") was created as an underground splinter from the PCB [Partido Comunista Brasileiro] in 1958, following Soviet leader Nikita Khrushchev's denunciations of Stalinist atrocities. The "PC do B" repudiated the new Moscow line and aligned itself with Maoism. . . . After the "PC do B" was

legalized in 1985, under the leadership of former deputy and
former guerrilla Joao Amazonas, it elected more deputies in
1986 and 1990 than its arch rival, the PCB. The "PC do B"
joined the FBP [Frente Brasil Popular, a leftist coalition] in

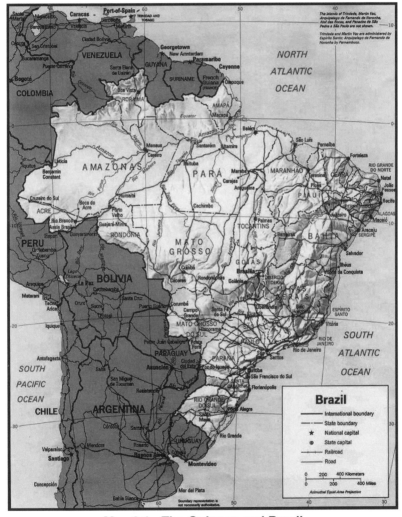

Map 3.1: The Guianas and Brazil
(Source: Courtesy of General Libraries, University of Texas at Austin, from their website for map designator "brazil_rel94.pdf")

support of Lula in 1989 and 1994. The "PC do B" doubled its delegation from five to ten federal deputies, representing nine states, in 1994. This feat resulted from "PC do B" domination of student organizations in most states and astute use of coalitions.[7]

— Lib. of Congress Country Study on Brazil, 1997

Lula sees himself as a negotiator, as opposed to an ideologue. He has attempted to befriend both Venezuelan President Hugo Chavez and U.S. President George Bush. But, in mid-January 2008,

Figure 3.1: Brazilian Infantryman
(Source: Courtesy of Orion Books, from *World Army Uniforms since 1939*, © 1975, 1980, 1981, 1983 by Blandford Press Ltd., Part II, Plate 103)

he traveled to Cuba and was televised during a very cordial conference with Fidel Castro. Thus, one suspects a preference for Marxist leaders. Lula comes from poor beginnings and is known to favor the redistribution of agricultural land.[8] "Land to the landless" was Che Guevara's chief rallying cry.[9] While wanting to take land from the rich and give it to the poor does not make Lula a Communist, it is still troubling. It could be a Socialist intention. Or, as in Zimbabwe, it might simply signal more Chinese cooperation.[10] Either way, Brazil bears watching. Having fought in Italy in WWII, its army is no stranger to combat. (See Figures 3.1 and 3.2.)

Figure 3.2: Brazilian Paratrooper
(Source: Courtesy of Cassell PLC, from *Uniforms of Elite Forces,* © 1982 by Blandford Press Ltd., No. 91)

In early 2008, a big enough natural-gas reserve was discovered off the coast of Brazil to make that country a world leader in energy exports.[11] To America's dismay, two left-leaning powerhouses were emerging side by side at the top of South America. Like Chavez, Lula has dramatically increased Brazil's defense spending over the last year. Because the two are such close friends, experts suspect a mutual defense pact.[12]

Within the notorious TBA at Brazil's western border lies Foz do Iguazu. *Hezbollah's* "al-Mukawama" training camp was allegedly on a farm outside this jungle city.[13] Just across a short bridge from Foz do Iguazu is Ciudad del Este, Paraguay. It was the site of the 2002 crime summit. While only half of the TBA's Muslims live there, almost all of its Chinese do. A few miles to the west is Hernandarias, Paraguay. This is where the Chinese Sung-I crime family is headquartered.[14] For whatever reason, most of the reactionary Chinese in the region seem to have been drawn to Paraguay.

Paraguay

Paraguay endured over 30 years of dictatorship under Alfredo Stroessner. Though he was ousted in 1989 and died in exile in 2006, the end to his iron-fisted rule failed to bring political stability to the country. Factional splits led to the assassination of a vice-president, the resignation of a president, and an attempted coup. Stroessner's party, the National Republican Association-Colorado Party, remained in power until April 2008.[15]

That Paraguay has for years served as a black-market conduit does not make its neighbors very happy. (See Map 3.2.) The U.S. supported the ouster of Stroessner and helped to resolve the crisis from Paraguay's contested 1998 election. Relations with the U.S. have improved as democratic reforms took hold. Economic ties between the two countries have also rebounded (after many years of decline during Paraguay's economic collapse). The U.S. remains committed to providing some economic aid to Paraguay and stopping all laundering of drug proceeds in the region. Paraguay remains the only South American country to still recognize Taiwan diplomatically.[16]

Paraguay's armed forces have conducted joint training exercises with those of America. In 2005, the Paraguayan government agreed to let U.S. troops enter that country for up to 18 months, ostensibly to monitor the TBA for terrorist activity. The U.S. troops have since been instructing their Paraguayan counterparts in ways to deter

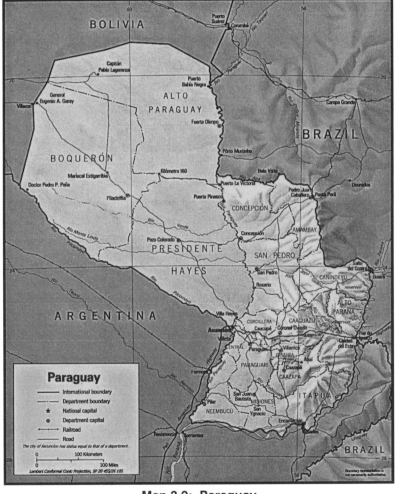

Map 3.2: Paraguay
(Source: Courtesy of General Libraries, University of Texas at Austin, from their website for map designator "paraguay_rel98.pdf")

drug trafficking, government corruption, and terrorism. Before being granted access by Paraguay, the U.S. troops were refused entry
by both Brazil and Argentina.[17]

There have been reports of Paraguayan National Police officers
being involved in drug-trafficking and human-kidnapping rings. The
Penal and Criminal Procedures Code of 2000 was designed to eliminate some of this corruption; but, despite a massive reorganization,
widespread government malfeasance still persists. Internal discord
remains more of a threat to Paraguayan progress than external
interference. The Colorado Party even wanted to amend the 1992
constitution to allow President Duarte to run for a second term in
2008. Paraguay's legacy of authoritarian government and violent
politics has not been completely erased. In 2004, the daughter of
a former president was kidnapped and killed, ostensibly by a radical leftist political group. Corruption in Paraguay's political and
financial sectors has resulted in the declining popular trust of its
government.[18]

Because Paraguay has traditionally been the best U.S. ally in
the region, the Communists have obviously targeted it. So far, their
"revolution" has been hard to spot in the midst of Paraguay's ongoing power struggle (Gen. Oviedo's erstwhile coups).[19] Its only real
footprint is FARC's implication in the kidnapping of an ex-president's
daughter, street demonstrations, and popular discontent. But that
revolution is nonetheless going on. Since 2004, peasants have staged a
series of land invasions and other protests, demanding redistribution
of agricultural land. Their leader appears to be Osmar Martinez.[20]
The link between drug trafficking and revolution is simple—money
helps with the politicization phase of the Maoist guerrilla method.
According to the father of 4GW, "the FARC and others find they
can use the drug trade for political ends."[21] Within Paraguay, as
in Brazil, the Communists' goal has been to get a leftist president
elected. According to documents from the Brazilian Agency of Intelligence, the ruling Workers' Party of Brazil received 5 million dollars from FARC-EP to be used by political campaign of candidates
in the 2002 election.[22]

Predictably, it happened in April 2008. The *Christian Science
Monitor* announced that Fernando Lugo had "won the presidency of
. . . Paraguay . . . ushering in another leftist government in South
America." With leftists already in control of Brazil and Argentina,[23]
that meant the TBA would continue to provide sanctuary to those

Map 3.3: The Tri-Border Region
(Source: Courtesy of General Libraries, University of Texas at Austin, from their website for map designator "paraguay_rel98.tif")

who would foment or fund revolution. It also meant that the U.S. had been paying too little attention to the electoral processes of the region.

Paraguay's Piece of the TBA

Ciudad del Este, Paraguay, has traditionally functioned as the hub of drug and arms transactions in South America. (See Map 3.3.) Of course, as more leftists are elected, there may be less need for the latter. Just to the southeast of Paraguay lies a country with a similar name but very different background—Uruguay.

4 Uruguay, Argentina, and Bolivia

- Of the three, is Bolivia the only leftist nation?
- In which countries were there government atrocities?

The Andes Have Many Strategically Important Minerals

(Source: DA Pamphlet 550-66 [1991], cover)

Uruguay Still Has Problems

Just below Brazil lies Uruguay. (See Map 4.1.) Generally thought to be more stable than its neighbors, Uruguay reflects the same disturbing trend—a recent shift to the left. Hours after Tabare Vazquez was sworn in as president in March 2005, he restored ties with Cuba, signed an energy deal with Venezuela, and announced a welfare package to tackle poverty.[1]

Tabare Vazquez, from the Broad Front coalition, became Uruguay's first left-wing head of state in March 2005. . . .

His win was part of a regional trend which had seen the emergence of left-wing governments in Brazil, Venezuela, Chile, and Argentina.[2]
— BBC *Country Profile*

Uruguay has a long history of both Marxist revolution and overzealous military response. Marxist Tupamaro urban guerrillas waged a campaign against the establishment throughout the 1960's and into the early 1970's. That campaign came to an abrupt end in 1973, when Uruguay's armed forces took over the country. Their rule turned repressive and lasted until 1985. During this period, Uruguay became known as "torture chamber of Latin America" and accumulated the largest number of political prisoners per capita in the world.[3] One of its neighbors suffered a similar fate at about the same time. Might different counterinsurgency advice from the U.S. have helped in both cases?

Argentina's Ongoing Inequity

Argentina also had to endure an overzealous military regime from 1976-1983. Its armed forces took over, not in response to a Marxist rebellion, but to a left-wing (Peronista) election victory. Juan Peron's first term of office from 1946 to 1955 had also ended in a coup. Then, starting in 1976, tens of thousands of people were killed in a seven-year "dirty war" against the military regime's civilian opposition. The bodies of many of the abductees—now known as the "disappeared"—have never been found.[4]

In October 2001, the Peronistas regained control of both houses of parliament in Congressional elections. Three months later, that parliament elected Peronista Senator Eduardo Duhalde as caretaker president. In May 2003, Nestor Kirschner was sworn in as Argentina's democratically elected president.[5] At the end of his term of office in late 2007, his wife Cristina Fernandez de Kirschner took over the office. Their leftist backgrounds are both a matter of public record.[6]

[S]he [Kirschner's wife] is also expected to . . . maintain close ties with other [leftist] Latin American countries such as Brazil and Venezuela. . . .

She has a long track-record as a politician. As a law student in the 1970's she was active in a leftist Peronist movement, later becoming first a provincial and then a national deputy.

Map 4.1: Uruguay and Argentina
(Source: Courtesy of General Libraries, University of Texas at Austin, from their website for map designator "argentina_rel_1996.pdf")

She supported her husband—whom she met at university in 1975—as he rose through the Peronist ranks, and in 1995 became a senator herself.[7]
— BBC *Country Profile*

In mid-December 2007, Madame Fernandez de Kirschner's innermost feelings became public. First, there were reports of U.S. authorities intercepting $800,000 of Venezuelan funds that were destined for her political campaign. Then, in response to this charge, she attacked U.S. foreign policy and pledged her support for Hugo Chavez's "Bolivarian" plan for the region. Finally, as a poorly thought-out aside, she admitted that Venezuela had contributed billions to Argentina's debt removal.[8]

Against so leftist a backdrop, *Hezbollah's* two Buenos Aires bombings in the early 1990's seem almost inconsequential. Nor is any current threat to regional peace posed by the Jamaat Tablighi Movement in Argentina. *Tablighi Jamaat* is little more than a Muslim missionary and revival effort anyway.[9] Communism and its too forceful repression remain the dual-threat in this part of the world. In March 2008, a laptop photograph was captured in Ecuador of an Argentinean Communist Party official in conference with a FARC chieftain.[10] Within Argentina's neighbor to the northwest may lie a much-needed clue to how this dual-threat can be handled.

Bolivia's Ongoing Nightmare

Bolivia has the second-largest underground reserves of natural gas in South America. (See Map 4.2.) In May 2006, its leftist president put that country's energy industry under state control. At the same time, he gave foreign energy firms six months to sell at least 51% of their holdings to the state or leave the country.[11]

Bolivia is also one of the world's largest producers of coca, the principal ingredient of cocaine. Any crop-eradication program—a past requirement for U.S. aid—would tend to anger Bolivia's poorest farmers who often depend on coca for their only source of income.[12] A large grant from the coca processors, on the other hand, might allow someone to do quite well in the democratic process.

Socialist leader Evo Morales, a figurehead for Bolivia's coca farmers, won presidential elections in December 2005, the first indigenous Bolivian to do so. He described himself as the candidate "of the most disdained and discriminated against." . . .

A few months later, in June 2006, he claimed victory in elections for a new assembly which will rewrite the con-

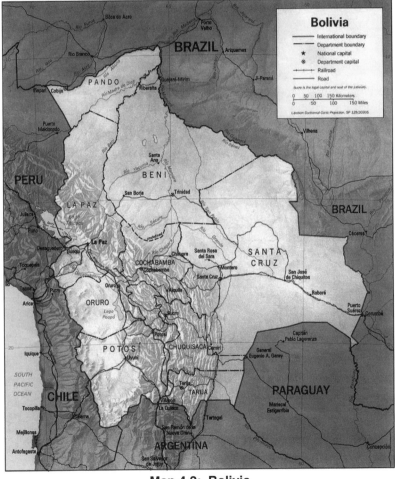

Map 4.2: Bolivia
(Source: Courtesy of General Libraries, University of Texas at Austin, from their website for map designator "bolivia_rel93.pdf")

stitution. He has campaigned for a new constitution to en-shrine the party's nationalisation and land redistribution programme. . . .

He pledged to raise taxes on foreign mining firms and re-distribute one-fifth of Bolivia's [rural] land to peasant farmers. . . .

. . . [His] promise to relax restrictions on growing coca, the raw material for cocaine, could make him a thorn in the side of the US. . . .

He is an admirer of two Latin American populist firebrands—Cuba's Fidel Castro and Venezuela's Hugo Chavez.[13]

— BBC *Country Profile*

A quick look at Bolivia's past may shed more light on what—ex-actly—has been happening there lately. Back in 1967, the U.S. helped its government to suppress a peasant uprising led by Ernesto "Che" Guevara. Then, from 1969 to 1985, there were a series of successful and aborted military coups in Bolivia. In 1989, leftist Jaime Paz Zamora became president. A year later, some four million acres of rain forest were allocated to Bolivia's indigenous peoples. Eight years elapsed, and Hugo Banzer was elected to the nation's highest office, fully intending to free Bolivia from drug trafficking. Just before his term ended, farmers rejected a government offer of $900 each per year if their coca crops were eradicated.

In August 2002, Gonzalo Sanchez de Lozada became president for a second time. His principal opposition had been "coca growers' representative Evo Morales." (See Map 4.3.) Three years later, Evo Morales (now admittedly Socialist) won the presidential election. He soon completed his gas nationalization program, giving the state control over the operations of all foreign energy firms. In August 2007, the leftist presidents of Bolivia, Venezuela and Argentina signed joint energy deals worth more than a billion dollars.[14] It would appear that drug money had helped to monopolize the region's petroleum, but to whose ultimate benefit?

So, in Bolivia, one finds an illustrative mix of drugs, oil, Social-ism, and carefully manipulated democratic process. Over a period of years, a Socialist candidate with a pro-cocaine platform had managed to win the presidential election in a country that borders five others. Now he has nationalized all oil operations and is using

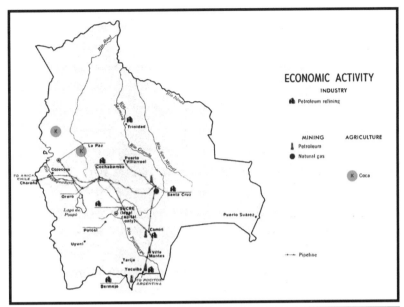

Map 4.3: Locations of Bolivian Petroleum and Coca
(Source: Courtesy of General Libraries, University of Texas at Austin, from their website for map designator "bolivia_econ_1971.jpg")

that asset for international leverage. Again, one wonders to what extent Morales had help. As of April 2008, an increasing number of Cuban and Venezuelan security agents and military personnel were reported in Bolivia to assist him.[15] Thus, an aspiring superpower with an expansionist record may have indirectly provided much of Mr. Morales' campaign advice. If so, that hidden mentor would be willing to combine drugs with politics elsewhere.

5 Chile, Peru, and Ecuador

- Are Shining Path guerrillas still active in Peru?
- What will Ecuador's leftist boss do with his U.S. airbase?

Coca and Poppies Grow Well Here

(Source: DA Pamphlet 550-88 [1994], cover)

Is Chile Still Leftist?

Many Americans know of Chile's past difficulties with General Augusto Pinochet. Following a bloody coup in 1973, his 17-year military dictatorship left more than 3,000 people dead and missing.

Chile is now relatively free of crime and official corruption. The authoritarian "Pinochet-era" constitution has been revised, and the judicial system overhauled. However, Chile's status as the world's largest producer of copper still makes it an international target.[1] (See Map 5.1.)

Michelle Bachelet has been Chile's duly elected president since 2006. A former health minister, and later defense minister, she is the fourth consecutive president from the Concertacion coalition that has led Chile since the end of military rule in 1990.[2] So, with a woman in charge, one would assume the old bugaboo of Socialism had finally departed. Unfortunately, this is not the case. A little of Chile's late-20th-Century history might help to dispel this illusion.

Pinocet had seized power from, and in fact killed, the world's first democratically elected Socialist president—Salvador Allende. Then, ten years after Pinochet stepped down, another Socialist—Ricardo Lagos—was elected president.[3] Madame Bachelet has since taken his place. During the Pinochet years, she worked undercover for the Socialist Youth.[4] So, there is little doubt that Socialism is again alive and well in Chile.

> 2005 December—Presidential elections. Socialist Michelle Bachelet gains the most votes but fails to win more than 50% support, forcing a second-round vote. . . .
> 2006 January—Michelle Bachelet wins the second round of presidential elections to become Chile's first woman president and the fourth consecutive head of state from the centre-left Concertacion coalition. . . .
> 2006 August—Chile and China sign a free-trade deal, Beijing's first in South America.[5]
> — BBC's *Timeline: Chile*

Here, like in Argentina, the army had countered a democratically elected Marxist regime, instead of a Marxist rebellion. Within Chile's northern neighbor, there is flagrant Communism in its most warlike form. There, Maoist guerrillas have been active since 1980.

Peru's Still Shaky Future

Like many other South American nations, Peru has alternated between democracy and dictatorship. (See Map 5.2.) The only difference is that some of its coups were by leftist army elements and some of its election victories were by rightist politicians. As the rest, Peru is deeply divided politically and economically. A minority

Map 5.1: Chile

(Source: Courtesy of General Libraries, University of Texas at Austin, from their website for map designator "chile_rel_1974.pdf")

elite of Spanish descent controls most of the wealth and political power, while indigenous citizens are largely excluded from either. Over the years, both Communist camps have attempted to exploit this imbalance. While the Marxist-Leninist Tupac Amaru's begin-

Map 5.2: Peru and Ecuador
(Source: Courtesy of General Libraries, University of Texas at Austin, from their website for map designator "peru_rel_06.pdf")

nings can be traced to Cuba (while still a Soviet proxy), the Maoist Shining Path's roots are decidedly Maoist. During Peru's brutal war against both sets of rebels in the 1980's and 1990's, more than 69,000 people were killed.[6] As early as 1982, deaths and "disappearances" at the hands of government agencies started to escalate. While unsuccessfully seeking a military solution to the growing terrorism, the Garcia administration allegedly committed human-rights violations that are still under investigation. Among them are the following: (1) the Accomarca massacre, where 47 campesinos were shot to death by Peruvian armed forces in August 1985; (2) the summary execution of more than 200 inmates during prison riots in 1986; and (3) the Cayara massacre in which some 30 peasants were killed and dozens more disappeared in May 1988. According to an official inquiry, an estimated 1,600 disappearances took place during Garcia's presidency alone.[7]

The Shining Path guerrilla campaign soon intensified. By 1990, some 3,000 political murders had been reported, and a driverless car had rolled up to and exploded within 100 yards of the American embassy. One U.S. State Dept. publication attributed the bombing to the Shining Path, while another credited the Tupac Amaru. Later that year, center-right candidate Alberto Fujimori was elected president on an anti-corruption platform. Though a devout rightist himself, he then took a page out of the leftist's playbook at the expense of the democratic process (and his public image). Six months after inauguration, he pushed through a constitutional amendment allowing the trial of all suspected terrorists by military court. Then, with army backing, he suspended all constitutional rights, dissolved the courts, and arranged the election of a new single-chamber legislature. The Shining Path's leader was eventually arrested and put in prison. By 1993, a new constitution had been adopted, enabling Fujimori to seek re-election. A year later, some 6,000 Shining Path guerrillas surrendered to authorities. In 1995, Fujimori was re-elected, and officials convicted of human-rights abuses pardoned.[8] But, the "good guys" had sent the wrong signal to the voting public, and that public would remember it.

It was not long before Tupac Amaru guerrillas had taken hostages at the Japanese ambassador's residence and then faced a nearly perfect building assault plan (from the inside out). By the turn of the century, the Peruvian human-rights ombudsman's office made it clear that no fewer than 4,000 people had "disappeared" since 1980 during the government's war against the left-wing rebels. Shortly thereafter, Mr. Fujimori was unceremoniously sacked as president by Peru's Congress and charged with dereliction of duty by its courts.[9]

In 2001, Toledo becomes Peru's first president of native origin. Within two years, Peru's constitutional court has struck down Fujimori's anti-terror laws and given more than 1,900 jailed Shining Path members the right to retrials by civilian court. At the end of 2006, Alan Garcia becomes president for the second time in 20 years after just barely defeating his left-leaning opponent—Ollanta Humala. Humala, an army officer, had attempted a coup against Fujimori but was later pardoned. By publicly endorsing Humala during the 2006 election, Venezuela's Hugo Chavez revealed to the world what part Humala was to play in the "Bolivarization" of South America. In late 2007, Fujimori was extradited from Japan on charges of corruption and human-rights abuses and jailed in Peru for six years.[10]

The Peruvian government has managed considerable gains against the Shining Path and Tupac Amaru guerrilla groups over the years. But, violence—in the form of murders and gang warfare—is still a big problem in Peru and undoubtedly linked to the drug trade. Peru is one of South America's biggest producers of coca—the raw material of cocaine. Facing the Pacific, it is also an important transportation link between Asia and Brazil.[11] That link is particularly important to the export of South America's considerable mineral wealth to aspiring superpowers.

Tupac Amaru's Cuban Affiliation

The Tupac Amaru Revolutionary Movement (Movimiento Revolucionario Tupac Amaru or MRTA) is a Cuban-inspired guerrilla movement that was most active in Peru from 1984 to 1997. Unlike the Shining Path, the Tupac Amaru is Marxist-Leninist in both ideology and combat method (preferring urban initiatives). As were the Soviet and Chinese factions in southern Africa in the 1980's, the Marxist-Leninist Tupac Amaru and Maoist Shining Path are marginally rivals. With Abimael Guzman Reynoso now in prison, Gabriel Macario is the Shining Path's top leader at-large. With Victor Polay in jail, Hugo Avalleneda Valdez is the MRTA's acting head.[12]

The Tupac Amaru received its initial support and training from Cuba. It also has ties to the Colombian FARC [before it became Maoist] and the Salvadorian FMLN. Some Tupac Amaru rebels are known to have fought with the FMLN in El Salvador.[13]

The Shining Path Was a PRC Initiative from Its Inception

The U.S. soldiers who helped to quell the Shining Path in the early 1990's knew its founder had been trained in China.[14]

He [Abimael Guzman] visited the People's Republic of China for the first time in 1965. After serving as the head of personnel for . . . [a] University, Guzman left the institution in the mid-1970's and went underground.

In the [late] 1960's, the Peruvian Communist Party splintered over ideological and personal disputes. Guzman, who had taken a pro-Chinese rather than pro-Soviet line, emerged as the leader of the [pro-Chinese] faction which came to be known as the "Shining Path" . . . He . . . [soon] began advocating a peasant-led revolution on the Maoist model. . . .

The Shining Path movement was at first largely . . . [limited] to academic circles in Peruvian universities. In the late 1970's, however, the movement developed into a guerrilla group centered around Ayacucho. In May 1980, the group launched its war against the government of Peru by burning the ballot boxes in Chuschi, a village near Ayacucho, in an effort to disrupt the first democratic elections in the country since 1964. Shining Path eventually grew to control vast rural territories in central and southern Peru and achieved a presence even in the outskirts of Lima, where it staged numerous attacks. The purpose of Shining Path's campaign was to demoralize and undermine the government of Peru in order to create a situation conducive to a violent coup which would put its leaders in power. The Shining Path targeted not only the army and police, but also government employees at all levels, other leftist militants such as members of the Tupac Amaru Revolutionary Movement (MRTA), workers who did not participate in the strikes organized by the group, peasants who cooperated with the government in any way (including by voting in democratic elections), and ordinary middle-class inhabitants of Peru's main cities. . . .

. . . [H]e declared Maoism as a "third and higher stage of Marxism," having defined Maoism as "people's war." In 1989, Guzman declared that the Shining Path (which he referred to as the "Communist Party of Peru") had progressed from waging a people's war to waging a "war of movements."[15]

There was more to bringing the Shining Path under control than death squads, and within its details may lie much of the solution for the future. The Peruvian army did not bother to outpost the villages that abutted the Shining Path's home ground. Instead, it armed their residents and periodically visited them by patrol. Called "Mesas Redondos," these villages loosely approximated a belt of defensive strongpoints.[16] The genius of this strategy may have been in its shifting of responsibility to resist the Shining Path onto the villagers themselves. In essence, the strategy obstructed the sea through which the Maoist rebels had to swim to attack the rest of Peruvian society.

The Shining Path Today

Unlike the Colombian FARC in its infancy, Peru's Shining Path has always been Maoist.[17] It emerged in Peru in 1980. FARC had been present in Colombia since 1964 but did not become a "people's army" of Maoist model until 1982.[18] Thus, it is quite possible that China took a more active interest in South America after its initial successes in South Africa, and before the demise of the Soviet Union.

The Shining Path, though greatly weakened in the 1990's by the capture of its leader Abimael Guzman, still has about 200 core members who receive funding through drug trade involvement. Its headquarters is thought to be in the upper Huallaga Valley.[19] That valley is well known for coca growing and drug trafficking to Colombia.[20] The Shining Path is also active in the Ene River and the Apurimac Valley of central Peru.[21] Unfortunately, the U.N. International Children's Emergency Fund (UNICEF) has found that most of the coca pickers in the northeast and southeast are children.[22] A much smaller Shining Path nucleus may now be using children to preclude another government attack. While good news for counterinsurgency "experts," it is less so for 4GW watchers. They are equally worried about the political and economic aspects of the Maoist method.

With Garcia now back in power in Peru, one can expect more Shining Path activity and more government excesses. But that activity may not be the same as before. There is likely to be just enough FARC-supported guerrilla activity to create a diversion for initiatives in the "non-martial" arenas of 4GW. In February 2008, seven Peruvians were arrested after returning from a meeting in Ecuador, at which FARC showed them how to "destabilize" Peru. Meanwhile, Hugo Chavez continues to fund Ollanta Humala's left-wing political party and other leftist activities, like a recent protest by farmers.[23]

Despite all the 4GW political emphasis, there will almost certainly be armed protection of the Peruvian coca fields. Not since a car bomb was detonated near Lima's American embassy in March 2002 has the Shining Path been suspected of major attack. While some terrorism experts have warned that it is now regrouping and recruiting new members, few Peru-watchers believe it can re-acquire its previous military scale. At last report, the Shining Path was attempting to rebuild the support and influence at the universities that it enjoyed in its infancy.[24] Peru's neighbor to the north no longer needs Communist guerrillas, because it has a new leftist president.

Ecuador's Fall

Ecuador has a long history of infighting among its top government echelons. In November 2002, leftist and former coup leader Lucio Gutierrez won the presidential elections. A month later, Ecuador's Congress replaced most of its Supreme Court. In April 2005, Congress voted to oust President Gutierrez, and Alfredo Palacio took his place. In October, former president Gutierrez was arrested on charges of endangering national security. Then, a few months later, those charges were dropped by a judge. About this same time, there were reports of Venezuelan soldiers training rebels in the mountains. Those "rebels" may have been Ecuadorian malcontents or just Colombian FARC personnel taking refuge on the Ecuadorian side of the border.

Venezuela's leftist government is training communist rebels in Ecuador, according to an Ecuadorian military intelligence report.

The El Comercio newspaper reported that the Alfarist Liberation Army has been operating since 2001.

The four-page report said a new subversive group was germinating in Ecuador and that certain of its members had sporadic contacts with members of the FARC . . . and had received training in Venezuela. . . .

According to the report in the Ecuador newspaper, Venezuelans are behind a military link with the group in Ecuador. . . .

"An armed group called the ELA has begun activities and its leaders are receiving strategic and military training from the FARC at a hacienda in north Ecuador," the report said.[25]

— *World Tribune,* 25 October 2005

Through it all, there was strong anti-U.S. sentiment in Ecuador. In 2006 March, nationwide protests erupted over a proposed free-trade agreement with America. Three months later, Ecuador canceled its operating contract with U.S. oil company Occidental Petroleum.[26]

Then, Rafael Correa managed to win the democratic election in November 2006. By promising a "social revolution to benefit the poor," he instantly joined the club of Latin America's most left-leaning leaders—Venezuelan President Chavez and Bolivian President Morales. Soon Correa had rejected the idea of a free-trade pact with the U.S., saying it would hurt Ecuador's farmers. And he further planned to keep the U.S. military from using its Manta air base on the Pacific for drug surveillance flights when that treaty expires in 2009. He was even opposed to Colombia's coca spraying along their common border, saying that the spray would drift into Ecuador and kill his crops.[27] He has a good point; Ecuador has its own coca fields.

On 3 March 2008, Colombian troops made a one-mile incursion into Ecuadorian territory to kill a top FARC leader. On his laptop computer, they found proof of the following: (1) $300 million in Venezuelan funds; (2) talks with Ecuador's Interior Minister about political legitimacy for the FARC (a claim later rescinded); and (3) FARC contributions to Correa's presidential campaign. Within days, the rulers of Venezuela and Ecuador had massed troops on their borders with Colombia and threatened war. Then, Nicaragua's ruler broke off diplomatic relations with Colombia. Not until President Uribe of Colombia had publicly apologized at a Dominican Republic summit, was the situation defused. The violent look on Rafael Correa's face during that apology spoke volumes.[28]

The President of Ecuador seems now to have adequately demonstrated his intention to support Venezuela's plans to "Socialize" the region. And like Chavez, he will allow Chinese interests onto his soil. However in Ecuador, the Chinese will have more than docks or oil fields. They will have their own air base.

Ecuadorian President Rafael Correa will not renew its [his goverment's] contract with the United States when the agreement for American use of the Manta airport base expires on 2009. But Correa offered the air base's concession to China during his state visit to the Asian country.

According to the Ecuadorian leader's website, the shift in contract partners is to make Manta China's gateway to Latin America. Correa had expressed during his presidential campaign [that] Ecuador needs to have more Asian investments to help the country upgrade its infrastructure requirements and to expand its international trade.

Business News America said a subsidiary of a Hong Kong-based company Hutchison Port Holdings, the Terminales del Ecuador, was given the Manta port concession.

It is not only Ecuador, which will benefit from the Chinese entry into Latin America. Brazil will likewise profit since Ecuador and Brazil inked an agreement building the Manta-Manaus link by rail. Aside from Terminales, other Chinese firms are interested in investing in the rail project. Ecuador also wants to connect highways with neighbors Colombia, Peru and Brazil. . . .

Manta is presently used by the U.S. Air Force's Southern Command to combat illegal cocaine trade in the region.[29]

— AHN News (Ecuador), 26 November 2007

61

The Chinese are obviously planning for Manta, Ecuador, what they are already doing in Lobito, Angola. There, the refurbished Benguela Railway helps them to extract the mineral riches of Zambia and the Congo. As did the "Tanzam Railway" at Dar es Salaam (Tanzania) in the 1970's, the Manta-Manaus line may also be used to transport arms and trained insurgents into the continent's interior.

In an April 2007 referendum, Ecuadorian voters supported President Correa's plan to form a citizens' assembly to rewrite the constitution. He intends to make about the same modifications as Chavez attempted in Venezuela.[30] That would make Ecuador a Socialist state.

The thought of a Chinese airbase in Ecuador is unsettling enough. Unfortunately, there is also a good possibility of a Chinese naval base in Panama (at what was formerly Rodman U.S. Naval Facility).

6 Colombia and Panama

- Is Colombia's FARC just another guerrilla group?
- What part does Panama play in the Communists' plan?

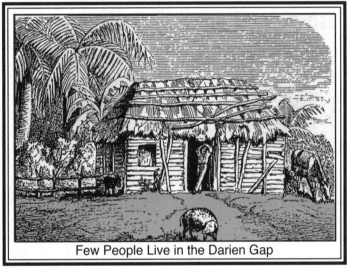

Few People Live in the Darien Gap

(Source: DA Pamphlet 550-36 [1991], p. 37)

Colombia in the Fight of its Life

Most Americans are aware of Colombia's trouble with drug traffickers and insurgents. What they don't realize is the tremendous influence those homegrown elements are now having on the rest of the region. Colombia has been the site of a protracted struggle against several large guerrilla factions. (See Map 6.1.) Three of these factions are leftist—FARC, ELN, and M-19. And one started out as a rightist paramilitary federation—the AUC. Of the four, the FARC is by far the most dangerous. If anything, its power in the rural departments of Colombia has increased over the years, despite the best efforts of the U.S.-supported Colombian military establishment. (See Maps 6.2 and 6.3.) The FARC still regularly targets rural outposts, infrastructure, and its political adversaries.

Then, there are Colombia's other three guerrilla factions. While the ELN has been talking with Colombian delegates in Cuba, it has yet to accept a formal peace process. The AUC did agree to demobilize its combatants, and some 23,000 have gone home. But, there have been cease-fire violations. They include mass killings, kidnappings, assassinations, illegal evictions, robberies, and the recruitment of children. Like the FARC, both the ELN and AUC use the Venezuelan side of the border as a safe haven to rest, secure logistical supplies, commit kidnappings, and trans-ship arms and drugs.[1] The M-19 that briefly appeared in the mid-1980's is not currently active.

To see how these various factions may be contributing to a Communist takeover attempt, one must investigate them in the reverse order of their inception.

The AUC

The AUC, or "paramilitaries," is an umbrella federation that was formed in April of 1997. Its original intent was to organize the various militias that sprang up to defend big-land owners and other pro-government segments of Colombian society. Unfortunately, the AUC soon replaced most of its counterguerrilla activity with drug trade involvement. Most of the AUC's military structure has been dismantled, and the majority of its top military chiefs are in jail. Over 31,000 members were demobilized between 2003 and 2006. But, like parts of Central America, Colombia now faces a few paramilitary groups that refused to disarm and gangs of demobilized personnel. Unlike the AUC, the new groups have made no attempt to fight guerrillas and are more interested in drug trafficking, other criminal endeavors, and controlling local politics.[2] They most closely resemble the *maras* of El Salvador.

While Colombia's homicide, kidnapping, and terror attack rates have decreased in recent years, those statistics are misleading. They are down largely because of temporary cease-fires and the AUC's demobilization. There has not been commensurate progress with other factions, like the FARC.[3]

When fully active, the paramilitary forces were strongest in northwestern Colombia's Antioquia, Cordoba, Sucre, Atlantico, Magdalena, Cesar, La Guajira, and Bolivar Departments. They also had affiliated groups in the coffee region, Valle del Cauca, and Meta Department.[4] That put some of the paramilitaries very

Map 6.1: Colombia
(Source: Courtesy of General Libraries, University of Texas at Austin, from their website for map designator "colombia_rel_2001.pdf")

65

near to the north end of the Panama border. Maps 6.2 and 6.3 tell an interesting story about the rest of that border. In 2002, there was a FARC corridor at its center that may have connected to a Tuira River resupply route through Panama or itself functioned as a swampy refuge. Then, in 2005, a FARC presence was noted in Colombia's Choco Department at the lesser-populated southern end of that border. This may mark its shift to an alternate resupply route or safe area inside Panama. The southeastern end of the isthmus and Gulf of San Miguel are still two of the wildest and most isolated places on earth.[5] That makes the tiny towns of La Palma and El Real very interesting to drug smugglers and guerrilla resuppliers alike. Neither town is connected by road to any other place in Panama or Colombia, but both have access to the Pacific Ocean and the tiny boats that ply its coast. El Real is additionally on the Tuira River.

M-19

In 1985, a shadowy group calling itself "M-19" brazenly attacked the Supreme Court at the Palace of Justice in Bogota. A Colombian army counterattack left all the rebels and 11 of the 25 Supreme Court Justices dead. Though much of M-19 remained intact after the raid, it was now without five of its leaders. In March 1990, it signed a peace treaty with the government. While its political affiliations can be traced back to Cuba, it was in part supported by drug traffickers.[6] Note the reference to a "people's army" in the following excerpt. M-19 may have been destined to become FARC's special operations branch.

> Cuba also was reported "to provide advice, communications, training, and some financial advice to several violent South American organizations." This included training the Colombian M-19 guerrillas, with the objective of establishing a "people's army." ("Cuba's Renewed Support for Violence in Latin America," *Dept. of State Bulletin,* Feb. 1982, 77) [7]
> — U.S. Congressional Report, 13 May 2005

After the first hours of the M-19 siege, a fire broke out and burned numerous court records on the fourth floor of the Palace of Justice, including the files of every extradition case.[8] Thus, the attack may

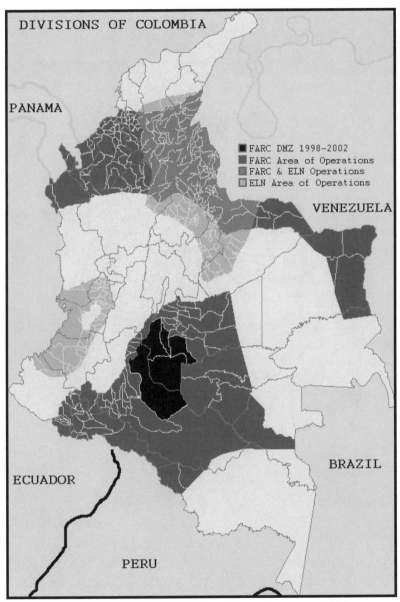

DIVISIONS OF COLOMBIA

PANAMA

■ FARC DMZ 1998-2002
■ FARC Area of Operations
■ FARC & ELN Operations
□ ELN Area of Operations

VENEZUELA

ECUADOR

BRAZIL

PERU

Map 6.2: Guerrilla Areas of Colombia, 1998-2002
(Source: Courtesy of Free Software Foundation (GNU Free Documentation License), from wikipedia.org s.v. "FARC," for map designator "Colombia_Rebel.png")

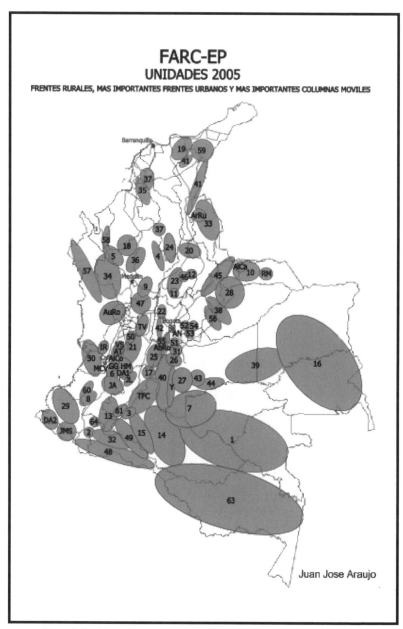

Map 6.3: Number and Location of FARC Units in 2005
(Source: Courtesy of Free Software Foundation (GNU Free Documentation License), from wikipedia.org s.v."FARC," for map designator "FARC%2C_unidades_2005.png")

have been to stop the extradition of FARC leaders arrested for drug trafficking, or simply to appear drug inspired. Either way, more deception occurred than in the average South American guerrilla attack. Thus, one of China's famous 36 Stratagems is suspected. Of course, organized greed can produce mixed signals. But M-19 appeared shortly after the Maoist Shining Path made its debut in Peru and the FARC went Maoist in method. Thus, M-19 may have constituted a part of the PRC's new strategy for South America. With what had happened in southern Africa, few would doubt that the Chinese had designs on Latin America. M-19's unique mix of tactical proficiency and ulterior motive would certainly suggest an Asian architect. The next outfit is less complicated.

The ELN

The ELN is a Colombian Marxist insurgent group that was formed in 1965 by Colombian devotees of Fidel Castro and Che Guevara. In fact, those founders had just come back from guerrilla warfare training in Cuba. Though rurally based, the ELN now has several urban units. It thus more closely follows the Marxist-Leninist model of city-oriented revolution than the FARC. The ELN conducts kidnappings, hijackings, bombings, and extortion; and it has minimal conventional military capability. It often takes for ransom the foreign employees of large corporations, especially those from the petroleum industry. While its traditional sources of income have been kidnapping and oil company extortion, it is now taxing the narcotics trade.

The ELN appears to target energy infrastructure. While it has inflicted major damage on both fuel pipelines and electricity grids, it has lost much of its capacity to launch such attacks in recent years. In December 2005, the ELN began preliminary talks with the Colombian government in Cuba, but it has yet to agree to a formal peace process.[9]

The ELN operates mostly in rural and mountainous areas of northern, northeastern, and southwestern Colombia, and the Venezuelan border regions. (Refer back to Map 6.2 and forward to Map 6.4.) It gets external assistance from Cuba in the form of medical care and political consultation.[10] While the ELN remains Marxist, the FARC has definitely turned Maoist.

69

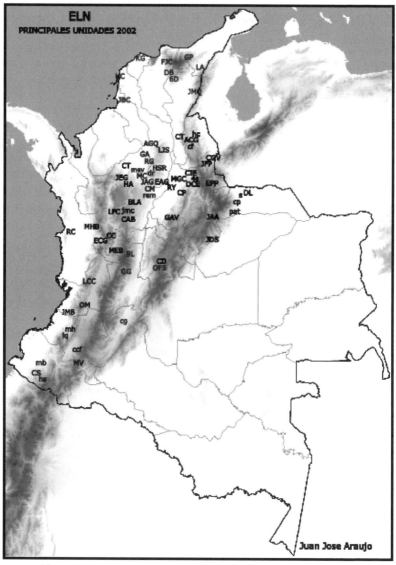

Map 6.4: Number and Location of ELN Units in 2002
(Source: Courtesy of Free Software Foundation (GNU Free Documentation License), from wikipedia.org s.v."ELN," for map designator "ELN%2C_principa...des_in_2002")

The FARC

The FARC may have had its roots in the 1950's friction between liberal and conservative militias. It was formally established in 1964 by the Colombian Communist Party to defend what were Communist-controlled rural areas.[11] It has since carried out bombings, murders, kidnappings, extortions, hijackings, and mortar attacks. It has also launched both conventional and guerrilla war attacks against martial, political, and economic targets.[12] The above references to "rural" and "conventional" may mean that the FARC has already worked through all three of Mao's martial stages.

Unlike the earlier forms of Marxism-Leninism in which the urban proletariat was seen as the main source of revolution, and the countryside was largely ignored, Mao focused on the peasantry as a revolutionary force which, he said, could be mobilized by a Communist Party with their knowledge and leadership. . . . Furthermore, unlike other forms of Marxism-Leninism in which large-scale industrial development was seen as a positive force, Maoism made all-round rural development the priority. Mao felt that this strategy made sense during the early stages of socialism in a country in which most of the people were peasants.

Unlike most other political ideologies, including other socialist and Marxist ones, Maoism contains an integral military doctrine and explicitly connects its political ideology with military strategy. In Maoist thought, power comes from the barrel of the gun, and the peasantry can be mobilized to undertake a "people's war." This involves guerrilla warfare using three stages. The first stage involves mobilizing the peasantry and setting up organization. The second stage involves setting up rural base areas and increasing co-ordination among the guerrilla organizations. The third stage involves a transition to conventional warfare. Maoist military doctrine likens guerilla fighters to fish swimming in a sea of peasants, who provide logistical support.[13]

The FARC enjoys safe havens just across Colombia's borders with Venezuela, Ecuador, and Panama.[14] While the latter has been confirmed,[15] it does not mean that the Panamanian government approves. The terrain and climate at southeastern end of the Panamanian isthmus are so inhospitable that few people can stand it. Colombian government forces have recently ventured deep into the FARC's southern base area, but their quarry still holds enough sway over the nation to make it a regional threat. To see how much that sway grew between 2002 and 2005, look back at Maps 6.2 and 6.3.

The FARC Is No Longer Just a Guerrilla Outfit

In December 2005, the FARC showcased its tactical prowess by successfully ambushing a sizable Colombian army column. Some 300 rebels trapped 80 government soldiers in an area sown with land mines southwest of Bogota and then opened fire with small arms, killing 29 soldiers. Six months prior to that time, the FARC had killed another 22 soldiers near their army base in the southern province of Putumayo.[16]

Unbeknownst to most Americans, the FARC is no longer a guerrilla organization. For over 20 years, it has been a Communist "people's army." It made that transition in 1982 after adding "EP" to its name. Its ideological leader at that time was Jacobo Arenas, the *nom de guerre* of Luis Morantes. A closer look at his beliefs reveals a distinctively Maoist outlook on revolution. There is no evidence, however, that Arenas ever traveled to China, as had the founder of Peru's Shining Path.

The FARC has openly sought to put in practice Communist theory from 1964 onward. One person believed responsible for this practice was Jacobo Arenas. . . . Many writings of Jacobo Arenas are about the adaptation of Communism into the Colombian socio-economic reality. . . .
Jacobo Arenas . . . loved what he referred to as the "peasant culture" in China, appreciating the role of the People's Liberation Army (PLA). He believed that the PLA were supporting their people's work, just as he considered that the guerrillas in Marquetalia were doing the same. He taught FARC cadres to have solidarity with China in the future.[17]

The role of Jacobo Arenas in FARC's military reorganization was significant. After the Seventh Guerilla Conference in 1982, Arenas started to work toward the goal of turning the FARC from a guerrilla organization to a rebel army (the "People's Army") [Ejercito del Pueblo].[18]

> Arenas . . . tried to implement a system similar to what the Chinese people and peasants were doing, as originally initiated by Mao Zedong. . . .
> . . . He taught FARC cadres to have solidarity with China in the future. . . . Arenas further taught his cadres that the foundations for a manufacturing culture in China were established by Mao Zedong, and that one day they would be the leaders in the field, by supplying anything required in the world.[19]

At the 1982 conference, the FARC added "EP" to its name as an expression of an expected progression from guerrilla into conventional warfare.[20] Like a national army, the FARC-EP has a military academy and a two-month basic training program, mainly involving infantry tactics. After basic training, guerrilla fighters are periodically re-assessed through evaluation and performance records. Those with the best records are sent to advanced training.[21] A few Angola veterans may still teach at those schools, but most likely the next generation of Asian-trained Cuban does. A widely circulated photograph shows several FARC fighters wearing uniforms of the same dark-brown woolen material once used by Chinese and North Korean armies.[22]

More on the 4GW Aspects of FARC-EP's Method

Attendees at the 1982 conference also agreed that FARC-EP would follow a traditional Communist strategy known as the "combination of all forms of struggle." Because that struggle could be either political or martial,[23] it partially resembled what is now known as 4GW.

Like the Mahdi Army in Sadr City and southern Iraq, the FARC-EP has created a "state-within-a-state" throughout much of rural Colombia. What funds that state are taxes.

> Now they [the FARC] tax every stage of the drug business, from the chemicals needed to process the hardy coca bush

into cocaine and the opium poppy into heroin, right up to charging for the processed drugs to be flown from illegal airstrips they control.[24]

— BBC News, September 2003

Prior to becoming interested in drugs, the FARC supported itself by collecting "war taxes" from the inhabitants, merchants, and landowners of the areas it controlled. During the 1970's and 1980's, it established its own schools, judicial system, health care, and agrarian economy. In essence, it had created its own *de facto* state in southern Colombia. While it had units throughout the country, it became strongest in Colombia's most remote rural areas, where it became known for improving health care, schools, and infrastructure.[25]

Paradoxically, the FARC-EP has not most heavily attacked Colombia's military, but rather its political and economic resources. Its target percentages from 1968 to late 2007 best reflect that unexpected agenda: (1) government—27%; (2) utilities—22%; (3) transportation—9%; (4) private citizens and property—9%; (5) police—8%; (6) businesses—7%; and (7) military—1%.[26] Instead of directly confronting the Colombian army, it has attempted to discredit Bogota's ability to govern and support its rural population. It may simply want enough chaos throughout the countryside to make its "state-within-a-state" appealing to the residents. By abducting up to 3000 people a year and holding another 3,000 in concentration camps, the FARC-EP effectively adds to that chaos while appearing to quell it.[27] Might it be using a 4GW variant of the Maoist method, wherein attacks on government forces are largely a feint? While all aspects of that variant must be considered, the economic is the most interesting.

Maoism emphasizes . . . village-level industries independent of the outside world.[28]

The village industry of most interest was drugs. (See Maps 6.5 and 6.6.) While the FARC began as a purely guerrilla movement, it got involved with drug trafficking in the 1980's (about the same time it became a people's army).[29] Now, it has ties with major drug cartels,[30] kidnapped children working in the fields, and other children protecting those fields.[31] But Arenas may have had in mind more of a militaristic state—like that of North Korea. Some say that, after he died in 1990, the FARC's leadership re-interpreted his ideology, to include the legalization of narcotics.[32] There is another possibility, of course. Jacobo Arenas may have been more interested in how North Korea was able to survive economically.

> Jacobo Arenas played an important role in key FARC financial matters. . . . He considered the example of North Korea as particularly useful. Kim Il Sung thus established a socialist state of North Korea, which to several Western analysts was a sort of "Secret State." . . . The term "secret state" was introduced as a way of describing that North Korea's economy and military build-up was mostly done by its own strength with relatively limited help from outside (coming from the Soviet Union and the People's Republic of China, for example). This would mean that North Korea's survival throughout the Cold War demonstrated that a policy of "standing on its own feet" was the only way to adapt to changing situations in the outside world.[33]

Jacobo Arenas envisioned an agrarian and Communist state with decentralized industry. How better could he achieve that vision than through thousands of tiny farms growing a high-value crop? He also saw how politics could be combined with warfare to overthrow a government.[34] Only drugs could bring in enough money to acquire high-level political favors. North Korea now has three sources of income—foreign assistance (mostly from China), missile sales, and drug trafficking.[35] It is the world's third largest producer of heroin, uses its ships to transport that heroin, and deals directly with the Hong Kong triads. The U.S. State Department cites "credible reports of North Korean boats . . . transporting heroin and uniformed North Korean personnel transferring drugs from North Korean vessels to traffickers' boats."[36] The prestigious *New York Times* has confirmed two examples. In 2003, Australian commandos stormed a freighter registered in Tuvalu, a tiny island nation in the South Pacific, after it was seen unloading 110 pounds of high-grade heroin. That vessel (the Pong Su) had sailed from North Korea to Singapore under a North Korean flag and then switched its registration to Tuvalu before sailing on to Australia. A year earlier, a Spanish warship

Map 6.5: Colombian Coca Growing Areas in 2006
(Source: Courtesy of General Libraries, University of Texas at Austin, from their website for map designator "colombia_cocoa_density_2002.gif")

Map 6.6: Colombian Poppy-Growing Areas in 2002
(Source: Courtesy of General Libraries, University of Texas at Austin, from their website for map designator "colombia_poppy_areas_2002.gif")

had stopped a North-Korean-owned freighter registered in Cambodia. Though purportedly carrying cement to Yemen, it turned out to have 15 Scud missiles on board.[37]

A warped 4GW strategy was thus born out the North Korean way of doing things. It provided a way for the downtrodden peasantry to make a subsistence living, while insuring an unlimited cash flow to the ruling party. With the people and cash, the FARC could then more easily get leftist candidates elected. If those candidates fell a little short at the polls, it could use those same two assets to fuel a rebellion.

As such a plan makes the FARC self-sufficient financially, it makes its proxy status much less apparent. Acquiring arms and training on the open market creates no trail back to its ideological mentor. The FARC helps to finance its operations through ransom and extortion but derives most of its income from drug trade taxation. It also targets anyone suspected of conspiring with the military or paramilitaries.[38] So, in essence, it taxes all drug-related activity, and then kidnaps or otherwise terrorizes anyone who objects.

The Tactical History of the FARC-EP

By the latter half of the 1990's, the FARC-EP had become strong enough to launch large multi-unit attacks against Colombian military installations. On 30 August 1996, it attacked the Las Delicias military base in the Putumayo Department, in which the Colombian army lost 54 dead, 15 wounded, and 60 captured. This surprise attack had been carried out at night after extensive intelligence gathering. Some 15 hours of subsequent fighting resulted in the complete destruction of the base. A week later, an attack on a military outpost in the Guaviare Department led to almost a month of fighting and 130 Colombian soldiers and civilians killed. In March 1998, some 700 FARC fighters ambushed the 52nd counterguerrilla battalion of the Colombian Army's 3rd Mobile Brigade. That battalion had entered the town of Penas Coloradas with the intention of damaging the FARC's infrastructure in the lower Caguan river. When the FARC counterattacked, the Colombian counterguerrilla battalion lost 62 killed, 43 captured, and 49 wounded. In August of that year, the FARC attacked and destroyed another military base in Miraflores in the southern Guaviare. Three months later, its fighters launched a military raid against the Mitu Department capital near the Brazilian border (which they briefly occupied for three days until Colombian reinforcements arrived). During the month of July 1999, the FARC launched another series of multi-unit attacks against military bases in Meta, Guaviare, Huila, Putumayo and Caqueta. In October 2000, it attacked and raided the town of Dabeida, killing 54 Colombian soldiers and policemen. That was the year FARC and ELN units joined forces to attack several paramilitary bases. As a result of this string of FARC victories, the (probably U.S.-trained) Colombian military was forced to abandon its rural-outpost strategy and create fortified strongholds closer to department capitals.[39]

Back in 1998, as an incentive to a cease-fire commitment, Colombian President Andres Pastrana had offered the FARC a de-militarized zone (DMZ) around its historic stronghold in southern Colombia. Comprising some 42,000 square kilometers, this DMZ had 120,000 residents. (Refer back to Map 6.2.) In effect, Colombia had ceded control of this huge region to the rebels. As apparent from the attacks already noted for this period, the people's army took full advantage of this opening. In February 2002, peace nego-tiations with the Pastrana administration broke down when FARC fighters hijacked a plane to kidnap a Colombian Senator. Then, on 7 August, the rebel group launched a large-scale mortar attack on the Presidential Palace where Alvaro Uribe was being inaugurated. From 2004 to 2006, President Uribe struck back with a new U.S.-supported offensive called "Plan Patriota." About 18,000 soldiers attacked the FARC's historical heartland in the south/southeast of Colombia, intending to kill or capture its main leaders. (See Map 6.7.) In response to the government offensive, most FARC forces strategically withdrew deep into their areas of influence. As their heartland is jungle covered and near the equator, they could easily establish new base camps and troop assembly points away from the Colombian Army concentrations. (See Map 6.8.) They also altered their attack strategy. The FARC's most recent attacks have been by "medium-size" unit groupings.[40]

In February 2005, the FARC attacked the Iscuande Marine base in southwestern Colombia, killing 16 and wounding 25 Marines. Later investigations disclosed that the guerrillas had gathered intelligence by either infiltrating the base or bribing its occupants. On 6 April, the FARC clashed with an elite counterguerrilla unit trained by U.S. Special Forces in the oil-rich Arauca Department, killing 17 of them during an attack on their military convoy. A week

79

later, the rebels attacked Toribio, a predominantly indigenous town in the Cauca department, and kept fighting at close quarters for a full month. Starting on June 24th, they attacked military positions in the location of Puerto Asis in the Putumayo Department, killing 25 and wounding 20 in a single operation. Within a month, the FARC had declared an "armed strike," and demanded that all transport over Putumayo's roads be halted. Towards the beginning of September, it supposedly blew up several key electricity towers in that department (though this sounds more like ELN). Then, on 17 December, the FARC launched a massive attack on the remote village of San Marino in the Choco department, killing six police officers and abducting 30. The ELN is believed to have actually participated in this attack. At the end of December, FARC fighters killed 28 Colombian soldiers in a heavily mined rural area near Vista Hermosa in the southern Meta province. The soldiers were part of a brigade tasked with protecting the workers destroying coca plants.[41]

While the FARC-EP's professed goal is to create a Communist agrarian state,[42] it may have a few urban cells. To date, their only activity has been car bombings, grenade attacks, and mortar barrages.[43]

The FARC-EP's Atheistic Signature

There is mounting evidence that the FARC has been kidnapping children to fill its ranks. During recent skirmishes between the Army and a FARC column, 19 of the 77 fighters captured were 15 or under. Of the 46 FARC fighters killed in those skirmishes, 20 were children.[44] As 30 percent of the FARC is female,[45] a fair share of those children were probably girls. If the FARC has been forcing children to fight, it has probably joined the Shining Path in using children to pick coca. This evokes nightmarish images of how the Lord's Army and other African guerrilla groups get children to do their bidding along the Ugandan and Congolese borders with Sudan. A full-blown "people's army" with this little regard for human rights must not be allowed to spread its debased methodology elsewhere in Latin America.

The FARC forcibly enlists any persons between the ages of 13 and 60 to work coca or poppy plantations, and serve in

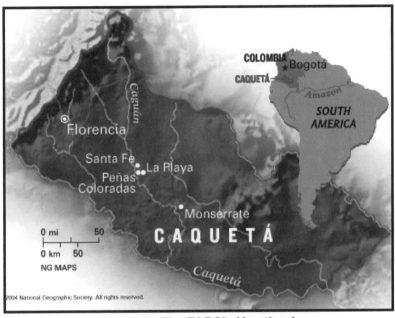

Map 6.7: The FARC's Heartland
(Source: Courtesy of Nat. Geographic Soc., from "An Illegal Cash Crop Sustains . . . 40-Year-Old Guerrilla Movement in Southern Colombia," © July 2004, "FARCzone.pdf.")

the military. The FARC have also targeted religious leaders and banned any spiritual expression.[46]
— PBS's Online News Hour, 2003

Evidence of the FARC-EP's Attempt at Regional Expansion

According to the Memorial Institute for the Prevention of Terrorism (MIPT), the FARC-EP may prefer its current "state-within-a-state" to taking over the Colombian government. Its degree of control over Colombia's countryside gives it enough political leverage to ensure a "relatively safe area" from which to attack the rest of Central and South America for quite some time. Whenever things get a little hot, it has only to hold peace talks.

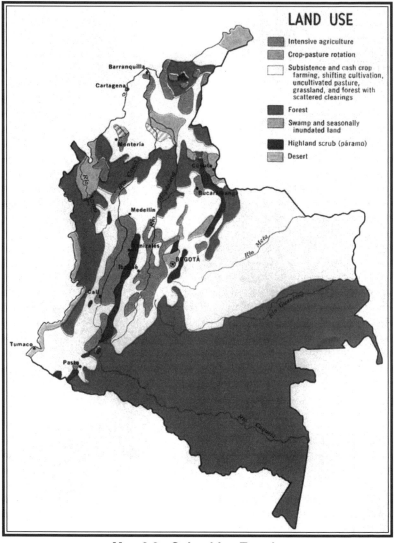

Map 6.8: Colombian Terrain
(Source: Courtesy of General Libraries, University of Texas at Austin, from their website for map designator "colombia_land_1970.jpg")

Today, the FARC's primary goal is territorial control within Colombia. . . .

The FARC's larger goals are a matter for speculation. For four decades the FARC has struggled to overthrow the Colombian government. This does not seem likely unless the FARC dramatically shifts its approach and increases its strength. The more likely outcome is that the FARC will continue to destabilize Colombian democracy but never actually overthrow the government. . . . The FARC aims to maintain its significant financial and *territorial* power (italics added).[47]

— Memorial Inst. for the Prevention of Terrorism

According to MIPT, Colombia functions only as the FARC-EP's base of operations.[43] That means its area of operations is much larger. In fact, FARC operatives have been spotted in no fewer than eight other Latin American nations.[49] Most worrisome to the U.S. are those in Mexico.

Besides a flagrant flow of arms from Venezuela (to include shoulder-fired surface-to-air missiles),[50] the FARC receives covert shipments through Panama and Brazil. In April 2005, the Honduran Security Minister intercepted an overland shipment of small arms from a Central American gang wanting to trade weapons to the FARC for narcotics.[51] Such a shipment would have had to move unobserved through pre-Ortega Nicaragua, Costa Rica, and Panama. The implication is disturbing—the smuggling routes have been so well established that they regularly funnel drugs and people north, and arms south. There will be more on this subject in Chapter 7. The FARC has also been receiving arms for drugs across the Brazilian border.[52]

[L]inks between crime syndicates in [the Paraguayan town of] Ciudad del Este and the FARC reportedly date at least from the mid-1990's. . . . Of three known FARC havens in Brazil, the biggest of them is located in the small city of Guaira in the southern part of Brazil's Parana State at the Paraguay border, only 100 miles (161 kilometers) north of Foz do Iguacu. . . . It is located on a 6,000-hectare ranch belonging to businessman Ahmad Mohamad, a Lebanese naturalized in Paraguay and arrested by Brazil's Federal Police in September 2002 [Godoy, "As Farc usam Brasil para

abrigar elite da guerrilha," *O Estado de Sao Paulo,*
1 March 2003].[53]
　　— Fed. Reseach Div., Lib. of Congress, July 2003

Criminal gangs in Paraguay also have ties to Colombia's
largest rebel group. Paraguayan officials arrested a Colombian citizen in Ciudad del Este last year as he tried
to arrange a cocaine-for-weapons swap on behalf of the
Revolutionary Armed Forces of Colombia (FARC). Links
between crime syndicates in Ciudad del Este and the FARC
date from the mid-1990's at least, when [Paraguayan] Gen.
Oviedo protected Brazilian drug trafficker Fernandinho
Beira Mar, who was captured in southern Colombia last
April while accompanied by FARC rebels.[54]
　　— *Washington Times,* 21 August 2001

What It Would Take to Stop the FARC-EP

There is no doubt that the FARC protects much of Colombia's
drug production, as it is known to operate throughout most of its
coca and poppy growing areas. (Compare Maps 6.2 and 6.3 to Maps
6.5 and 6.6). According to National Public Radio (NPR) in December 2007, cocaine production has risen despite massive U.S. aid to
fight both insurgency and drugs.[55] That means the FARC and any
affiliates will continue to be adequately funded unless major modifications are made to the U.S. strategy for the region. America has
traditionally tried "top-down" solutions to such problems. So, what
undoubtedly needs to be changed is how those guerrillas and drug
traders are combatted at the local level. A FARC chieftain has been
extradited to the U.S. on drug trafficking charges,[56] but what has
been done with his town bullies?
　　Because the rural peasantry of most Latin American countries
has been shortchanged by the urban elite, only a 4GW modification
to America's traditional style of warfare will work. It must be long on
miscreant apprehension and short on bystander duress. In a high-
stakes drug environment, things like raising the salaries of local
policemen becomes as important as their training. Further, there
must be enough U.S. supervision at the local level to prevent any
recurrence of "death squads." Yes, they have occurred in Colombia
as well.

The FARC briefly flirted with a political route to power in the late 1980's, when it established its own party—the Patriotic Union (UP). But the UP was decimated by right-wing death squads (allegedly sponsored by drug traffickers with links to government security forces). Some 3,000 UP members were murdered, including the UP's 1990 presidential candidate, Bernardo Jaramillo Ossa. As the political route was thus effectively closed to FARC members, they returned to the military way. As late as 2003, the FARC was blamed for a car bombing inside Bogota but denied responsibility.[57] Very possibly, that bombing was conducted by the more city-oriented ELN. The two groups have worked together, but not always wholeheartedly.

> The ELN has . . . operated with the FARC-EP. . . . "During 2004, the FARC-EP and the ELN carried out a series of attacks against the civilian population, including several massacres of civilians and kidnappings. . . . There were occasional joint actions by the FARC-EP and the ELN." (Human Rights Commission Report, 28 Feb. 2005)

In mid-2006, mutual rivalries between local FARC and ELN forces escalated into hostilities in Arauca, along the border with Venezuela. According to the BBC, "the FARC have for some years moved to take over ELN territory near the Venezuelan border, and the smaller rebel army reacted by killing several FARC militants." A statement posted on FARC's homepage accused the ELN of "attacks that we only expected from the enemy." (BBC, "Colombian Rebels Turn on Allies," 12 June 2006) [58]

The occasional combat between FARC and ELN is further proof that, like the Chinese and Soviet proxy armies that converged on Rhodesia, they have different mentors and ideologies. Only one of the two guerrilla factions has been spotted in the nation just to the west of Colombia.

Panama Is Still this Hemisphere's Main Trading Hub

As shown in the Introduction, America was more worried about Panama becoming a Cuban-backed Socialist state than a narco-state when its forces invaded that country in 1989. Manuel Noriega's

85

renaming of his national guard the "Panama Defense Forces" was further proof of what he intended. The revolutionary government of Sudan calls its ideology police the "Popular Defense Forces." Panama was of interest to the Cubans and Soviets in 1989, and it is now of interest to the Cubans and Chinese. Otherwise, Hutchison Whampoa (a "Chinese military company"[59]) would not have bought up Rodman Naval Station and most of the docks at both ends of the canal.[60] Panama is, quite simply, the most logical place from which to coordinate revolution in Central America. That's why the U.S. Special Forces launched their regional counterguerrilla operations from there. A nearly impenetrable jungle forms the Darien Gap between Panama and Colombia. It creates not only a long break in the Pan-American Highway, but also a perfect refuge for guerrillas. (See Map 6.9.)

Panama Still Figures Prominently in the Drug Trade

According to the BBC, Panama is "still known as a major transit point for U.S.-bound drugs and illegal immigrants, and a haven for money-laundering."[61] As late as 13 December 2007, the *CIA World Factbook* called Panama a "major cocaine trans-shipment point and primary money-laundering center for narcotics revenue." It further said that "organized illegal narcotics operations in Colombia operate within the remote border region with Panama."[62]

The Panamanian government is friendly to the U.S. and among the handful of nations still recognizing Taiwan. But it has no army and far too few police concurrently to watch the world's biggest drug cartels and spy organizations. (See Figures 6.1 and 6.2.) Still, Panama combats the narcotics-and-arms trade as best it can, considering its proximity to cocaine-producing nations and role as commercial crossroad. Of course, America has helped. The government of Panama has signed agreements with the U.S. on maritime law enforcement, counter-terrorism, counter-narcotics, and stolen vehicles. A three-year investigation by its Drug Prosecutor's Office (DPO), the PTJ (Policia Tecnica Judicial), and other regional agencies made possible the May 2006 arrest in Brazil of Pablo Rayo Montano. Montano was a Colombian-born drug boss whose cartel owned many assets in Panama. Panamanian authorities seized those assets after his indictment by a U.S. federal court in Miami. In March 2007, the U.S. Coast Guard, in cooperation with local agen-

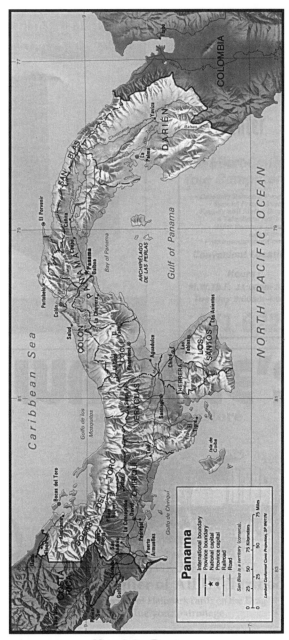

Map 6.9: Panama
(Source: Courtesy of General Libraries, University of Texas atAustin, from their website for map designator "panama_rel_1995.pdf")

87

cies, seized over 38,000 pounds of cocaine off the coast of Panama.[63] Like gambling houses, drug smugglers play the odds to guarantee a profit. If a shipment that large got intercepted, how much more got through?

Is Panama Now the Northern Equivalent to the TBA?

FARC-EP uses the remote areas of eastern Panama as a sanctu-

Figure 6.1: Now Gone Panamanian National Guardsman
(Source: Courtesy of Orion Books, from *World Army Uniforms since 1939*, © 1975, 1980, 1981, 1983 by Blandford Press Ltd., Part II, Plate 101)

ary,[64] and FARC operatives have been spotted in other parts of the country.[65] Combine this FARC presence with the following circumstances, and the U.S. may have a much bigger problem in Panama than it would like to admit. Panama City is at the south end of the canal and a modern, high-rise metropolis that easily provides all the luxury and decadence that any drug trader or foreign emissary could want. Tiny Colon is at the north end of the canal and a free-trade zone in which much money gets laundered.[66] (See Map 6.10.) Many of Noriega's former allies are still in power in Panama,[67] and official

Figure 6.2: Now Gone Panamanian National Guard Paratrooper
(Source: Courtesy of Cassell PLC, from *Uniforms of Elite Forces*, © 1982 by Blandford Press Ltd., No. 90)

corruption is an ongoing problem there.[68] Its communities of Muslims and East Asians are among the largest in the region.[69] While both Russian and Chinese organized-crime families have made Panama their respective bases of operation,[70] only the latter has been spotted in TBA.[71] Thus, in terms of regional stability, these Panama canal cities may have become the northern equivalent of Ciudad del Este. From the latter, all the drug trade and revolution gets coordinated for South America; and, from the former, the same thing may be happening for Central America. Both are in countries that have been traditionally friendly to the U.S. And both contain Chinese triads that orchestrate the regional pillage. But, it would be foolish to think that all the Chinese in Panama are there to make money. Unlike the TBA, Panama sits atop the two most important transportation conduits in the Western Hemisphere—the canal between oceans and land bridge between continents. And, unlike the TBA, Panama has enough Chinese immigrants to obscure a small army of PRC operatives.

> Many Chinese immigrated to Panama from southern China to help build the Panama Railroad in the 19th century; their descendants number around 50,000. Starting in the 1970's, a further 80,000 have immigrated from other parts of mainland China as well. (Jackson, "Panama's Chinese Community . . . ," *The Panama News,* May 2004) [72]

With all this potential for Central American subversion from Panama, one wonders how close Daniel Ortega may be to creating a Socialist state in nearby Nicaragua.

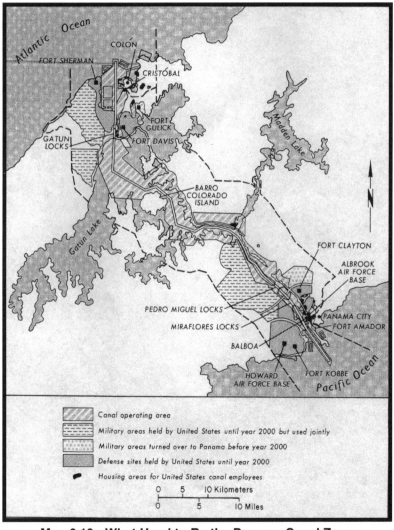

Map 6.10: What Used to Be the Panama Canal Zone
(Source: DA Pamphlet 550-46 [1989])

7 Costa Rica, Nicaragua, _____ and Honduras

- Is Costa Rica as stable as it was?
- How much effect has Ortega had on Nicaragua?

Most of the Population Are Poor

(Source: DA Pamphlet 550-33 [1989])

A Word of Warning

The reader is now entering into a part of Central American history in which so much evil occurred in the name of "combatting Communism" that its details will hurt. While the U.S. military did not directly generate this evil, its "kill-oriented" 2GW counterinsurgency advice did too little to stop it. That advice must now be altered. If it isn't, America will have little chance of reversing that region's recent decline. To be part of a "legitimate" war, a military defense must not produce disorders graver than those to be eliminated.[1] The people of Honduras are still suffering from what happened twenty years

93

ago. At that time, their country was the region's U.S. bastion and host to very little Communist subversion of its own. Now, there is so much dissatisfaction with how its army handles teenage unrest that a leftist will almost certainly be elected. Before confronting the Honduran nightmare, one must look at the first country through which U.S.-bound drugs must pass after leaving Panama. (See Map 8.1.)

Central America's Least Likely Drug Conduit

Costa Rica is a democratic republic that has remained relatively stable throughout most of Central America's turmoil. Oscar Arias Sanchez was elected its president in 8 May 2006. When Mr. Arias first held that office from 1986-1990, he won the Nobel Peace Prize for his role in ending two civil wars in the region.[2] As rebellions raged elsewhere, Costa Rica remained neutral. That's not quite the same as being a staunch U.S. ally. Arias resisted pressure from the U.S. to weigh in against the Sandinistas in Nicaragua and intervened against the activities of U.S.-backed Contras on Costa Rican soil.[3] Now, Arias is again both chief of state and head of the Costa Rican government. That government also has a democratically elected Legislative Assembly and legislature-appointed Supreme Court. But none of those officials appear to come from that country's Communist Party.

At present, there are 300,000-500,000 Nicaraguans in Costa Rica (only some legally), and almost 10,000 refugees from Colombia. While the situation appears calm, the CIA still lists Costa Rica as trans-shipment country for cocaine and heroin from South America to the United States. Like Panama, Costa Rica has no military forces of its own, only various policing agencies.[4] Thus, it is ill-prepared to take on the corrupting influence and strong-arm tactics of a world drug syndicate. While a narcotics conduit can be easily established through bribery, it cannot usually be eliminated without force.

> While relatively free of crime, Costa Rica has been used as a transit point for South American cocaine, and there have been allegations that drug-tainted money has found its way into the coffers of the two main political parties.

Once dubbed the "Switzerland of Central America," the country's self-image was badly shaken in 2004 when allega-

tions of high-level corruption led to two former presidents being imprisoned on graft charges.[5]
— BBC *Country Profile*

Since 1949, at least two of Costa Rica's presidents have pursued Socialist policies. They both came from the National Liberation Party (PLN)—the same political organization of which Arias is currently a member. In June 2007, Costa Rica switched its diplomatic allegiance from Taiwan to China in a bid to attract PRC investment. Three months later, a national referendum favored ratifying the

Map 8.1: Nicaragua and Northern Costa Rica
(Source: Courtesy of General Libraries, University of Texas at Austin, from their website for map designator "nicaragua_rel_97.pdf")

95

Central American Free Trade Agreement (CAFTA).[6] While the CAFTA is generally thought to help the U.S., it also facilitates all kinds of imports. That the agreement includes a single (and quite distant) Caribbean nation—the Dominican Republic—seems very suspicious. Why aren't the other island nations included? As already documented, almost all the cocaine to enter America's East Coast comes through the Dominican Republic. Of course, CAFTA also applies to the now Marxist Nicaragua. (See Map 8.2.)

Nicaragua's New President

On 10 January 2007, Daniel Ortega of Sandinista fame was elected Nicaragua's new chief of state and head of government for the next five years. Having a decidedly Marxist past, Mr. Ortega is likely to maintain close ties with regional Socialist leaders, particularly those in Cuba and Venezuela.[7] In November 2006, the Sandinista National Liberation Front (FSLN) also won 38 out of the 92 National Assembly seats in Nicaragua.[8]

A little of the FSLN's background might help to explain the threat to the region posed by Ortega's election. In 1979, a military offensive by the FSLN had caused the ouster of President Somoza. Eventually, Daniel Ortega's FSLN government would nationalize (and turn into Communist cooperatives) all of Somoza's lands. But a full two years before doing so, it was able to legitimize its hold on power in the 1984 elections. That's when the U.S. opted for counter-revolution. It armed and financed thousands of "Contras" who attacked Nicaragua from bases in Honduras. Only after Washington had to face World Court condemnation for mining Nicaragua's harbors did those hostilities end. In 1990, the Sandinista political party was finally defeated by the U.S.-backed (and now defunct) National Opposition Union in elections that were a part of the peace agreement.[9]

While Nicaragua has an army, navy, and air force, it spends very little of its gross domestic product (GDP) on supporting them. In fact, Nicaragua doesn't have much of a GDP and must rely on international assistance even to meet its debt-financing obligations.[10] In essence, Nicaragua's legacy of a dictatorship, war, and natural calamity has made it the second poorest nation (after Haiti) in the Western Hemisphere.[11] This makes Nicaragua as vulnerable to Chinese manipulation as was Zimbabwe. The *CIA World Factbook* lists Nicaragua as a trans-shipment point for not only "cocaine destined for the U.S.," but also "arms-for-drugs" shipments headed south.[12] What comes through Nicaragua going north must also transit Honduras. (Refer again to Map 8.2.)

Honduras' Uncertain Future

Honduras is where most of the Contras were based, and where gang-like *maras* have recently grown strong. In late December 2004,

Map 8.2: Honduras
(Source: Courtesy of General Libraries, University of Texas at Austin, from their website for map designator "honduras_rel_1985.pdf")

members of one of those *maras* machinegunned a bus, killing over 20 people, just to protest the anti-*mara* policies of the Honduran government.[13]

Natural disaster, wealth differential, criminal activity, military rule, and official corruption have all turned Honduras into one of the least developed and least secure countries in Central America. Until the mid-1980's, it was dominated by a defense establishment that enthusiastically supported U.S. efforts to stem revolutionary activity in the region. Since that time, civilian leaders have sought to curb the power of that defense establishment. Some army officers have been charged with human-rights abuses, but many others have still to be prosecuted for 1980's violations. Chronic unemployment and drug trafficking have contributed to a crime wave by youth gangs known as "*maras.*" Those *maras* are said to have tens of thousands of Honduran members and use threats and violence to control the poorer districts of towns and cities. Meanwhile, according to the BBC, "the police are thought to have been involved in the murders by death squad of youths and street children."[14]

Manuel Zelaya, from the Liberal Party (PL), won Honduras' hotly-contested presidential election in November 2005. His main rival was the National Party's (PN) Porfirio "Pepe" Lobo Sosa, a former Communist.[15] Within Honduras' 128-seat National Congress (last elected in November 2005), the PN now holds almost as many seats as the PL.[16]

Mr. Zelaya, a big landowner and centrist, has proposed to double the number of police officers and to jail murderers and rapists for life. Upon taking office, he appointed a former military general to combat the gang violence and announced plans to rehabilitate former gang members.[17] While the latter intention is commendable, it is doubtful that a U.S.-trained military man would also qualify as a corrections specialist. A brief look at Honduran history may help to construct a more viable 4GW counterinsurgency strategy.

The Unforgiving Past

While Honduras was blessed in 1981 with its first civilian government in more than a century, its armed forces chief General Gustavo Alvarez retained considerable power. The U.S. military may have exploited his presence to bypass diplomatic channels.

Shortly after the election, U.S.-run camps for training Salvadorians in counterinsurgency appeared on Honduran soil. Then, in 1982, U.S.-backed Nicaraguan counter-revolutionaries began to launch attacks against their homeland from Honduras. Before long Honduras was experiencing more political unrest of its own. General Alvarez responded to it by ordering the detention of "trade union activists and left-wing sympathizers." During this same period, Honduran government death squads purportedly eliminated subversive elements.[18]

By the end of 1984, General Alvarez had been deposed amid anti-American demonstrations in Tegucigalpa. The U.S.-run training camps for Salvadorian counter-revolutionaries had also been shut down. But, the Honduran government continued to cooperate with America's anti-Sandinista activities in return for substantial economic aid. In 1987, that government granted amnesty to military men and left-wing guerrillas alike for abuses committed during the first part of that decade.[19]

In February 1988, an Amnesty International report warned of an increase in human-rights violations by armed forces and right-wing death squads in Honduras. Six months later, the Inter-American Court of Human Rights found the Honduran government guilty of "disappearances" of Honduran citizens between 1981 and 1984. By February 1989, the Summit of Central American presidents in El Salvador had reached agreement on demobilizing the Nicaraguan Contras who were based in Honduras.[20]

In November 1993, Liberal Party candidate and veteran human-rights activist Carlos Reina was then elected president. Reina pledged to reform Honduras' judicial system and limit the power of its armed forces. Over the next two years, he ended compulsory military service and charged the first military officers with human-rights abuses. Four years later, Carlos Flores of the Liberal Party was elected president. He too pledged to restructure the armed forces. In 1998, control over Honduras' police was transferred from military headquarters to civilian authorities, but reports of rights abuses continued. After another year, the armed forces were placed under civilian control.[21] Sadly, none of these initiatives seemed to do much good. The Honduran security apparatus still appeared to be overly abusive.

Then comes the shocker from which all military men, however impassioned with their own causes, must learn. In January 2001, the Honduran Committee for the Defense of Human Rights quanti-

99

fies the extent of the continuing nightmare—more than 1,000 street children had been murdered during the previous year by police-backed death squads. By August of 2001, the United Nations itself had called on Honduras' government to prevent the extrajudicial killings of children and teenagers.[22] According to a U.N. report a year later, a total of 1,000 youngsters had been murdered between 1998 and 2002 (mostly by security forces). Though 500 more youths were reported killed in 2003, Amnesty International claims that few, if any, of the perpetrators throughout the entire five-year span had been brought to justice.[23]

Desperate to eliminate the trouble's cause, the Honduran government had re-established diplomatic ties with Cuba after 40 years in January 2002. Resolving a maritime-boundary dispute was the only reason ever officially given. However, Communist collusion with the *maras* may have been suspected. Needless to say, bargaining with Cuba could do nothing to remove the evil that had taken root within Honduras' own security establishment. In May 2004, a prison fire at San Pedro Sula killed more than 100 inmates, many of them *mara* gang members. As 2007 approached, Honduras' president found himself under attack from opposing directions—first from the suspected Communist subversives, and then from his own heady security personnel. To combat the former, he ordered all radio and television (TV) stations to carry government propaganda for two hours a day for 10 days to counteract what he called a misinformation campaign.[24] The latter posed more of a problem. While several other Latin American nations had experienced something similar (most notably, Argentina, Uruguay, and Peru), it was not unique to the region. Before the Surge, Iraq also suffered from government-sponsored death squads. The only link between such widely separated regimes is where they get their counterinsurgency advice. They were all trying a 2GW solution to a 4GW problem.

The interior of Honduras has now become exceedingly dangerous for all journalists. The reason for this again evokes images of Iraq.

> One area we have been investigating particularly is the private security companies which appeared in Honduras after the Cold War of the 1980's when our country was nicknamed the "backyard of the USA."
> They were mainly formed by landowners and people

who had violated human rights during the war, and who suddenly found themselves without the protection of the army.

There are more than 350 such companies in Honduras. They employ seven times more people than the whole of the national police force.

They are overflowing with weapons and the state has little control over them.[25]

— BBC News, 4 July 2007

In effect, Honduras reflects the worst that can happen from a botched reaction to suspected Communist influence. According to the *CIA's World Factbook,* it is still a "trans-shipment point for drugs and narcotics," site of government "corruption," and location of "money-laundering activity."[26] Unlike before, Honduras is now definitely part of the problem.

What Went Wrong and Further Research

It's clear from what has transpired in Honduras that the U.S. counterinsurgency method of the 1980's did not have enough of the 4GW attributes to work over the long term. It undoubtedly relied too much on killing the foe, and not enough on eliminating his dissatisfaction. The rural peasants of Central America have been long abused by elitist city dwellers, big land owners, and more than one U.S. corporation. While that makes them more susceptible to the false promises of Communism, they are more lovers than fighters. Until the U.S. military learns more about 4GW and projecting minimal force, it should not try to provide assistance. Never again must the following be allowed to pass for "bringing liberty to a region."

During the 1980's, the United States established a very large military presence in Honduras with the purpose of supporting . . . anti-Sandinista Contras fighting the Nicaraguan government . . . [and] the El Salvador military fighting against the FMLN guerrillas. The U.S. built the airbase known as Palmerola, near Comayagua . . . so that C5-A cargo planes could land there, rather than at the public airport in San Pedro Sula. The U.S. also built a training base near Trujillo which primarily trained Contras and the Salvadoran military, and in conjunction with this, developed Puerto Castilla into a modern port. The United States built many airstrips near the Nicaraguan border to help move supplies to the Contra forces fighting the Sandinistas in Nicaragua. Though spared the bloody civil wars wracking its neighbors, the Honduran army quietly waged a campaign against leftists which included extra judicial killings and forced disappearances of political opponents by government-backed death squads, most notably Battalion 316 (Cohn and Thompson, "When a Wave of Torture . . . Staggered a Small U.S. Ally," *Baltimore Sun,* 11 June 1995).[27]

Rare Details of the Aftermath

When Honduran Security Ministry forces intercepted a *mara's* shipment of small arms headed south to the FARC-EP in April 2005,[28] they may have been standing atop a main drug conduit. The organized-crime syndicate behind the smuggling has allowed MS-13 to protect its overland drug conduit in Mexico.[29] If MS-13 also protects the Guatemalan, Honduran, and Salvadorian legs of that conduit, it may have tried to back-ship arms along it. Though somewhat dated, the following excerpt may thus contain little-known details about the route. And some of its references (like to the Panamanian segment) may be of significant intelligence value. Of note, Nicaragua was deeply involved in the two-way smuggling operation long before it became officially Sandinista.

Last 6 August [1999] the National Association of Former Fighters of the Farabundo Marti National Liberation Front [ANECFM/LN], that represents nearly 600 former [FMLN] combatants reinserted into civilian life in El Salvador, sent the U.S. State Department . . . a sealed envelope. . . . The association was denouncing the sale of weapons to the FARC by some former guerrillas. It also noted that a group of FARC fighters had been trained to handle these tools of war in Central American territory. . . .
. . . On the other three documents sent to the State Department, Monge [ANECFM/LN National Coordinator] told Semana [a Bogota newspaper] that these were on FARC

purchases of heavy . . . [weapons] in Nicaragua. "Our men have firsthand knowledge of the acquisition of 16 land-to-air missiles, known as SAM 16, 14, and 7, that are used for shooting down planes and combat helicopters." . . . According to Monge's report, these missiles were bought in Nicaragua in mid-May and two weeks later they were loaded onto shrimp fishing boats headed for the coasts of Panama. There the Machos del Monte insurgent group received them. This group has had close relations with the FARC for several years. Along with FARC leaders in the border area, the Panamanian movement was in charge of moving the weapons into Colombian territory. . . .

. . . "Nicaragua has become the axis for the weapons black market. There the big traffickers operate, running a business that is fed to a good degree by American weaponry. And the best client in the warfare industry is the FARC," an investigator with the Salvadoran Office of the Prosecutor General, who asked to remain anonymous, said. The demobilization of the guerrillas in El Salvador and Guatemala and the Sandinistas arrival in power took place almost a decade ago. A good part of the weapons that remain from these war years wound up in the hands of the Colombian subversives, but the reality of the matter is that these [weapons] ran out. The distributors, therefore, contacted the major suppliers in the United States and Libya and put them in charge of supplying the market with the latest weapons and most advanced technology, seeing as Central America continues to be the epicenter of the market for South American guerrillas. . . .

The latest of these reports was given to the State Department last 16 August. The document features a concrete denouncement: FARC guerrillas are being trained in Nicaragua at Lake Xilao, located to the north of Lake Managua. Three groups of 36 guerrillas have gone there and have remained for 45 days, receiving instruction in how to handle the missiles. Those that run the weapons business have developed a sophisticated system to sidestep the zone's controls. They use the great navigability of the Nicaraguan and Honduran rivers to move large quantities of weapons. For these trips they use fast boats with lots of cargo space that can also be taken out onto the high seas to

103

the Atlantic Autonomous Region, off the shores of Honduras and Nicaragua. There they make their trans-shipment
onto the shrimping boats. Another strategy . . . is to take
the weapons on a roundabout route. A ship may go to Venezuela, return to Nicaragua, where it passes the island of
San Andres or to Panama and then finally enter Colombian
territory.[30]

— Bogota newspaper (FBIS translated), 1999

The "Machos del Monte" mentioned above were the most fa-
natical of Manuel Noriega's Defense Forces.[31] A commissioned
U.S. special operator has described them as specially trained for
jungle and irregular warfare, heavily indoctrinated in nationalist
rhetoric, and inclined to hold out as long as possible.[32] As proven
in the last chapter, they had probably embraced both Marxism and
the drug trade. After the U.S. invasion, they were hopefully eliminated from Panama's new security apparatus. But that would not
preclude them from going to work for someone else. That someone
else would most likely have Marxist leanings—like the Chinese
organized-crime syndicate known to use Panama as a base of operations.[33] The Machos del Monte may now serve as that syndicate's
local enforcement branch, much as "Los Zetas" do for one of Mexico's
biggest drug cartels.[34]

8 El Salvador, Belize, Guatemala, Mexico

- What is the *mara's* role in cocaine smuggling?
- How trustworthy is the Guatemalan Army?

Indigenous Peoples Have Been Largely Ignored

(Source: DA Pam 550-78 [1984], cover)

The Crux of the Matter

Thus far, the research has suggested a 4GW assault on America by some foreign entity. While that entity's ultimate objective may be destabilization through drug smuggling and associated corruption, its ongoing reward has been massive profit and easier espionage. In essence, the conduits for people and dope coming into the U.S. can also be used for spies and technology leaving the U.S. Where stolen-car-packed shipping containers can get out, so too might a complete military assembly. Luckily, blocking the entry routes should also lower the outflow.

Some of the cocaine has been reaching the East Coast via the Dominican Republic, Haiti, and Bahamas, but up to 92% has been coming through Central America to the southwest border.[1] Asian heroin has historically joined the procession in Acapulco,[2] but some may now be crossing Hutchison Whampoa's Panamanian docks. Only certain is that a drug conduit (or series of conduits) now runs through (or along the coast of) every Central American country bordering the Pacific.[3] Mexico's new Pacific seaport and Texas' north-south turnpike are both Chinese trade initiatives,[4] but the PRC's role in the assault has yet to be determined. A *mara* controls major segments of Mexico's rail system,[5] and drug cartels compete for the rest of the country. Of course, there are also FARC operatives in Mexico.[6] They have been showing the cartels and *maras* how better to protect the Colombian cocaine on its way to market. That's tantamount to providing them with light-infantry training. To make matters worse, Mexico has been facing the old Communist choice between armed revolution and leftist "reform." After a Marxist uprising at its southern end in the mid-1990's, its last presidential election was nearly won by a Hugo Chavez crony. (See Map 8.1.)

China's Degree of Involvement

Mao is gone, but PRC's politburo is still somewhat paranoid. It almost certainly blamed America for the financial and political collapse of the world's only other Communist power in 1990. To avoid the same fate, that politburo's members may have decided to go for America's throat. To do so, they would need only a trade-and-democracy-oriented 4GW sequel to their traditional guerrilla format. The PLA does now depend, after all, on much of its funding from civilian corporate extensions.[7] There's big money to be made from the international trade in drugs. That's why the government of North Korea so openly participates in it.[8] What if one of those PLA extensions were a triad that its intelligence service had infiltrated or created? Part of that triad's profits could then go toward targeted nation political "assistance," trade arrangements, and/or Maoist insurrection without leaving any trail back to China. Did not the CIA ask the Mafia to kill Fidel Castro? Why couldn't the PLA's triad enlist cartels, *maras,* and a nearby "people's army" to so fortify the drug routes into the U.S. that they couldn't be blocked?

106

In combination with a Chinese buyout of American businesses and debt, all that drug money might significantly alter the U.S. government's perspective on international issues. An administration that routinely looked the other way would be of more use to the Chinese than a puppet regime.

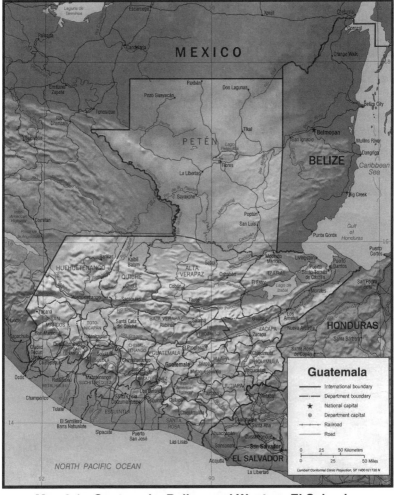

Map 8.1: Guatemala, Belize, and Western El Salvador
(Source: Courtesy of General Libraries, University of Texas at Austin, from their website for map designator "guatemala_rel00.pdf")

For those seemingly disjointed activities at the top of Central America even to have a mutual instigator, many links must be established between them. All the tunneling beneath the U.S. border certainly suggests Asian military advice, but no hard proof of that yet exists. Mexico is obviously of strategic significance to the PRC, but that value could have as much to do with petroleum as its adjacency to the U.S. Yet, Mexico's southern neighbors have been experiencing far too much trouble after civil wars that ended 20 years ago. Theirs is a predominantly Catholic region in which evil must be fanned to survive. Any evidence of Communist subversion would be buried in the constant turmoil of narcotics and human smuggling. Still, chaos is an integral part of a well-known style of Asian warfare. In a rash of incidents, those of strategic value cannot be fully countered. Chaos also works well in a 4GW setting. Then, to a harried population, a leftist candidate can seem the only alternative to open revolt or military excess. Chaos can be quickly generated by converting the targeted nation into a narco-state. Afghanistan already qualifies, as does Colombia. Until their drug problems are controlled, neither will be their insurrections or governmental ineptitude. Enough drug money can buy the best arms and highest officials. How much more trouble would America have if Mexico were also to become a narco-state?

Before Mexico can be discussed in depth, its southern neighbors must be closely examined. Again, the reader is warned. What is to follow will not be pleasant for most Americans to hear. Within El Salvador, a Honduras-like nightmare is still underway. (Refer back to Map 8.1.)

El Salvador's Troubles

El Salvador is a tiny nation on the Pacific southeast of Guatemala. (See Map 8.2.) The most densely populated in Central America, it's more industrialized than the others. But it also has one of the saddest histories. In the 1980's, El Salvador was ravaged by a bitter civil war. That war was in part generated by the ongoing inequality between wealthy elite (who dominated both government and economy) and remainder of the population (who lived in poverty). It left 70,000 (one of every 100 citizens) dead in a country only slightly bigger than New Jersey. In 1992, a U.N.-brokered peace deal ended the civil war, but natural disasters followed.[9]

El Salvador's economy now largely depends on what little money its immigrants to the U.S. can send home. And its society is among the most crime-ridden in the Americas. Like Honduras, its teen-age gangs have become a great problem. Also like Honduras, its government doesn't seem to know what to do about it. The right-wing National Republican Alliance (ARENA) party has enjoyed four consecutive election victories. Unfortunately, it has also been linked to civil-war-era death-squad murders, and the current president of El Salvador has refused to revoke the amnesty of those persons involved.[10]

Map 8.2: Mexico

(Source: Courtesy of General Libraries, University of Texas at Austin, from their website for map designator "mexico_rel97.pdf")

Within the sufferings of the Salvadorian people may lie proof of how much long-term harm can be done by a 2GW solution to a multifaceted revolution. But then, how much more proof is really necessary after almost a million civilians were mistakenly killed in Vietnam,[11] and their descendents still suffer from agent orange poisoning? A viable 4GW counterinsurgency portfolio would contain infantry tactics that might have succeeded with less bloodshed and civil-action programs that might have precluded the gangs. Most certainly, "friendly" government forces must never again be given 2GW training—without subsequent supervision—in countries where indigenous populations have long been suppressed.

The Chinese are just as interested in dominating the world as were the Soviets, but more from the standpoint of economics than ideology. Thus, there may no longer be much Communist agitation in El Salvador. Armed revolution is, after all, the Communists' preferred strategy of the past! The new strategy may involve an attack so subtle that it could be launched—with few repercussions—against the U.S. heartland itself. If that attack looked on the surface like a police problem, America's political leaders would be unlikely to deploy enough military assets to solve it.

El Salvador's Slide into Anarchy

Turn back the clock to 1977. That's the year General Carlos Romero is elected president of El Salvador. Soon guerrilla activities by the left-wing FMLN intensify amid reports of increased human-rights violations by government troops. Those violations allegedly include death squads. Within two years, Romero is ousted in a coup by reformist officers who install a military/civilian *junta*. Not unexpectedly, this fails to curb army-backed political violence. Soon, Jose Napoleon Duarte becomes head of the *junta* and first "civilian" president since 1931.[12] In 1980, Roman Catholic Archbishop of San Salvador and human-rights campaigner Oscar Romero is assassinated while performing mass. The Salvadorian military is soon implicated,[13] and the spark to a civil war has been struck.[14] Between 1979 and 1981, 30,000 people are killed by army-affiliated death squads.[15] The FMLN launches an all out attack against the Salvadorian regime on 10 January 1981. That attack brings that regime immediate military aid and advisers from the United States.[16] Later that year, both France and Mexico recognize the FMLN as a legitimate political entity. Still, the U.S. continues to assist a government in which right-wing death squads are known to be backed by the army. Then, in 1982, the ARENA party wins its first parliamentary elections. Soon, Duarte has used the democratic process to acquire his presidency. He will eventually seek a negotiated settlement with the FMLN but never actually gets it. In 1989, as FMLN attacks intensify, another ARENA candidate, Alfredo Cristiani, becomes president in voting that is widely believed to be rigged. After two years, the Salvadorian government finally recognizes the FMLN as a political party. Then, representatives from it and the former rebel faction sign a U.N.-sponsored peace accord.[17]

One would think El Salvador's problems solved at this point in her history. They aren't. In 1993, its leaders declare amnesty for all those implicated by the U.N. commission on human-rights atrocities. A year later, ARENA candidate Armando Calderon Sol is elected president. By 1997, the FMLN has made progress in parliamentary elections, and leftist Hector Silva becomes the mayor of San Salvador. However, former guerrilla Facundo Guardado is decisively defeated in the next presidential election by ARENA candidate Francisco Flores.

Through it all, the unadjudicated wounds of a civil war continue to fester. In March 2005, the OAS human-rights court re-opens an investigation into one of the worst atrocities of the war—the massacre of hundreds of peasant farmers in the village of El Mozote. In January 2007, 21 inmates are killed in a riot at a maximum-security prison west of the capital. These killings may be another example of government excess, or simply a dispute between *maras*. The very next month, three members of the governing ARENA party are murdered in Guatemala. While an organized-crime syndicate is suspected of the killings,[18] no one knows for sure. There are now far too many variables to be easily connected. All that is certain is that the traditional mix of revolutionary and overzealous patriot has been joined by two new players—the *maras* and international organized crime.

The Legacy of the Salvadorian Counterinsurgency Effort

The most difficult to decipher of the Central American aberrations is the *mara*. Despite a later influx of deported Los Angeles (LA) street gang members, the *maras* of El Salvador initially grew out of their government's response to local insurgency.

In 1989, the Mara Salvatrucha, or MS-13, appeared in Honduras, and in the early 1990's, . . . M-18, surfaced. Both gangs were the result of the migration of refugees fleeing increasingly deadly engagements between rebel groups and government forces and the heavy-handed actions of state security apparatuses (Mara Prevention Unit of Honduras; interview with advisor to ex-President Maduro).
. . . Their [the LA refugee gangs'] . . . encounters with the law resulted in a great many members being imprisoned and later deported to their countries of origin, a process that saw an upswing in 1998 and 1999. The deportees rapidly became gang leaders in their home countries. . . .
[The most destructive] Mara activities, especially those of the Salvatrucha and M-18 gangs, . . . [then] began in El Salvador and Honduras, and a little later in Guatemala.[19]
─ *Military Review*, July/August 2007

From the outset, MS-13 was different from its rival M-18. The difference lay in MS-13's closer ties to organized crime. To smuggle drugs into America, an organized-crime faction would need a single *mara* that could operate on both sides of the U.S. border. While both *maras* have now extended their activities from El Salvador to Honduras and Guatemala,[20] MS-13 appears dominant in Mexico.

[In Los Angeles] M-18 was an existing gang made up primarily of Mexican youths, while immigrants who had fled the fighting in El Salvador formed MS-13. These nationalities gave the gangs their identities, although both gangs later added immigrants from Honduras and Guatemala, and some Mexican youths also joined the MS-13.
Clear lines demarcated the territorial turf in Los Angeles of local gangs and the immigrant gangs from Mexico and Central America. Leaders who controlled the latter gangs called themselves the Mexican Mafia [a California prison gang], an organization that continues to influence the policies that guide the MS-13 and the M-18 in Mexico and Central America. . . .

The growth of mara membership and reach seems to rely on very careful planning that could include some form of support from other organizations, such as organized crime syndicates. . . . The level of organization achieved, especially by MS-13, has facilitated stronger links with narcotics-trafficking cartels.[21]
— *Military Review*, July/August 2007

Soon the *modus operandi* of the rejuvenated *maras* would become painfully clear. They would tax whoever or whatever moved through their areas of control.

[T]he gangs devised a "war tax," a form of extortion in which they demanded payment for the right to move freely through their areas without being molested or assaulted.[22]
— *Military Review*, July August 2007

There are now indications that MS-13 has become more organized than it could have on its own. Its current gang members are prohibited from taking drugs. And it has greatly expanded over the last four years despite the best efforts of local governments. As of March 2004, MS-13 was believed to possess 25,000 members across the full breadth of Central America, though anyone with a gang tattoo could be arrested in El Salvador.[23] As of January 2005, some estimates put the gang's total membership in El Salvador alone at over 40,000.[24]

Though El Salvador's outlawing of gang membership has led to thousands of arrests, the gangs still appeal to its youth. The government's hard-line approach has failed to reduce gang violence, but seems popular with the voters. Apart from a few Catholic programs, no viable solution has been tried.[25] The government has yet to realize that it was its own heavy handed approach that led to the birth of MS-13 almost 30 years ago. MS-13 was, in large part, joined by orphans wanting to defend themselves. Teenagers with parents now join for the same reason. Compulsory military service in El Salvador has made little difference.[26] (See Figure 8.1.) Most likely, it is an international organized-crime syndicate that has helped MS-13 to grow so fast without losing cohesion. The CIA still lists El Salvador as a trans-shipment point for cocaine.[27]

Background and Associations of the FMLN

The FMLN was no haphazard collection of malcontents. In 2006, the funeral of its former commander Shafik Handal was attended by 100,000 red-shirted mourners.[28] Of obvious Cuban mentorship (while still Soviet), the FMLN was even reinforced by a few Tupac Amaru volunteers from Peru.[29] One of the reasons the U.S. launched a counterrevolution in Nicaragua was to stop the Sandinistas from supporting FMLN.[30]

The FMLN was a decidedly Marxist-Leninist movement that fought El Salvador's military from 1980 to 1992. Its goal was to overthrow the military dictatorship that had ruled that country since the 1930's and replace it with a Communist government.[31] In 1970, the General Secretary of the Communist Party of El Salvador, Cayetano Carpio, left that party to form a new organization that could wage an armed struggle against his nation's military dictatorship. That organization was the principal forerunner of the FMLN.[32] In 1980, with Cuban backing, the FMLN formed an umbrella federation over five leftist groups. Those groups were to follow the Soviet style of revolution—i.e., bombings, assassinations,

Figure 8.1: Salvadorian Soldier
(Source: DA Pam 550-150 [1995], p. 195)

economic sabotage, arson, and other attacks that were both urban and rural. Since 1988, the FMLN has increased the level of urban terrorism in the Salvadorian capital.[33]

U.S. support for El Salvador began with Jimmy Carter's approval of a military aid package to fortify the "anti-subversive brigades." Then, a week after entering office, Ronald Reagan approved more military aid and 54 advisers. With most of the Salvadorian operations now monitored by those advisers, the war started to escalate. Though contemporary counterinsurgency tactics from the Vietnam War were applied, what ensued was one of the bloodiest conflicts in Latin American history. Before its end, 80,000 lives would be lost.[34]

The FMLN's largest offensive occurred in November 1989. It caught the regime completely off guard by taking control of large sections of the country and parts of the capital. Once inside San Salvador, FMLN fighters quickly entered many of the poor neighborhoods. To evict them, Salvadorian planes dropped bombs in densely populated areas. Many analysts point to the FMLN's show of strength in this 1989 offensive as the turning point of the war. That's because it forced the rightist regime to admit to itself that it could not win militarily. After that offensive, the U.S. also started to push for a negotiated settlement, whereas before, it had pursued a policy of militarily confrontation with the FMLN.[35] After peace accords were signed in 1992, all armed FMLN units demobilized and their core personnel became a political party. Today, the FMLN is one of El Salvador's two biggest parties.[36] And it is still supported by Cuba's Marxists and Nicaragua's Sandinistas. It even has an office in Managua.[37] Obviously, most of that support now takes the form of political advice and funding.

At some point, an FMLN candidate will almost certainly be voted into presidential office in El Salvador. As of March 2003, that party had already won 100 of the 262 mayoral races including that of the country's capital. At that time, it was also projected to increase its share of the 84 congressional seats from 25 to 31, with ARENA taking only 29.[38]

More on the *Maras'* Affiliations

El Salvador's *maras* have no ideological or political motivation; they simply sell protection to smugglers. That MS-13 is starting to resemble an organized-crime family may mean it has now affiliated with a Chinese or Russian syndicate. Once former L.A. gang members arrived in El Salvador, Honduras, Guatemala, Nicaragua, Panama, and Mexico, they quickly put to work what they had learned in prison. Many locals subsequently joined. Some estimates put their overall number in Central America at over 100,000. In El Salvador alone, there are 15 municipalities that are marginally under their control.[39]

While this may be hard to believe, the military history and current predicament of Guatemala are even more discouraging. Of particular importance to the research will be any unseemly aftereffects of U.S. military assistance.

Guatemala Is Still in Turmoil

To this day, Guatemala is in chaos. That chaos is due in part to its *maras* and government. Gang members staged simultaneous riots in at least seven Guatemalan prisons in August 2005. With nearly military precision, they launched coordinated attacks against rival groups with grenades, guns and knives. Those attacks left 31 inmates dead.[40] What the *maras* have managed along the Guatemala's border with Mexico is the most troubling. There, they decide how many humans, drugs, and arms move along the smuggling conduits.[41]

In 1996, Guatemala emerged from a 36-year-long civil war that had pitted leftist, mostly Mayan, insurgents against the army. That army—with U.S. military assistance—had waged a vicious campaign to eliminate those guerrillas. More than 200,000 people (most of them noncombatants) died or disappeared. Despite an official finding that 93% of all atrocities had been committed by security forces, moves to bring those responsible to account got off to a slow start. Guatemalans still live in one of the most inequitable societies in the region. There is considerable poverty throughout the countryside and among most indigenous communities. Organized crime and violent street gangs add to the misery. The CIA describes Guatemala as is a "major corridor for smuggling drugs from South America to the United States." [42]

Unfortunately, Guatemala's pain in ongoing. Official police figures confirm that 5,885 of its residents died by violence in 2006, 500 more than in 2005, and a 60% increase over 2003. The 2006 murder rate is higher than the average number of people killed in each year of the civil war. "The cause is the dramatic increase in organized crime, which is taking over the country," says Frank LaRue, director of the Presidential Human Rights Commission.[43] Guatemala's role as a transit point for large cocaine shipments has grown. So too have the *"maras."* Some estimates put their membership at more than the 19,000-strong police force.[44]

That these *maras* have been extorting sexual favors from refugees headed north is only the tip of a very ugly iceberg. As of June 2005, 1,500 women had been murdered over four years in Guatemala. Many of those deaths were thought to be sexually motivated with very little chance of their perpetrators ever being caught or convicted.[45]

Guatemala has inexorably slipped toward Colombian-style anarchy since the peace accords of 1996, according to former president Oscar Berger.[46] The *machismo* that tends to emanate from kill-oriented 2GW training may be part of the problem. All members of Guatemala's compulsory military are now restricted to their barracks on election day and not allowed to vote.[47]

National Unity for Hope (UNE) candidate Alvaro Colom Caballeros is Guatemala's new president. Colom has been described as a "center-leftist" by the BBC.[48] Luckily, UNE only controls 33 of the 158 seats in the unicameral legislature.[49]

Not until January 2006 were large petroleum reserves discovered in Guatemala. They will make it much more appealing to the Chinese. While only 526 million barrels of oil have been found so far, so has 2.96 billion cubic meters of natural gas.[50] According to the CIA, both cocaine and heroin move through Guatemala from the south. As of 2005, it also had 100 hectares of its own opium poppies (enough to produce one metric ton of pure heroin per year). Its proximity to Mexico makes it a major staging area for drugs bound for the U.S. Money laundering is also a problem there, as is the official corruption that too often accompanies drug trafficking.[51]

The Tragic Details of Guatemala's Civil War

Though officially supported by the U.S., the Guatemala's security establishment committed so many human-rights abuses during its civil war that it was at least twice disowned by the American military.[52] Thus, that military cannot be directly blamed for what happened. Yet, how it might have prevented those abuses could prove useful in the future. That something horrific occurred is a matter of public record. In December 2005, investigators found all the old files of the National Police—a force with a reputation so bad that it had been disbanded as part of the 1996 peace settlement.[53] The contents of those files point to a need for future U.S. advisers to closely monitor all host-nation police activity. They also paint a less-than-glorious history of Guatemala.

Guatemala is the leftists' first real foothold in Central America. The land reforms of President Jacobo Arbenz Guzman are what brought Che Guevara there to preach Marxism in the early 1950's. After Korea, the U.S. is none too happy with these developments, and its CIA is generally thought to have backed the *coup d'etat* that removes Arbenz.[54]

Then, in 1966, moderate Mendez Montenegro gets more votes than the incumbent military regime's candidate, but not the majority needed for election. Congress only elects him after making a pact with the outgoing regime that undermines his authority. Soon, military and paramilitary operations by Col. Arana Osorio and others substantially lower the rural guerrilla threat, but urban guerrilla activity worsens. This may be the period in which 400 native villages are razed.[55] Four years later, Guatemala's military regains the presidency and appears to embark on a program to eliminate left-wingers altogether. That program results in at least 50,000 deaths.[56]

> The 1970 elections were held in an atmosphere of fear, which polarized the population and drove a frightened middle class to vote for the candidate of the army and the right. This was Colonel Arana Osorio, dubbed by his critics the "Jackal of Zacapa" because he had condoned the ruthless antisubversion campaign in that department that had cost the lives of thousands of peasant bystanders. . . .
>
> Once in power, Arana acted forcefully. . . . *Le Monde* quoted foreign diplomats as estimating that right-wing terrorists committed 15 assassinations for every one committed by left-wing guerrillas. Another estimate was of 15,000 deaths from political violence during Arana's first three years in office. In response to criticism . . . , Arana replied that "if it is necessary to turn the country into a cemetery in order to pacify it, I will not hesitate to do so."

. . . In 1974, Arana rigged the presidential elections, forcibly prohibiting demonstrations of protest.[57]
— Dept. of the Army Pamphlet 550-78 (1984)

As hard as it is to believe, the military repression actually worsens in the 1980's. During 1981 alone, around 11,000 people are killed by death squads and soldiers in response to growing anti-government guerrilla activity. In 1982, General Rios Montt gains power following a military coup. Shortly thereafter, he is ousted in another coup by General Mejia Victores, who declares an amnesty for guerrillas. After two more years, Cerezo Arevalo is elected president, and the Guatemalan Christian Democratic Party wins the legislative elections under a new constitution. In 1989, an attempt to overthrow Cerezo fails, and the civil war toll since 1980 reaches 100,000 dead and 40,000 missing.[58]

Then, peace talks between the government and rebels of the Guatemalan Revolutionary National Unity begin in 1994, and right-wing parties retain a majority in the legislative elections. Within a year, those rebels have declared a ceasefire, and the U.N. and U.S. formally accuse Guatemala of widespread human-rights abuses. After Alvaro Arzu is elected president in 1996, he conducts a purge of senior military officers and signs a peace agreement with the rebels, ending 36 years of civil war.[59]

One might also think the problem in Guatemala resolved at this point. But, as in El Salvador, it wasn't. In 1998, Bishop Juan Gerardi, a human rights campaigner, is murdered. A year later, a U.N. commission blames security forces for 93% of all atrocities in a conflict that had claimed 200,000 lives. It also stipulates that senior officials had overseen 626 massacres in Mayan villages. The government tries to make amends for the abomination, but those amends are too little and too late. In December 2001, President Portillo pays U.S. $1.8 million to the families of 226 men, women, and children killed by soldiers and paramilitary personnel in 1982 at the village of Las Dos Erres.[60]

After conservative Oscar Berger wins the presidential election in late 2003, he makes major cuts to the army. Several bases are closed, and 10,000 soldiers are retired. By the end of 2004, the U.N. mission monitoring the peace process, says that Guatemala still suffers from crime, social injustice, and human-rights violations. In November 2005, Guatemala's leading anti-drug investigator is arrested in the U.S. on charges of drug trafficking. A year later, the

119

Guatemalan government and U.N. agree to create a commission to identify and dismantle "powerful clandestine armed groups."[61] Such a phrase might apply to a militia, or to the paramilitary wing of a crime syndicate.

During August of 2007, there is a high murder rate among candidates and activists alike in the run-up to Guatemala's September elections. Two months later, Alvaro Colom of the center-left UNE Party wins the presidential election with nearly 53 percent of the vote.[62] Thus, the two factors that had originally brought Guatemala to ruin seem still present—a downtrodden people and leftist promises. Only time will tell how Colon will do. Guatemala's military has been a threat not only to its own people, but also to those of a northern neighbor.

Belize's Challenge

Belize has more in common with the Caribbean island-states than with its Central American neighbors. Formerly called British Honduras, it has been independent since 1981 and is now one of the British Commonwealth of Nations. Its parliamentary democracy enjoys relative stability. However, Belize does have a problem with violent crime, much of it drug related, and with the trafficking of narcotics to the U.S.[63] The CIA notes an unsustainable foreign debt, high unemployment, growing involvement in the South American drug trade, and increasing problem with urban crime.[64] With newly discovered oil reserves,[65] Belize may now be experiencing the unsettling influence of more foreign attention. In April 2005, rioting broke out in Belize's capital during a wave of anti-government protests.[66]

Belize has a small army,[67] but because of previous boundary disputes with Guatemala, that army probably now watches the Guatemalan border more closely than the one with Mexico. This creates additional opportunity for smugglers who have received their merchandize by sea.

In 2006, the U.S. State Department included Belize on its slate of countries doing too little about human trafficking.[68] The CIA also describes Belize as a place of cocaine transit and money laundering.[69] And so, the discussion finally arrives at the final stopgap nation before such things impact the U.S.

A Clear and Present Danger from Mexico

After 2,500 drug-trade-related deaths in 2007,[70] Mexico's new president Calderon dispatched "more than 24,000 military and security forces to pacify areas overrun by 'drug gangs'." Yet, violent crime remains a major concern throughout that country. In fact, Mexico has one of the highest kidnapping rates in the world. While the killings are generally attributed to cartel turf wars,[71] many may have more to do with keeping local residents quiet along key drug routes.

According to the CIA, Mexico is the principal trans-shipment point for South American cocaine, with at least 90% of all U.S.-bound product coming through it. Mexico's own drug cartels control most of this action and enjoy a fair amount of local money laundering. To make matters worse, Mexico is also a major supplier of heroin, marijuana, and methamphetamines to the U.S. market.[72] Its own cultivation of 3,300 hectares of opium poppies in 2005 yielded the equivalent of eight metric tons of pure heroin. Though the Mexican government conducts one of the largest crop eradication programs in the world, it has yet to control the problem.[73]

Mexico is also a source, transit, and destination country for human beings being trafficked for sex and labor. Some of the victims are from South America, the Caribbean, Eastern Europe, Africa, and Asia, but most are from Central America. Through promises of employment and threats of violence, women and children are brought from the countryside to the city for sexual exploitation. Pervasive corruption among state and local police officials makes all of this possible.[74]

What happens in Mexico will eventually affect the United States. That's why U.S. leaders have traditionally monitored all events south of the border. Now that NAFTA, CAFTA, Mexican-truck leeway, and the north-south Texas turnpike are all in place, illicit goods can more easily reach middle America. As of February 2008, Washington was further pursuing free-trade agreements with Panama and Colombia.[75] The "economic cooperation" between nations is undoubtedly beneficial, but it also means more U.S. imports to inspect for contraband.

While the Mexican border is too porous and long to be completely blocked by a 2GW barrier system, such a barrier would help to slow the smuggling. At present, half a million unauthorized immigrants

121

still cross it yearly. Yet, the U.S. Senate still refused in July 2007 to fund all the fencing and intrusion devices mandated by the Secure Fence Act of 2006. With the added prospect of an Asian tunnel at any points along the frontier's 1,950-mile length,[76] the chances of totally stopping the flow of narcotics flow to a willing market are not good. Totally to shut off that flow, the U.S. would have to get more involved in what happens just across the border. How it might do so will be discussed in Part Three.

The ongoing crime wave in Mexico is more than coincidental. The Maoist people's army from Colombia has been helping to keep the northern legs of the cocaine conduit open. Among other things, it has provided military training to MS-13 and the Mexican cartels. At the end of 2005, the Mexican Secretary of Interior admitted to FARC "cells" in several Mexican states.[77] The FARC's ties to organized crime and regional/international drug rings are well known.[78]

> Arrests made by Mexican authorities in November 2000 established links between the FARC and Mexican cocaine traffickers. Evidence showed that the FARC had tried to supply cocaine to the Mexican Tijuana cartel in exchange for cash and possibly weapons. The Cardenas-Guillen cartel of northern Mexico is known to have maintained a pipeline for Colombian cocaine, which the group shipped across the border into the United States. In May 2003, AUC and FARC operatives reportedly had arrived in Mexico to maintain Mexican drug routes after the arrest of key Mexican figures.[79]
> — Library of Congress Study, October 2003

The *maras* have been instrumental in the movement of dope between Guatemala and Mexico. Instead of carrying the drugs, they have probably been hired by a crime syndicate to just protect the routes. MS-13 is said to control most of the rail lines heading north. That control has more to do with who rides than with what they are carrying.[80]

> The Maras flourished in the corrupt environment along the Guatemala-Mexico border in the Mexican state of Chiapas. There they rule over considerable portions of the smuggling networks that transport people, drugs and weapons between

the two countries and into the north of Mexico, by means of a cargo railroad that departs the border city of Tapachula.[81]
— Jamestown Foundation, 13 January 2005

The Mexican train routes (both east and west) are the primary means for illegal immigrants to transit Mexico on their way to the U.S. Up to 99% of these are freight and not passenger trains. The Mara Salvatrucha is controlling eastern Mexican train route Transportacion Ferroviaria Mexicana (TFM) . . . which runs from Chiapas to Tabasco through Veracruz to northern Mexico. Rumors are that they are also beginning to control the west coast train route Transportacion Maritima Mexicana (www.am.com). Salvatrucha members extort sexual favors or money from the illegal immigrants in order to allow them to board the empty freight cars. If the "taxes" are not paid, the immigrants could be beaten, thrown off the train, or even killed (www.univision.com). In addition to their control of the train routes, Salvatrucha members are known to be working as protection for drug cartels as they smuggle their contraband into the U.S. (www.cronica.com.mx) [82]
—Jamestown Foundation, 17 November 2005

Almost No Possibility of *al-Qaeda* Involvement

The above-mentioned contraband arrangement is clearly not part of a worldwide Muslim plot. *Hezbollah* hit men did once enter Mexico to attack its officials.[83] And *al-Qaeda* operative Adnan El Shukrijuman has been seen in Sonora.[84] But there is very little evidence of Muslim extremism in Mexico. Of course, its people-smuggling network has not been totally ignored by the Islamists. Some have even forged a few new branches.[85]

If there is a hidden instigator in Mexico, it is more probably one of the PRC's two intelligence services. They almost certainly have links to China's many triads. And "Chinese mafias" have already been implicated in Mexico's trade in illegal aliens.

In April 2005, the Honduran Director for Immigration Affairs was arrested for involvement in human trafficking. He worked with Chinese "mafias" to smuggle Chinese,

Afgha[n], and Pakistani citizens into Honduras and then into the U.S.[86]
— Jamestown Foundation, 17 November 2005

Of late, China has had more strategic reasons to be interested in Mexico. Not only is Mexico right next door to the PRC's only real opposition to world domination, but it is also petroleum rich. Mexico is both a major producer and exporter of oil. Nearly one-third of its revenue comes from that industry.[87] This, in itself, makes Mexico of utmost importance to the natural-resources-strapped PRC. In January 2006, Mexican oil production was estimated at 3.42 million barrels per day and oil reserves at 12.51 billion barrels. As of that same date, its natural gas production was 41.37 billion cubic meters with a reserve ten times that large.[88] Those are significant quantities.

As much of the Mexican crude is bought by the U.S.,[89] one might expect local guerrillas to discourage U.S. oil companies from operating there, just as they have in Nigeria. But so far, all attacks have been against Mexico's own state-run oil company. With compulsory military service,[90] Mexico has enough soldiers to deal with the problem, but not if it follows the Guatemalan and El Salvadorian counterinsurgency models of the 1980's.

Mexico's Tenuous Political Situation

Felipe Calderon, from the conservative National Action Party, won the July 2006 presidential election by less than one percentage point over his left-wing rival, Andres Manuel Lopez Obrador. Calderon had vowed during his campaign to tackle violent crime, tax evasion, and corruption. To this end, he promised to raise army salaries to limit the number of crime-related bribes. He also predicted the fight against drug gangs would take longer than his six-year term in office.[91]

Andres Manuel Lopez Obrador is from the Party of the Democratic Revolution (PRD). He has been described as a "center-leftist." After the election, he held several mass rallies in downtown Mexico City to try to force a general recount. On 31 July, in an act of civil disobedience, his supporters blocked 12 kilometers of one of the most important thoroughfares in the capital, Paseo de la Reforma. For about two hours on 9 August, they also took over the toll booths on four federal highways into the city. Finally, hundreds of Lopez Obrador supporters surrounded the main offices of four foreign banks, closing them for several hours. They claimed that the banks "ransack the country" and "widen the barrier between rich and poor." Their leader had just sent a message to the press, explaining the reasons for his blockades and other "peaceful civil resistance." At a subsequent rally, Lopez Obrador called for the establishment of a parallel government and shadow cabinet. Like Peru's opposition candidate, he professes to be the indigenous people's candidate. And like Humala in Peru, Lopez Obrador was "supported" by Hugo Chavez.[92] To see how all of this might fit into a Communist conspiracy involving Mexico, one must review that nation's recent history.

A Detailed Look at Mexico's Not-Too-Distant Past

Mexico has long been beset by Communist influences. It was from Mexico, after all, that Fidel Castro relaunched his guerrilla campaign against the Batista regime in Cuba.

[Che] Guevara arrived in Mexico City in early September 1954, and shortly thereafter renewed his friendship with Nico Lopez and the other Cuban exiles whom he had known in Guatemala. In June 1955, Lopez introduced him to Raul Castro. Several weeks later, Fidel Castro arrived in Mexico City after having been amnestied from prison in Cuba, and on the evening of 8 July 1955, Raul introduced Guevara to the older Castro brother. During a fervid overnight conversation, Guevara became convinced that Fidel was the inspirational revolutionary leader for whom he had been searching, and he immediately joined the "26th of July Movement" that intended to overthrow the dictatorship of Fulgencio Batista. . . . Guevara [then] participated in the military training alongside the other members of the 26J Movement. . . .

When the cabin cruiser Granma set out from Tuxpan, Veracruz for Cuba on November 25, 1956, Guevara was one of only four non-Cubans aboard. . . . Attacked by Batista's military soon after landing, about half of the expeditionaries were killed or executed upon capture. . . . Only 15–20 rebels survived as a battered fighting force; they re-grouped and fled into the mountains of the Sierra Maestra to wage guerrilla warfare against the Batista regime.[93]

Throughout the 1960's, the Mexican government suppressed any dissatisfaction among the peasants and laborers over the unequal distribution of wealth. During the Olympic Games of 1968, its security forces fired on a student demonstration in Mexico City, killing hundreds of protestors.[94]

Then, in 1976, huge oil reserves were discovered beneath Mexico's offshore waters, and the Cantarell field became its mainstay of oil production.[95] This greatly increased the country's chances of foreign intrigue. Realizing this, the Mexican government continued actively to discourage any behavior that seemed the least bit subversive.

Finally, in 1994, there was a overt rebellion in the state of Chiapas (next to Guatemala) by the Zapatista National Liberation Army (EZLN). Though ostensibly populist, this rebellion was brutally suppressed by government troops. Then, Mexico's leaders revised their position and recognized the EZLN as a political entity. In November 1995, they and EZLN representatives reached an agreement on greater autonomy for the indigenous Mayans of Chiapas. But soon the southern insurgency rekindled when the Popular Revolutionary Army (EPR) joined the fight. As the EPR was more obviously Marxist, one can start to see how its sudden bolstering of the EZLN may be part of an overall Communist plan.[96] After all, the Zapatistas did fly a flag with a red star in a black field. And their principal aim was to gain benefits for the peasantry—e.g., land reparations for the poor. Central to Zapatista ideology was "bottom-up" instead of "top-down" politics (an Asian, though not necessarily Communist, concept). Still, that ideology did contain elements of Marxism. And the EZLN's initial declaration of war against the Mexican government pledged more than just support for the indigenous peoples of Chiapas. It extended its cause to "all the exploited and dispossessed [peoples] of Mexico." Most disturbingly, it offered to provide material aid to similar movements in Cuba, Bolivia, Ecuador, and elsewhere. Like Peru's early Communist factions, the Zapatistas had created autonomous communities with collective programs. Their influence would soon extend as far north as Mexico City.[97]

During December 1997, 45 Indians were killed by paramilitary gunmen in a Chiapas village. The incident created such an uproar that President Zedillo was forced to investigate it. A month later, the Governor of Chiapas resigned. Peace talks with the Zapatistas were resumed but soon broke down. In March 2001, the Zapatistas—led by Subcomandante Marcos—staged a march from Chiapas to Mexico City to highlight their demands. Within a month, the Mexican parliament has passed a bill increasing the rights of indigenous peoples. However, Marcos rejected the bill, claiming it would leave the Indian population worse off than before. He also warned that the uprising in Chiapas would continue.[98]

In November 2001, President Fox appointed a prosecutor to investigate the disappearance of left-wing activists during the 1970's and 1980's. Seven months later, millions of secret security files were released to the public. Within those files was evidence of the torture and killing by security forces of hundreds of political activists in the 60's and 70's. President Fox soon announced that his government would prosecute those responsible. Within a month, former President Luis Echeverria had been questioned about the massacres of student protesters (when he was interior minister in 1968, and again when he was president in 1971). In September 2002, three army officers were charged with first-degree murder of 134 leftists in the 1970's.[99]

Throughout this leftist activity, Mexico had been experiencing a steadily worsening drug-trafficking problem. At the start of the 21st Century, it had four main drug cartels that each controlled parts of the U.S. border: (1) Tijuana (Arellano Felix Organization); (2) Juarez; (3) Sinaloa; and (4) Gulf. Those cartels regularly competed, and the Gulf and Sinaloa cartels would eventually become the most powerful.[100]

As the new century progresses, it's hard to tell which crimes are leftist, and which drug inspired. In January 2005, six prison officers are murdered, and all top-security jails put on high alert amid escalating tension between authorities and drug gangs. Finally, in July of 2006, the Mexican people get a break. Conservative candidate Calderon just barely defeats his leftist rival. Three months later, the U.S. president signs into law a plan to build 700 miles of double fencing along the U.S.-Mexico border. For whatever reason, Mexico's leaders do not want the barrier. In December 2006, they create a new federal police force to tackle the drug cartels, and thousands of troops are deployed to the western state of Michoacan as part of an anti-drug drive.[101] Michoacan just happens to be the site of Mexico's new Chinese-built Pacific seaport.

The EPR

The EPR is the most likely of Mexico's leftist guerrilla movements to have traceable foreign ties. Though it originated in the state of Guerrero (Acapulco's location), it has also conducted operations in Oaxaca, Chiapas, Guanajuato, Tlaxcala, and Veracruz. The EPR first announced its existence on 28 June 1996, as the EZLN was about to make a peace deal with the government. The EPR has a more obviously Marxist ideology than the EZLN, and openly advocates Socialist revolution. Subcomandante Marcos has tried in communiques to distance his group from the EPR, but the EPR insists on supporting the Zapatistas. The EPR has further founded its own militarized political wing—the Popular Revolutionary Democratic Party (PDPR-EPR). Though not quite the same as Obrador's "Party of Democratic Revolution," the likeness is remarkable. The PRDP does not function in the political arena independent of the EPR, and does not appear on the ballots of any local or federal election.[102]

The EPR has had many armed clashes with Mexican authorities since 1996. In July of that year, that country's military intelligence service concluded that it was better equipped and organized than the EZLN. In August of 1996, the EPR launched a coordinated multi-state attack against army, police, and government targets in the states of Oaxaca, Guerrero, Puebla, and Distrito Federal (Mexico City). Its guerrilla forces also blocked roads in Chiapas and seized a radio station in Tabasco. In July 2007, it claimed responsibility for several attacks against PEMEX (Mexico's state-owned petroleum company) oil facilities in the Bajio region. Two months later, PEMEX reported sabotage-like explosions at several major pipelines in the key energy-producing state of Veracruz and farther inland at Tlaxcala. Following those attacks, President Calderon deployed 5,000 special troops to secure not only the pipelines, but also dams and power plants. Shortly thereafter, the Centro de Investigacion y Seguridad Nacional (Mexico's intelligence service) leaked a report that "Venezuela's Hugo Chavez was believed to be supporting the EPR with materials, armament, and training."[103]

The EPR had originally been a conglomeration of factions. It subdivided again after some internal squabbling in 2000. Former members created the Insurgent People's Revolutionary Army, Revolutionary Armed Forces of the People, and other small groups. Several became marginally active in southern Mexico. In December 2000, President Vicente Fox offered the EPR amnesty as part of an effort to calm the southern insurgency. To this day, the group issues public statements and appears to be reemerging. Mexican officials claim it played a role in the 2006 mass protests in Oaxaca and bombing in Mexico City. To capitalize on Mexico's ongoing tension, the EPR may engage in future, small-scale attacks. Its probable allegiances are again evident from its flag—a red star with crossed rifle, hammer, and machete in a green field.[104]

The Concurrent Drug War

While the inner workings of the various drug routes are well beyond the scope of this book, the following excerpt should provide some insight into their operation.

[When] U.S. and Colombian authorities began closing smuggling routes through the Caribbean in the late 1980's and 1990's, Colombian criminals began smuggling cocaine and heroin through the Central American isthmus and Pacific routes. Both . . . led them to Mexico.

In the world of organized crime, an individual who wants to smuggle an item into the United States knows he can count on his Mexican counterparts. With an intimate knowledge of the terrain, lists of corrupted officials on the payroll, and decades of perfecting smuggling skills, Mexicans can smuggle just about anything into the United States for the right price. The U.S.-Mexican border is a "soft underbelly" and a porous border. As a result of the important trade relationship between the United States and Mexico, the border cannot be closed.

The Colombians began heavily relying on Mexican smuggling prowess in the 1990's. . . .

Since the Colombians began selling cocaine at the wholesale level to Mexican organized crime, rival factions have battled over control of the downstream revenue, largely dictated by points of entry into the United States, such as Nuevo Laredo, and points of reception from Colombia, such as Acapulco. . . .

. . . Two factions of organized crime, known as the Sinaloa Cartel and the Gulf Cartel, have risen to the top and battle over trafficking routes that span the length and width of Mexico, from Cancun to Acapulco, and from the Guatemalan border to Nuevo Laredo. . . .

Acapulco is a straight shot north from Buenaventura, Colombia, the country's largest Pacific port. Many of Colombia's drug trafficking organizations, including the . . . (F.A.R.C.), used the Buenaventura port to smuggle loads of pure cocaine north. The lack of coastal patrols along the Central American isthmus facilitates the route. Speed boats regularly take illicit products north to Acapulco, where they are loaded onto trucks destined for Nuevo Laredo. . . .

. . . Acapulco happens to be the most logical reception point for both cartels because it avoids the better patrolled waters that surround Mexico's Yucatan peninsula in the Caribbean. Unfortunately for Mexico, Acapulco is not big enough for more than one criminal organization.

Two well-organized and ruthless security details propagate the battle between these two criminal factions. El Chapo [head of Sinaloa Cartel] maintains a group called "Los Pelones," while the Gulf Cartel maintains a group called "Los Zetas." Members of both groups use high-powered automatic rifles, grenades, and ruthless tactics to eliminate the enemy.

The necessary involvement of police officials at the local, state, and national levels, and the Mexican military, complicates the battle over turf. Corruption pollutes well-intentioned policemen and soldiers. The law of "plata o plomo," a choice between accepting a job on a criminal payroll or accepting a bullet in the head, perennially compromises members of the Mexican security forces at all levels.

Due to constant demand for cocaine, heroine *(sic)*, . . . and other drugs, the Mexican criminal enterprise earns more than US$50 billion a year. A considerable amount of this money makes its way back to Colombia to purchase pure cocaine and heroin. Millions of dollars a year land in the hands of policemen, intelligence agents, mayors, port masters, pilots, and many other officials who face the infamous "plata o plomo" decision.[105]

In essence, Mexico is fast becoming a narco-state, just as Colombia did. That means the Mexican government will have about as much chance of controlling its rural areas. A Maoist people's army now uses much of the Colombian countryside as a safe haven from which to subvert the rest of the region. Little imagination is required to see how Mexico's future will affect the United States.

Cross-Border Coordination

Besides NAFTA and CAFTA, there have been other trade arrangements between Central American countries. On 12 July 1998, the leaders of Honduras, Guatemala and El Salvador agreed to a $2-billion rail network between their nations and Mexico.[106] Such a network would help illegal immigrants to move north, because MS-13 already controls the main rail lines in Mexico.[107] Unfortunately, MS-13 also protects the drug conduits.

That MS-13 maintains a presence on both sides of the U.S. border must greatly facilitate the smuggling of drugs across it. As of January 2008, there were estimated to be 10,000 MS-13 gang members inside the U.S.[108] Of course, there are many more in El Salvador, Honduras, and Guatemala.

In a train station near Mexico's border with Guatemala, a gun battle erupted between rival street gangs in September 2004. Investigators say the shoot-out was part of an ongoing turf battle between MS-13 and M-18. Both are trying to control the rail yards where thousands of undocumented Central Americans slip into Mexico *en route* to the United States. (See Map 8.3.) Authorities in Chiapas claim the shoot-out occurred at the Islamapa station in the community of Tuzantan. Gang violence has become quite common in southern Mexico as members work to solidify their hold over local smuggling routes.[109] The *maras* already control key sections of the drug-and-weapon smuggling networks.[110] Like the FARC and ELN in Colombia, they may simply tax all contraband that passes through their zones of "protection."

Considering the Zapatista uprising in Chiapas, MS-13's control over the Guatemalan border may be no coincidence. Still, its architect is far from clear. There has even been Muslim versus Christian violence in Chiapas.[111] Mexico's National Center for Investigation and Security reports no FARC cells in Chiapas and says they are more likely in the following locations: (1) the U.S. border states of Nuevo Leon and Coahuila; (2) Queretaro, Mexico, and Distrito Federal (around Mexico City); and (3) Oaxaca (Chiapas' neighbor).[112] Yet within Chiapas, both revolutionary and *mara* activity have occurred, and they may be part of a foreign strategy.

Map 8.3: *Maras* Control Main Rail Lines
(Source: Courtesy of Instituto National de Estadistica de Mexico, in General Libraries, University of Texas at Austin, from their website for map designator "railroads.gif)

Chinese Nationals in Mexico

A recent visitor to Tijuana saw far too many Chinese restaurants.[113] While such a sighting may seem ludicrous to those obsessed with *al-Qaeda*, it doesn't to PRC watchers. China has identified its ties with Mexico as one of the four "strategic partnerships" its ruling party has designated for Latin America. Allegedly, those ties have to do only with the transfer of goods to the United States.[114] But, the word "strategic" usually has more of a military connotation. One cannot help but wonder which goods might have 4GW significance.

Many of the Chinese aliens to enter the United States have crossed Mexico's boundary with Belize under the auspices of a Chinese organized-crime faction. In China, all factions that smuggle human beings are called "snakeheads."[115] While "snakeheads" often cooperate with triads, their exact relationship has yet to be determined.

Since the late 1980's, hundreds of thousands of illegal immigrants from China's Fujian province have been smuggled into the United States. The business of human-smuggling has evolved as security has tightened in the U.S. And the smugglers, called by Chinese as "snakeheads," have become more sophisticated. . . .

With Mexico to the north, Belize has become a stopover for smugglers traveling by land from Latin America to the United States.

Residents of Douglas in Belize know their village is a popular spot to smuggle goods and people into Mexico. The village lies next to the Rio Hondo River, which divides the two countries.

Belize has a surprisingly large Chinese population, making up more than 3 percent of the country's total population of 300,000. Those familiar with the trade say the smugglers are local Chinese-Belizean businesspeople. . . .

After the Chinese cross into Mexico, they travel north and are smuggled across the border into America. Every week, 50 to 100 Chinese nationals are caught trying to cross the U.S.-Mexican border.[116]

— NPR's Morning News, 20 November 2007

How the Cartels and *Maras* May Be Linked to the PRC

Vowing to topple all drug cartels in Mexico, President Felipe Calderon has deployed thousands of troops to fight the drug gangs. The bloodiest gunfight recently occurred along the border with Arizona when armed assailants killed 22 people, including five policemen, in a five-hour gun battle.[117] If the cartels trust MS-13 to protect their drug shipments, then where did MS-13 learn so much about light-infantry tactics? FARC cells are suspected in the border states of Coahuila and Nuevo Leon.[118] And FARC-EP is known to idolize the North Koreans and have Cuban and Venezuelan advisers. But MS-13's tactical advice may be coming from an even higher source.

There have been reports of Chinese military contingents operating with Mexican army units that help with the drug smuggling.[119] Whether those contingents are part of some joint training exercise is unknown. Chinese military assistance was undoubtedly offered to Mexico during a visit by members of the Poliburo Standing Committee of China's ruling Communist Party in 2005.[120] While the initial news release can no longer be located (possibly by *The Washington Post),* a tiny North Korean military contingent was killed to a man on Mexican soil in the late 1980's.[121] The North Koreans may have been tunnel engineers, but more likely they were from that country's Light-Infantry Training Guidance Bureau.

It's clear from past history and recent elections that both Mexico and Peru are still Communist targets for subversion. Only still under discussion are which Communists. The other targeted nations are believed—by a Venezuelan observer—to be El Salvador, the Dominican Republic, Jamaica, and more subliminally Panama.[122] Notably absent from the list is Colombia. That government's lack of control over its own countryside must be to the Communists' advantage.

There have only been hints of what the PRC's overall strategy for the region might be. It does not revolve strictly around oil. In addition to Venezuela, Bolivia, Ecuador, and Nicaragua, China appears most interested in the nations that can either grow/produce illicit drugs or trans-ship them to market. Only the most naive of Americans would believe that the PRC's reasons are strictly monetary.

The PLA—through its intelligence service—is probably the

brains behind this drug-related assault on America. Wherever the PLA is involved, so too are its known extensions—Hutchison Whampoa and COSCO. COSCO's ships have long been suspected of the massive smuggling of weapons, drugs, and illegal aliens.[123]

China's Probable Goal in this Hemisphere

Hutchison Whampoa helps to fund the PLA. That it now runs Dar es Salaam's main container terminal will come as no surprise to those who remember that China supported southern Africa's rebels through that same port in the 70's and 80's.[124] Hutchison Whampoa's Western Hemisphere ports may now serve the same purpose. Its website claims operations in Argentina, Ecuador, Panama, the Bahamas, and Mexico. At Freeport in the Bahamas, it has a "deep-water container port . . . serving as a trans-shipment centre for the eastern seaboard of the Americas and the principal East/West . . . haul routes throughout the region." On Grand Bahama island, it has the "world's largest privately owned airport . . . capable of handling the world's largest aircraft." In Mexico, it runs container unloading facilities at Manzanillo on the Pacific and Veracruz on the Gulf of Mexico. After greatly expanding its Ensenada port facilities (just south of San Diego), it plans "an 85-hectare deep-water, greenfield site with 1,350 metres of berth length" at Lazaro Cardenas south-west of Mexico City.[125] With everything else that has happened in Mexico, the PLA's newfound enthusiasm for free trade seems a bit suspicious. So does its ability to forestall any serious resistance from north of the border.

By any analysis, this company [Hutchison Whampoa, Ltd.], headed by Li Kashing is an interesting operation:

* Hutchison has worked closely with the China Ocean Shipping Co. (COSCO). . . . COSCO, you may remember, is the PLA-controlled company that almost succeeded in gaining control of the abandoned naval station at Long Beach, California.
* Li Kashing has served on the board of directors of China International Trust and Investment Corp., a PLA-affiliated giant run by Wang Jun whose name may ring a bell.

Yes, the very same Wang Jun enjoyed coffee at the White House in exchange for a modest donation to the Clinton-Gore 1996 slush fund.[126]
— *Washington Times,* Nat. Wkly. Ed., 1 March 1999

Mexico's Border Region Has Become an Open War Zone

On 23 March 2008, the police chief of a Mexican town along a previously quiet sector of the U.S. border fled to New Mexico after his deputies abandoned him. A few days earlier, heavily armed men had kidnapped several people and executed two of them.[127] This was far from an isolated incident. In May, a five hour gunfight had left 22 people dead, including five policemen, along Mexico's border with Arizona.[128] Within this context, reports of people in full military regalia occasionally straying into U.S. territory seem much more believable. Some of those people were even thought to have Chinese advisers.[129]

Fortified Drug Conduits Pose a 2GW Risk to the U.S.

In late March 2008, a 66-pound block of uranium (of undisclosed grade) was confiscated near Bogota, Colombia. Its location had been learned from a FARC leader's laptop computer that was captured during a raid into Ecuador's border region on 1 March. As FARC probably lacks the expertise to make its own "dirty" bomb, it may have wanted to sell the uranium to fund future operations.[130] One first wonders where the FARC could have gotten such a thing. Then there is the question of where the buyer would have taken delivery. If tons of cocaine can annually make it across the U.S. border, then so too could 66 pounds of uranium.

Of course, there is also the problem of advanced technology leaving America. One could "back-ship" fully assembled military hardware along the largest of the smuggling conduits (those often arranged through corrupt officials). In April 2008, even the conservative *Washington Post* admitted that the U.S. government had grown increasingly concerned about the growth in size and sophistication of the PRC's intelligence-gathering effort. There was now proof that Chinese agents had infiltrated at least four military programs (nuclear missiles, submarine propulsion, night vision, and pilot training). All could help China to develop countermeasures or its own capabilities. And that was not the extent of the bad news. One of the 4GW arenas, after all, is economic. "While military technology appears to be the top prize, the Chinese effort is also aimed at commercial and industrial technologies."[131]

Finally, there is the problem of information about America's ongoing war effort leaving the country. Drugs provide another way to collect it. Just as *Hezbollah* has been using dope dealers to entrap Israeli soldiers,[132] so too could China get U.S. security personnel to divulge secrets. Once the quarry had been enticed into a lucrative narcotics transaction, he might be forced by drug habit or blackmail to provide details on deployments, commanders, or electronic systems.

While the overall threat to America may seem unified and daunting, it occurs across a network so convoluted as to defy blockage. Thus, it must be uniquely countered at many places at once. That suggests something simple in method, yet locally modifiable.

The Answer Lies in Tiny Security Detachments

That this subliminal assault on America is being supported, if not orchestrated, by a foreign military power means that it is most properly handled by the U.S. military. To do so effectively, the American defense establishment will have to step away from its tightly controlled 2GW comfort zone and come to rely more on decentralized 4GW initiatives. Latin America is already so far gone, that reversing the trend will take hundreds of U.S. squad-sized elements working with local counterparts in Combined Action Platoons (CAPs) in isolated locations. A string of CAPs along the Guatemalan border with Mexico would help, but the narrowest chokepoint to overland cocaine flow is in eastern Panama. Because the Communists have chosen a drug-trade format, those U.S. soldiers or Marines who would man those CAPs must first learn the basics of law enforcement. They must also be taught enough about UW to be able to melt into the jungle whenever seriously threatened with annihilation.

Then, as the human, drug, and arms smuggling routes are progressively blocked, so too will be the funds for gang, organized-crime, and revolutionary activity in Latin America. All of this has to be accomplished in a much less "militaristic" fashion than was tried last time, or the leftists will simply win all the elections. Part Two will develop the specific parameters for this new 4GW approach to counterinsurgency.

Part Two

The Urgent Need for a New U.S. Strategy

"Victory attained by violence is tantamount to a defeat,
for it is momentary."
— Mahatma Gandhi

(Source: Mahatma Gandhi, "Satyagraha Leaflet No. 13," 3 May 1919, as found at http://www.quotationspage.com/quotes/Mahatma_Gandhi/)

The 4GW Difference in Latin America

9

- Why is this Western Hemisphere crisis so hard to solve?
- How many things are in play in each of the 4GW arenas?

Rural Residents Will Need Alternative Sources of Income

(Source: DA Pamphlet 550-82 [1993], p. 65)

4GW's Roots

As all armed insurrections have political, economic, and psychological overtones, most pose 4GW-like problems. Traditional Maoist revolution is no exception. To embrace "all means of resistance," it includes "politicization" and "labor collectives." The only difference between it and a modern 4GW conflict is its lack of intra-arena coordination. In 4GW, any initiative can be intended to screen some activity or need in another arena. Throughout Iraq, for example, acts of violence have diverted the Coalition's attention from more important issues of governance and infrastructure.

Where there is too little armed revolt, the purveyor of 4GW might try a nonmartial diversion. Of all the economic excesses, drug trafficking would be the most disruptive. It could function not only as a feint, but also as a fund raiser. Most Communist regimes have so little concern for human rights, that narcotics easily qualify as a legitimate trading commodity. Only Western governments consider such things a police matter. As such, they would never deem drug trafficking as part of a 4GW agenda.

That the U.N., Britain, and U.S. have been trying to turn all armed insurrection into political strife is an admirable ambition. Violence—for whatever reason—does tend to spawn additional violence. But an extremist winning an election can be as detrimental to world peace as a successful rebellion. Hitler was confirmed as overall leader of Germany by 84% of the electorate in a 1934 plebiscite.[1] And there are more recent examples. Did *Hamas'* winning the Gaza election help to stabilize the Near East? Neither would a political victory by *Hezbollah* in Lebanon be in the best interests of the Free World. Thus, every nation's politics are to some extent America's business. Productively to enter into those politics, the U.S and other countries need only obey the democratic process and host-nation rules.

Once an Islamist or Marxist is elected, a U.S.-sponsored invasion, insurrection, or military coup will only make things worse. Any Western response must necessarily precede the election and consist of more than just political advice and funding. There are alternatives to heavy-handed interference and underhanded subversion. One of the best is foreign assistance at the local law enforcement level. With fewer violent crimes and governmental atrocities would come less fear at the polling place. In the most volatile regions, specially trained infantry squads would have a better chance of providing this kind of service than police advisers. There is, after all, a clear correlation between infantry tactics and police procedures. It is most obvious at the squad and special-weapons-assault-team (SWAT) level. With a different way of projecting force, the U.S. military could create enough local security in distressed nations to insure truly fair elections.

Then, to elect a democracy-oriented conservative, the people in each area would only need two things: (1) a livelihood that is not guerrilla or drug related; and (2) rightist-regime interest in local infrastructure. Otherwise, they might find the Islamist or Marxist promises of land redistribution and alternate governance more appealing. To fulfill the first requirement, each U.S. contingent could bankroll a few small business or farming initiatives, like the Marines have done in Iraq's Anbar Province with their "micro-loans."[2] It could offer a small stipend to community watch volunteers. And, it could create a few public-works jobs like Franklin D. Roosevelt did with his Civilian Conservation Corps of 1933.[3] This third choice would additionally suffice for the second requirement—upgrading local infrastructure.

The U.S. military would only have to provide three things: (1) more training and trust for the noncommissioned officers (NCOs) involved; (2) a small slush fund; and (3) an engineer and medic for each contingent. Within developing nations, a few U.S. dollars can go a very long way at the grass-roots level. In many of those nations, roads are still repaired the old-fashioned way—with rock chippers, shovels, and sweat equity.

The Inevitable Iraq Comparison

Vietnam and post-Vietnam eras are ancient history. Most U.S. counterinsurgency ability assessments are now based on the post-Iraqi-Surge period. One of the most obvious consequences of that Surge was less media coverage. To the new field commander's credit, neighborhood police departments were finally augmented with U.S. troops. But, instead of street barricades between districts, tall walls were built. While their impact on infiltration was probably dramatic, so too was their effect on resident freedom. The number of U.S. military detainees was also doubled. By mid-January 2008, that number had risen to 24,000. Still, the U.S. military seemed to realize the 4GW risk. The detainees' cases were reviewed every six months by a military panel. Their efforts to rehabilitate themselves were considered at those hearings. Hard-core inmates were separated from those suspected of lesser crimes. And, unlike in the overloaded U.S. penal system, all inmates were offered rehabilitation programs.[4] As of 22 February, more suspects were being released than picked up.[5] By mid-April, the number in U.S. prison camps stood at only 20,000. Still there was the little matter of 26,000 more in extended Iraqi police custody. Most had not been officially arraigned, and some were still disappearing.[6]

As in Peru in the early 1980's, holding suspects for an indeterminate period of time without due process of civilian law tends to alienate the voting public and lessen the chances a long-term solution. Because of the near chaos before the Surge, America's new counterinsurgency plan may have been justifiable over the short term. But how it is now amended will determine whether U.S. forces succeed in Iraq.

Latin America Is More Like Afghanistan

Many parts of the world have drugs, and others 4GW; but few have both at once. In this sense, Latin America has become like Afghanistan. There, despite America's best efforts, heroin production has more than tripled since 1992. Afghanistan now produces 93% of the world's opium poppies, while President Hamid Karzai's regime has only managed to control 30% of the countryside.[7] Not until 12 December 2007 was the key heroin-producing town of Musa Qala finally wrested from the Taliban in Helmund Province.[8] Though the Taliban has been largely funded by heroin, U.S. troops were for many years told that drug interdiction was not part of their mission.[9] Only if they don't intend to win, is it not part of their mission. However, Afghanistan does not abut the United States. The extent to which drug trafficking has created conduits into the U.S. heartland is what makes Latin America unique. Those conduits could be easily used for other things—like spies, saboteurs, or military contraband. As such, Latin America constitutes a far more important theater of war. What happens there must be now viewed as narcotics-oriented 4GW.

Islamic radicals have no intention of adding parts of Central and South America to a Muslim empire, or of attacking American interests there. Almost all of their activity has been to raise funds for other theaters. U.S. leaders who have grown too fond of chasing *al-Qaeda* must concede that point. For the last 50 years, Latin America has been a Communist target. Only different now is the attack's instigator. It is no longer the Soviet Union, but another hungry giant with a style of revolution that is better suited to the region. For plausible deniability, this new giant must depend more on its proxies.

Cubans [emphasis added] . . . and even advisors from the

leftist government of Venezuela are . . . active in the [rebel-held] area [of Colombia].[10]
— John Moore
former DOD counter-terrorism analyst
in Congressional testimony, 9/14/2001

Commodities Are Contested in 4GW's Economic Arena

The above-mentioned giant is obviously interested in South America's natural resources. Uniquely, two of the continent's traditional crops can be locally refined and easily traded. That makes all kinds of expansionist activity possible without implicating its instigator.

Within Colombia and its neighbors, U.S. drug-enforcement and special-operations personnel have been valiantly struggling against some of the world's most sophisticated criminals for over 20 years. Now that a clear correlation has been proven between drug trafficking and leftist takeovers, those brave young Americans deserve some good-sized reinforcements.

An Objective Look at Past U.S. Efforts in Latin America

In this part of the world, two things are clear. Leftists are starting to win all the elections; and, while in office, rightists allow too many governmental excesses. This dynamic is still at work in Peru. Its residents are again being ruled by an old-time rightist boss, but they will at some point opt for a leftist replacement. Though generally credited with bringing down the Shining Path and MRTA, Fujimori is in prison. He has had to learn the hard way how much long-term resentment can be created by martial law. When he dissolved the Peruvian Congress, courts, and constitution in 1990, he effectively alienated his people. In the last presidential election, the next generation came very close to picking Hugo Chavez's candidate—Ollanta Humala. Thus, one can safely say that overriding a civilian criminal justice system is not a good way to counter rebellion.

Such a discussion becomes more controversial when one considers where Fujimori probably got his advice. That America's counterinsurgency efforts in Iraq and Afghanistan still allow for bom-

145

bardment of populated areas shows too little aversion to collateral damage. That so many people are still at Guantanamo shows too little respect for due process. That the CIA even considered water boarding shows too little regard for civilized behavior. Such things are particularly counterproductive in a predominantly Christian region. In a 4GW environment, all police and military operations must be carefully integrated. When civilian factors are in play, the same rules apply to American soldiers as to big-city policemen. There can be no more inadvertent shelling of innocent bystanders, condoning of local death squads, or entrapment by ill-conceived stings. GIs can only apply lethal force when their lives or those of others are at immediate risk. None of this will be possible at isolated CAP outposts, unless the U.S. squads have been trained in criminal investigative procedure and UW. Their job will be to help local authorities to curtail criminal activity without having to resort to extrajudicial measures.

After 50 years of the traditional American approach to Communist expansion, the situation in Central and South America is now deteriorating. The U.S. government has supported and trained Contras in Nicaragua and looked the other way in several other countries while government death squads freely operated. Most of those countries are being lost, not through guerrilla warfare, but through leftist campaign victories. Succeeding at 4GW takes minimal force and closer attention to public opinion.

The "Haves Versus Have-Nots" Syndrome

In the Preface, the Mexican persecution of priests was mentioned only as a warning of the extremes to which Latin America's ruling elite have been willing to go to dominate their indigenous populations. As any recent traveler to Argentina can attest, there are still glaring indicators of this syndrome.[11] One of its most recent examples is the killing of a Catholic nun by a rich land owner in Brazil. Her only indiscretion was to protect the rain forest and minister to the poor.[12] Where harmless nuns are being killed, indiscriminate death squads cannot be far behind. The only sure way to stop this kind of thing—in a counterinsurgency or 4GW setting—is to discourage killing.

The 2GW Syndrome for Latin America

Whenever a military force is on the offensive in second-generation warfare, it attacks enemy strongpoints head on with overwhelming firepower. While those strongpoints are under siege, any unit that attempts to reinforce or leave them is likewise bombarded. As enemy troop concentrations are generally associated with strongpoints, many opposition soldiers get killed. That's why 2GW-oriented armies tend to measure their degree of success through body counts. Every time they lose 100 while killing what they perceive to be 1,000, they figure they have done a good job. If they really have or not depends on many things. Among them are whether that strongpoint ever had any strategic value, and whether each of the 1,000 was confirmed to be an actual combatant and counted just once.

For whatever reason, this way of gauging battlefield success produces more than just inflated casualty totals in Latin America. There, it creates atrocities—and not just those of 20 years ago. There is now evidence that they continue today in the place where U.S. leaders would least want to find them. A 2GW-trained Colombian Army has apparently been a little too eager to wrest the momentum away from the FARC. When dealing with a people's army that is largely made up of children, such eagerness easily equates to abusing youngsters.

Human rights groups estimate that nearly a thousand Colombian civilians have been executed during the army's six-year offensive against FARC rebels. Members of some rogue army units are accused of executing [teenage] civilians and dressing them up in rebel uniforms so they can be counted as rebels killed in battle.[13]
— NPR's "Morning Edition" News, 14 April 2008

4GW Requires a Different Approach

The Marines' difficulties in Anbar Province stopped the day they began to see every Sunni as part of the solution rather than part of the problem. They had discovered a crucial axiom of 4GW—that it is more important to convert one's foe than to kill him. Little did they know that killing, *per se,* has never been an essential ingredient of war. They had needed their weapons for self-protection, not to make a strategic difference.

War Hasn't Been about Killing for Quite Some Time

For those who have lost a friend or fought for their very lives in war, such an idea seems ridiculous. It's true that U.S. soldiers and Marines must sometimes kill or be killed in the most obscene of man's inventions. But "killing," *per se,* does not win wars. There have been any number of wars won by the side that took the most casualties. It often fought unconventionally. Among the most recent examples are the following: (1) the NVA/Viet Cong in Vietnam; (2) the Communists in southern Africa; and (3) the Sandinistas in Nicaragua.

Many Americans still do not realize that their assault forces have taken more casualties at short range than quarries who could move rearward through tunnels. The enemy casualty totals have been amassed at high altitude or long range through standoff weaponry with too little concern for whether all targets were combatants. Even the outcome of a conventional war depends more on strategic-asset differential than kill differential. With this in mind, it's easier to see why the unconventional wars of the future must be won by some way other than expert snipers and pinpoint bombing. The name of the game is no longer to kill as many foes as possible, but rather to sway the allegiance of as many as possible. Otherwise, the number of mothers mistakenly killed alone will ensure enough *jidahist* zeal to keep the War on Terror going for generations.

In essence, the political, economic, and psychological factors have become as important as the martial. To excel at 4GW, one must be better at converting one's foe than killing him. As most insurgencies and 4GW's are bottom-up evolutions, this conversion must take place across a wide expanse of territory at the bottom echelon. Until U.S. tactical doctrine changes to embrace this reality, that doctrine itself may prevent U.S. forces from winning any more wars.

A Solution Emerges

U.S. infantry squads trained in mantracking, criminal-investigative, and UW procedures could turn the tide in Latin America, providing they were sufficiently trusted and funded. (See Figure 9.1.) Operating from isolated CAP platoons, they would help indigenous sister squads to do the following: (1) disrupt smuggling and guerrilla routes; (2) apprehend smuggling and guerrilla leaders; (3) discourage gang activity; and (4) reestablish local infrastructure. Though a loose extension of the local government, those U.S. squads would immediately report any extrajudicial action by indigenous forces (including sister squads) to an American headquarters. They would live on, and generally resupply themselves from, the local economy. With an engineer and medic attached, each would establish a clinic, public-works projects, and micro-loans for local entrepreneurs. To further interact with the community (and keep unemployed youth productively occupied), each would start and play in a soccer league.

> [Central American] communities should build sports and cultural facilities and programs that encourage youth participation. The more organized these efforts are, the higher the probability of success, as evidenced by such programs as "Safer Communities" and "Citizen Safety Assemblies."[14]
> — *Military Review,* July/August 2007

Thus, the U.S. infantry detachment's role would have more to do with community service than killing or being killed. Still, where drug cartels and Maoist people's armies are involved, that "community service" could at times turn risky. During any serious annihilation attempt, the GIs would simply revert to escape and evasion (E&E) or guerrilla warfare. That would preclude any need for a collateral-damage-producing rescue.

Further Applicability of the Method

While this book has been investigating what to do in Latin America against the FARC, many of its conclusions would also work in Afghanistan against the Taliban. As both organizations now acquire most of their funding through drug production, both can only be dried up through drug interdiction.

Those who don't agree should imagine the entire Free World under drug-oriented 4GW assault. With almost all of its cocaine

PROBLEM	SOLUTION
TOO LITTLE LOCAL SECURITY FOR FAIR ELECTIONS	GIS HELP TO RESTORE ORDER THROUGH CAP UNIT OUTPOSTS
DRUGS TRANSITING CAP ZONE	GIS HELP TO LOCATE AND INTERRUPT DRUG CONDUITS
COCA OR POPPIES BEING GROWN IN CAP ZONE	GIS HELP TO LOCATE AND ERADICATE ILLICIT DRUG CROPS
DRUGS BEING PROCESSED IN CAP ZONE	GIS HELP TO LOCATE AND DESTROY DRUG FACTORIES
TOO FEW OTHER LIVELIHOODS FOR DRUG WORKERS	*GIS PROVIDE MICRO-LOANS FOR NEW CROPS OR BUSINESSES*
GUERRILLAS TRANSITING CAP ZONE	GIS HELP TO LOCATE AND INTERRUPT INFILTRATION ROUTES
GUERRILLAS RECRUITED/TRAINED IN CAP ZONE	GIS HELP TO IDENTIFY AND ARREST RECRUITERS/TRAINERS
GUERRILLAS BASED IN CAP ZONE	GIS HELP TO LOCATE AND DESTROY BASE CAMP FACILITIES
TOO FEW OTHER JOBS FOR PROSPECTIVE GUERRILLAS	*GIS GIVE SUBSISTENCE WAGE TO COMMUNITY WATCH VOLUNTEERS*
PEOPLE BEING SMUGGLED THROUGH CAP ZONE	GIS HELP TO NAB "COYOTES" AND CARE FOR HUMAN CARGO
YOUTH GANGS OPERATING IN CAP ZONE	GIS INSURE GANG MEMBERS ONLY WATCHED
TOO FEW ALTERNATIVE ACTIVITIES FOR YOUTH	*PUBLIC-WORKS JOBS CREATED AND SOCCER LEAGUES STARTED*
GOVERNMENTAL SECURITY EXCESSES IN CAP ZONE	GIS REPORT ALL EXTRAJUDICIAL ACTIVITIES TO U.S. HDQTS.
TOO LITTLE INFRASTRUCTURE	*GIS RUN LOCAL CLINICS AND START PUBLIC-WORKS PROJECTS*

Figure 9.1: 4GW Initiatives by CAP Platoon in Latin America

coming from Colombia and 92% of its opium from Afghanistan,[15] what chance would that Free World have without first curtailing their production in both places? Drugs have the power not only to fund insurgency, but also to corrupt governance. It takes lowering their supply to win such a conflict.

Thus, U.S. leaders must stop drawing too fine a distinction between military and law enforcement matters. Otherwise, their efforts in Afghanistan may have less success than those in Iraq. (See Figure 9.2.) Luckily, the ultimate instigator in Latin America is more apparent. So, there, non-*jihadist* issues will more likely be considered.

Figure 9.2: Same Plan Would Work on Drug-Funded Taliban
(Source: DA Pam 550-65 [1986], cover)

10 Undermining the Proxy Coalition

- On what do all of Latin America's troublemakers depend?
- How might that thing be disrupted?

The Common Tie between Disruptive Elements Is Drugs

(Source: DA Pam 550-33 [1989], cover)

Multiple Foes—All Linked to the PRC?

Communist China has already documented its willingness to use terrorism as a military strategy. In the PLA's 1999 publication *Unrestricted Warfare,* two of its colonels proposed precisely that.[1] So the Latin American chaos is certainly within the PRC's sphere of capability. For deniability, it would only require various strings of proxies and ways for those proxies to support themselves. There would be politico-military proxy strings emanating from allied nations: such as (1) Iran—*Hezbollah*—*Hamas*; or (2) Cuba—Venezuela—FARC.

153

Relations between China and Venezuela should be at the highest strategic level, and in the front lines of the battle-field.[2]

—Hugo Chavez, 1 January 2008

There would also be commercial proxy strings with Hutchison Whampoa, COSCO, or some other PLA-connected business at their head. With China's differing view of morality, some might amount to criminal proxy strings (like a PLA-influenced triad coordinating cartels and *maras* from the TBA and Panama). Finally, there would be combinations: e.g., North Korean Bureau 39 dealing directly with the Hong Kong triad that ships heroin and methamphetamines to a Mexican distributor.[3] While such a proxy web might seem improbable to Americans, it is nevertheless possible. Even Western criminals will sometimes create elaborate schemes to escape detection. By following the famous 36 Stratagems, China may well have manipulated both the Islamist and Judao/Christian worlds. That would make the PRC into "Terror International," with Iran only the most active of its Islamic surrogates.

In Iraq, Nigeria, and the Southern Philippines, China hides its quest for oil behind Islamic insurrection. In the mostly Christian Western Hemisphere, its only screen for expansion is a drug war. While drug trading creates the diversion, Marxists get elected or rebellions launched. Within Latin America, COSCO brings natural resources out, and guns or heroin in. Farther north, it takes technology out, and drugs or people in. In essence, the PLA adapts smuggling channels to 4GW use. Then, on-the-spot proceeds fund the choice between PRC candidate and disruption.

In a loosely controlled "bottom-up" evolution, people's army, cartels, *maras,* and voting masses all play vital roles. U.S. leaders take note. Winston Churchill once said, "No matter how involved a commander may become in the elaboration of his own thoughts, it is sometimes necessary to take the enemy into account."[4]

The Glue That Holds the Proxies Together

Among all the proxies, dope is the common thread. *Hezbollah* and *Hamas* get funded by dope. FARC and the *maras* protect dope. The triads and cartels distribute dope. Dope creates the diversion, and dope funds the main attack. That attack is the unfortunate choice between three evils: (1) a ruling rightist's oppression; (2) a leftist candidate's election; and (3) an armed rebellion. Once the flow of drugs abates, so too will the proxies' power. There is little doubt that Cuban-backed Venezuela has been coordinating the political and revolutionary parts of that equation. And it has concurrently done far too little to stem the flow of narcotics. As of April 2008, 250 tons of cocaine were passing through Venezuela annually, almost twice the rate of the late 1990's. Under the pretext of participating in the drug war, Venezuela has installed Chinese-made radar throughout much of the country. And so, once again, there is telltale PRC involvement.[5]

The Criminal Proxy Coordinator

Some will say Part One only proves that various organized-crime factions have conspired to milk the Americas. If that were true, one of the Colombian cartels or FARC would be overseeing the project, with the Mexican cartels and MS-13 only cooperating.

Originally, there were four cartels in Colombia: (1) Medellin; (2) North Coast; (3) Cali; and (4) Norte del Valle. The Medellin cartel declared war on the Colombian government in 1989, so it may have had something to do with M-19's Palace of Justice raid. After many of its leaders were killed or captured in the early 1990's, it ceased to exist as a unified faction. Vigilantes financed by the Cali cartel helped to bring it down.[6] Though the North Coast cartel also had many of its leaders eliminated around the turn of the century (some by Norte del Valle), it still marginally manages to function.[7]

The Norte del Valle cartel principally controls the northern part of Colombia's Valle del Cauca Department (home to the Pacific seaport of Buenaventura). It rose to prominence in the late 1990's after the Medellin and Cali cartels became fragmented. For a while, the Norte del Valle group was the single most powerful cartel in Colombia. According to a 2004 U.S. Government indictment, it was shipping cocaine to Mexico and employing AUC to protect its facilities and routes.[8] By late 2007, many of its leaders had also been killed or captured by Colombian agencies, the DEA, U.S. special-operations units, or drug-trade rivals.

Meanwhile, the Cali cartel was operating out of the lower part of the Valle del Cauca Department. Its leaders preferred to bribe Colombian officials, diversify into heroin, and pioneer drug routes through Panama. It clashed with the FARC in the early 1990's, but that animosity may not have lasted. Most of the Cali cartel's leaders were later arrested. Because it had originally been a confederation of smaller elements, it continued to operate at a reduced capacity. Around 2000, it was accused of "socially cleansing" its home town of hundreds of prostitutes, street children, petty thieves, homosexuals, and homeless.⁹ One hates to think who more probably did this.

Thus, none of Colombia's cartels are strong enough to be coordinating the Central American onslaught. Either FARC has added another dimension to its already besieged role, or an Eastern syndicate is officiating. As busiest triad in Latin America and alleged PRC instrument, Sun Yee On is the most likely candidate. But if the PLA itself is managing, more than one triad may be involved.

Most of these Chinese criminal enterprises have worked with criminal groups of other ethnic and racial backgrounds, such as . . . Hispanic.¹⁰
    — recent FBI study for U.S. State Dept.

It's clear from Colombian-cartel history that America's principal strategy has been to remove dope trade kingpins. Because the Cali and Norte del Valle groups had so little organizational structure, that strategy didn't work on them. Nor will it work on the triads. Like 14-K, many are made up of individual chapters—each of which operates autonomously.¹¹ Some other way must be found to discourage triad interest in the Colombian-cocaine market.

Smuggling to Southern U.S. Border Directed from Panama

Chinese organized crime has made Panama its base of operations, and PRC intelligence mans an office there.¹² But, where's the proof that the PLA has been using organized crime as a strategic instrument? Here's more evidence from a very reliable source.

The growing anti-U.S./NATO "strategic partnership" of China and Russia poses an increasing threat. There is a well-documented history of both Russian and Chinese organized crime organizations working as tools of their governments.¹³
    — American Foreign Policy Council Report

Now, the search boils down to which of China's organized crime factions are present in Panama. Their identity can only be narrowed to "triad gangs." Given the dynamics of "criminal turf," most of those gangs probably serve the same triad. Interpol has linked 18 Chinese gangs throughout Central America to the obscure Fa Yen triad.[14] But Sun Yee On is more probably the lead player.

> The massive smuggling of illegal aliens from the People's Republic of China into Panama's ports is . . . problem. . . . The alien smuggling . . . is conducted by Chinese *triad gangs* on commercial ships (italics added).[15]
> — American Foreign Policy Council Report

Removing the Proxies' Purpose

Problems are best handled at their source. While the U.S. demand for drugs may be the most logical objective, those more tangible will have to suffice. With regard to cocaine, the best remaining option is the coca fields. Those fields cannot all be eradicated through aerial spraying. For many, their initial demise will take troops on the ground, and their long-term removal will take subsidized crop rotation.

After crop elimination, the next best target is the cocaine-producing facilities. Most are probably now underground. Finding their entrances would take locally stationed mantrackers.

Third most productive in removing the proxies' purpose would be blocking the drug conduits. Like infiltration routes in guerrilla warfare, they again would only be evident in normal terrain to skilled mantrackers. Unless carefully sabotaged, they would be relocated. Two-ton bombs from 10,000 feet would serve only to kill unsuspecting mules and local wildlife. Technology would be of more help where fast boats leapfrog up Central America's Pacific coast. Always possible, of course, are aerial legs over the areas most heavily contested. (See Figure 10.1.)

Most difficult would be stopping the cocaine at the Texas, New Mexico, Arizona, or California borders. There, hollow imports, hang gliders, and deep tunnels could easily breach the most sophisticated of barriers. So much money would be in play that local corruption would be endemic. If officials could not be bought, they would be blackmailed with compromising photos, implicated in crimes they

157

Figure 10.1: Part of the Route May Be by Air
(Source: FM 5-103 [1985], p. 4-39)

didn't commit, or otherwise squeezed. Against that which is triad-coordinated, no countermeasure would be foolproof. Its members will be among the most expert criminals in the world.

　　Chinese criminals are quite familiar with the investigative techniques (i.e., wiretaps, undercover agents) and strategies used by the U.S. law enforcement agencies and are innovative in devising methods (i.e., cloned cellular telephones, using codes during telephone conversations) to evade detection by law enforcement officials. . . .
　　With reduced trade barriers, it is even easier for them to move their base of operation to another country if market conditions there are more favorable, such as more demands for their merchandise, and fewer risks (i.e., lack of law enforcement presence).[16]
　　　　　　— recent FBI study for the U.S. State Dept.

　　With FARC available to train cartels and *maras* in light-infantry tactics, a PLA-managed criminal coalition would be far too formidable for the international law enforcement community to handle alone. That community would need more help from the U.S. military in Colombia, Peru, and Central America. And this help must be quite different from the anti-Communist "assistance" of the 1980's.

11 __ A Quasi-Military Solution Required

● What military procedures might prove counterproductive?

● Could civilian regimens take their place?

Tension Reduction Programs Are Not New to the Military

(Source: Courtesy of Sorman Information and Media, from Soldf: Soldaten i falt, ©2001 by Forsvarsmakten and Wolfgang Bartsch, Stockholm, p. 394)

Latin America Is No Longer a Low-Level Sideshow

As any American policeman can attest, drug traffickers are the most dangerous of all criminals. They will kill anyone who informs on them and routinely ambush or assassinate law enforcement officials.[1] To this add a full-blown Maoist people's army, and one can readily see how the hinterlands of Colombia could be every bit as dangerous as Iraq. Mexico is quickly moving in the same direction. Doubters of that should dust off their passports and dodge kidnappers for a while in Mexico City.[2] Any GI wanting to assist either country will need more light-infantry skill than most U.S.

commandos had at the height of the Vietnam conflict. As the next paragraph will demonstrate, time has done little to dampen this unfortunate truth.

21st-Century Wars Will Be Won by Dismounted Infantry

While everyone was watching Iraq, there elsewhere occurred an epochal shift in the evolution of warfare,[3] according to one of America's best military thinkers. That momentous occasion may have come as part of a Chinese and North Korean experiment.[4]

> Conclusive proof that another epochal shift had occurred came last year in the small village of Bint Jbiel, just over the Israeli-Lebanon border, and nearby in the defile of Wadi Saluki, where Hezbollah fighters ambushed and destroyed a battalion's worth of Israel's blitzkrieg heavy tanks. . . .
> . . . The . . . parallel disasters of Bint Jbiel and Wadi Saluki became laboratories for teaching how a well-trained insurgent force exhaustively drilled, carefully dug in, camouflaged and armed with the latest precision anti-tank weaponry could utterly devastate a modern, technologically superior Cold War armored force, even if that force commanded the air absolutely. . . . [B]oth of these battles strongly suggest that weapons from the second precision revolution in the hands of diabolically skilled infantry will eventually make heavy, mounted warfare a relic of the machine age.
> . . . Our own experience in Iraq and Afghanistan tells us that we have no choice but to meet him [the enemy] on his terms, on the ground in the close and all-too-often fair fight.[5]
> — M.Gen. R.H. Scales (Ret.), *AFJ*, December 2007

There is compelling evidence that *Hezbollah's* defense line was of Chinese and North Korean design. The Chinese helped to arm it, and the North Koreans helped to dig it.[6] Just as German designers had tested new aircraft during the Spanish Civil War, Communist tacticians may have been looking for new ways to stop a Westernized assault in southern Lebanon. Such an assault would be "high-tech," mechanized, and fully supported by aircraft. One way to obstruct it would be with the "remote-control killing of modern tanks" from a below-ground matrix of defensive strongpoints.[7] With Chinese assistance, Iran had just developed a 333-mm rocket that could be fired remotely.

> Industry sources said the [Iranian] effort, reportedly aided by China, was designed to turn the Fajr-3 [possible misprint] into a more mobile and accurate system. . . . An earlier version of the Fajr-5 [rocket], which contains a high-explosive warhead, was supplied to Hizbullah in Lebanon. . . . Each battery contains a command post vehicle, with each launcher equipped with a mission computer and capable of being fired via remote control from a distance of one kilometer.[8]
>
> — *Geostrategy-Direct,* 31 May 2006

What Such a Development Means to the U.S. Military

To meet an insurgent "on his terms, on the ground in the close and all-too-often fair fight," U.S. infantrymen must first dismount their vehicles. Then, they will need more surprise—not firepower— to defeat "well-trained . . . [and] carefully dug-in" fighters. The key to that surprise is how close they approach the state of the art with their tactical technique. Tactically advanced squads, fire teams, and individuals have enabled poorly endowed Eastern armies to stymie or destroy Western phalanxes since 1953. Unfortunately, the same people who helped to dig the *Hezbollah* defense line also instruct every inductee in guerrilla warfare and likely have the world's second best small-unit tactics. (North Vietnam still reigns supreme in this field of endeavor.)

Insurgency Already Poses a Big Enough Problem

More often than not, Western counterinsurgency methods have failed to bring a lasting peace to rebellious regions. At great cost and effort, the British were finally able to defeat Boer guerrillas at the turn of the last century. But they cut so many corners in the process (like putting all Boer families into concentration camps [9]) that they lost popular support and had to leave.

161

The British were also able to defeat ethnic Chinese guerrillas in Malaya some 60 years later. Yet, Malaya had only one tiny overland frontier and enough jungle to conceal government tracking teams. Again, the British gathered almost all the rural Chinese families into "protected" enclaves.[10] Now the former battlefield is the Islamic nation of Malaysia. Its court system has become increasingly *sharia* based,[11] and its border regions offer safe haven to trans-national guerrillas.[12]

Through tiny long-distance forays, Rhodesia's Selous Scouts and South African Reconnaissance teams also did a good job of combatting Communist guerrillas in the 1980's. Still, they failed adequately to compensate for the past oppression of indigenous peoples and over-relied on killing their enemies. After a U.N.-brokered peace agreement, the Communists were soon able to win most of the elections. Now Zimbabwe can only survive with PRC help,[13] most of Angola's natural resources are destined for China,[14] and South Africa too often mirrors Chinese policy in the Congo.

Within a few short years, something similar was occurring in Latin America. Only this time, it was government forces committing the atrocities, and leftist candidates being elected because of it. The only thing even close to a lasting success occurred in Peru where whole villages were armed at the edge of the Shining Path's heartland, and government troops routinely patrolled into them. Sadly, the ruling regime also jailed thousands of people unjustly. Though most were later civilly tried and released, the long-term damage had been done. Still painfully reminded of the rightist regime's excesses, Peru's people came very close to picking an avowed leftist in the 2006 election.

At the start of this century, U.S. "search-and-destroy" operations were enjoying about as much success against Iraqi insurgents as they had in Vietnam. In a rush to create a democratically elected government, America's interim managers had allowed Tehran to pad the elections.[15] Of course, that was before Iran had been positively proven to be fanning the unrest. Still, the oversight did little to help U.S. forces. Not only was enemy violence increasing, but so too was host-government excess. In a last desperate attempt to stabilize the situation, U.S. military leaders finally decided to take back the only strategic ground in this type of war—the neighborhoods. To do so, they used a variation of the Marine "Combined Action Platoon" (CAP) concept from the Vietnam War (GIs and Iraqis serving together in district police stations). With citizen support far from certain, those

U.S. leaders also walled off many neighborhoods and jailed huge numbers of suspects.[16] In places where GIs could only occasionally visit, they wisely formed Concerned Local Citizens (CLC) groups to act as armed-community-watch elements. In 2008, they planned to increase the number of CAP outposts in Baghdad from 75 to 99, and to assign public-works projects to 80,000 CLC members throughout the country.[17]

By 1 March 2008, Baghdad's level of violence had fallen, but a cease fire with al-Sadr was largely the reason. His Mahdi Army had now controlled Basra, the only Iraqi outlet to the sea, for almost three years.[18] On 23 March (after probable urging from the U.S.), Iraq's pro-Iranian prime minister launched a half-hearted military attempt to retake Basra. Despite U.S. air and British artillery support, Iraqi security elements soon became so hard pressed that some changed sides.[19] Then Baghdad's Sadr City became restive, and from there Iranian-made rockets began to rain down on the Green Zone. When Iraqi security forces responded, some again traded all weapons and vehicles for their lives.[20] On 30 March, al-Sadr announced to the al Jazeera news service that the U.S. would be "defeated just the way they were defeated in Vietnam" and that his militiamen were on the path to "liberation."[21] A day later, the Iraqi government brokered a deal with al-Sadr through Iran's "clerics." In return for a reported promise to cease all raids/arrests and set free all uncharged detainees, al-Sadr ordered his fighters off the streets.[22] On 4 April, al-Maliki again vowed to continue the crackdown on Shiite radicals inside Baghdad. One day later, bowing to al-Sadr's demands (and the original agreement), the Iraqi president put a nationwide freeze on all raids against Shiite militants. When rockets began to land on a U.S. base as well as the Green Zone, American forces got involved. Their ground units helped the Iraqi Army to blockade Sadr City, and their helicopters overflew it looking for launch sites. Then, the Americans began slowly to push the militants out of areas from which rockets could reach the Green Zone. Each major advance was preceded by tank fire and consolidated with another wall segment. Through it all, al-Maliki did little more than warn the Sadrists that their candidates might be banned from the upcoming elections if the rockets did not stop.[23] In late May, a deal was struck with al-Sadr through Iran, wherein Iraqi Army troops alone were able to enter the centers of Basra and Sadr City without encountering any resistance.

163

One of two things had just happened in Iraq. Either the U.S. military had once again tried a 2GW solution to a 4GW problem, or it had been hoodwinked. Either way, its claim to be fighting mostly *al-Qaeda* became as tenuous as its initial refusal to admit any insurgency at all. On 12 April 2008, the Bush Administration for the first time admitted that Iran posed a bigger threat to Iraq than *al-Qaeda*. A day later, the prestigious *60 Minutes* disclosed that the "insurgency and militias" controlled many of Iraq's corrupt ministries, and that this was fully known to—and tolerated by—Iraq's prime minister. To make matters worse, al-Maliki had created a law that gave him personal immunity to any corruption charge.[24]

In effect, the Iraqi government had just strengthened al-Sadr's political position, and U.S. leaders needed to start thinking about Iraq's upcoming elections. Yet to be seen will be the long-term effect on voter opinion of U.S.-applied martial law, prison-like neighborhood dividers, and inner-city helo-missile strikes. At some point, all detainees must be judged by civilian courts, all walls replaced with vehicular/pedestrian checkpoints, and all bombing from whatever source banned. Otherwise, the voters may finally opt for the public aid and false promises of their Islamist candidates, and the whole U.S. effort will have been for nothing. To see how Iran and *al-Sadr* are expelling U.S. forces from Iraq, one must only look at how Iran and *Hezbollah* dealt with the Israeli Defense Forces' (IDF's) 1982 invasion of Lebanon. Of particular note was the Communist presence in the alliance.

> In response to this IDF incursion, the National Lebanese Resistance Front *[Hezbollah]* was formed on 16 September 1982. It brought together varying Communist, Socialist, Shiite, Sunni, and Palestinian militias and . . . represented the first time collective Lebanese resistance took precedence over civil war.[25]
> — *Marine Corps Gazette,* June 2003

> There is no Sunni or Shia resistance; there is only an Iraqi Islamic resistance.[26]
> —Al-Sadr in *Newsweek* interview, May 2006

Just as *Hezbollah* has done in southern Lebanon and parts of Beirut, al-Sadr has created a quasi-state in southern Iraq and Sadr

City. Amidst self-induced chaos, both provide relief to residents in the form of education, loans, grants, health care, and security. Al-Sadr already controls most of Iraq's basic-service ministries.[27] Until U.S. leaders fully awake to the ultimate threat in that country, one has only to look at Lebanon to see Iraq's future.

Thus, one realizes that the most innovative of the Western approaches to counterinsurgency have lacked the political, economic, and psychological sophistication to succeed over the long haul. Yet, important lessons have been learned from which to build a more viable model.

- Actively pursuing only perpetrators
- Giving them full legal consideration when caught
- Outposting the worst neighborhoods and villages
- Arming community watches at the edge of enemy refuges
- Occasionally patrolling into such places

Also clear from Africa, as well as Iraq, is the main prerequisite for long-term success—local security. Without it, Communist or Islamist commissars will simply coerce the vote.

The Next "Counterinsurgency" Effort in Latin America

Those who think the Western Hemisphere problem hugely different from that in the Middle East, must remember that the Communists were allied with *Hezbollah* in Lebanon in 1982.[28] That gave them an early voice in the region. That lone voice has since evolved into three: (1) North Korean construction advice for *Hezbollah's* southern defense line;[29] (2) PRC political advice for *Hezbollah's* Occupied Territories' proxy *(Hamas);*[30] and (3) probable Chinese political advice for *Hezbollah* itself.

Americans, who don't yet see their nation under attack from the south, must stop thinking in terms of conventional warfare. There can be Communist expansion without armed revolution. 4GW thinkers have warned that 21st-Century wars will be largely fought in nonmartial arenas. An enemy victory can just as easily be achieved through elections. Within Latin America, the facts are as follows: (1) four Marxists are already in power in Venezuela, Ecuador, Bolivia, and Nicaragua; (2) seven left-leaning presidents rule Costa Rica, Guatemala, Brazil, Uruguay, Paraguay, Argentina, and Chile; and (3) two Chavez favorites just barely lost the elections in Mexico and Peru. Many had the benefit of external funding and Cuban political advice. While much of that funding was undoubtedly from Venezuelan oil, some came from other commodities at stake in the economic arena of 4GW. This was particularly true in Bolivia, where President Evo Morales is and always has been the coca candidate.[31]

Needless to say, China's revolutionary government is also interested in politics and trade. With neither does it pay much attention to human rights. So with regard to Latin America, the PRC may have a foreign policy that is quite different from that of the U.S. The Japanese managed considerable infiltration of this region between 1900 and 1941.[32] Thankfully, they never thought of politics-and-trade-oriented attack or of a self-supporting people's army.

The Future of Counterinsurgency

In the southern Philippines, Iraq, Djibouti, and Paraguay, U.S. soldiers and Marines have had great success with adopting local customs and improving community infrastructure. Both will be also necessary in the most volatile regions of Latin America. There, local security must necessarily include drug route suppression. And there, host country police and soldiers must not be allowed to resort to death squads or torture. Finally, something must be found for the area's misguided teenagers to do, as if quelling gang violence in East L.A. Among the options are intramural sports leagues and public-service jobs.

Whoever the instigator of the chaos in Colombia and Central America, the U.S. will not be able to stop it without doing something momentous, different, and soon. Massive 2GW intervention has already been tried in this region. That leaves the Pentagon with two options: (1) outposting hundreds of U.S. squads with enough skill to survive alone; or (2) training indigenous forces in something its own manual-writers don't fully understand. As the next chapter will again demonstrate, the vast majority U.S. infantry and special-operations units still lack the small-unit tactical sophistication to accomplish either.

Luckily, there is a fully tested method that will allow underqualified instructors to arrive at world-class tactical technique. To the mediator or scientist, collective wisdom and experimentation seem a perfectly logical way to solve problems. But to the U.S. military establishment, they are alien concepts. Its infantry organizations do not function by democratic process, nor are their published procedures meant to be locally modified. The new method supplants firepower with surprise, so that those who use it can more often abstain from killing. (See the Appendix.) That makes it the perfect vehicle for training U.S. or indigenous squads in how to excel at a 4GW assignment.

12 What's Not in the Military Manuals

- What counterinsurgency skills must be self-developed?
- Would adding them to the manuals ensure victory in war?

Western Manuals Divide Every Issue into Subsets

(Source: FM 10-76Z/CM [1977], cover)

How American Infantry Manuals Are Written

The U.S. military approaches learning quite differently from a college, research lab, or business enterprise. As such, its manuals cannot be reasonably compared to textbooks, research reports, or profit plans. They are more about obeying doctrine than adjusting to ongoing circumstances. And they have two other big strikes against them from the outset. The first is that all are written from the top down. The overall subject is divided into its most logical parts, and then each subsequent part is dissected into subsets. Because the larger categories can only be addressed in philosophical terms, a manual's authors often assume the rest must be visionary as well. Unfortunately, esoteric edicts don't easily translate into squad maneuvers. The second problem is that the manuals are so heavily staffed that little tactical detail survives the procedure. Most of their writers have had no enlisted experience with detail, and only that on which everyone can agree gets included. So the troops end up with vast strings of definitions that do little to do help them survive in combat.

The Effect of Existing Manuals

Young officers often see themselves as protectors of a system that has created a magnificent heritage. All of America's service branches do enjoy a fine heritage, but much of that heritage has come from individuals having to supersede their respective systems. Their heroics were often the only way to compensate for a tactical deficiency. Plenty of examples exist. One of the most interesting involves Marine Cpl. Tony Stein. More easily to assault Japanese pillboxes in WWII, he single-handedly fashioned a precursor to the modern squad automatic weapon (SAW). If the Marines had known more about "stormtrooper tactics,"[1] Tony would not have had to amend their procedure.

> Then there was . . . Cpl. Anthony Stein. . . . Tony had been a Golden Gloves boxer, set pins in a bowling alley and pulled a stint working a shovel for the Civilian Conservation Corps before becoming a machinist. Tony had been at Guadalcanal, Bougainville, [and] Vella Lavella. He had gone home in July 1944, married his sweetheart, and headed back to the South Pacific after a three-day honeymoon. Now, Stein was in the Fifth Marine Division—A Company, 1st Battalion, 28th Marines. . . . Because of its accuracy and firepower, the Browning automatic rifle was a favorite with the troops, but it weighed 23 pounds. . . .
>
> On one of the islands where Tony had soldiered, he had come across a downed U.S. Navy fighter plane. From one of its wings, he had taken a light-weight .30 cal. air-cooled machine gun, which he took apart and put in his pack.

When afforded the time, he fiddled with it, and turned it into a hand-carried, belt-fed, personal weapon he called his "stinger." It had quite a sting, and it burned up ammo fast.

When the 28th hit Green Beach at Iwo Jima, the landing spot closest to Mount Suribachi, the 1st Battalion was to drive straight across the island with the 2nd Battalion following part way and then turning toward the volcano [Suribachi]. . . . When A Company moved out, Tony Stein was in the lead, and he headed right for a Jap pillbox. With his stinger, he suppressed the Jap fire and a demolitions team consisting of Sergeant Merritt M. Savage and Corporal Frederick J. Talbert blew up the emplacement. That worked so well, they did it all morning. In the first hour of the advance, Stein personally slew at least 20 Japs, then he ran out of ammo. We have seen how hard it was to run or even walk in the sandy volcanic ash of Iwo, so Stein took off his shoes. Then he took off his helmet. He grabbed a wounded Marine and hustled him off to the beach, grabbed as many ammo boxes as he could carry and ran back to his outfit. He made that round trip eight times that day, each time getting a wounded man to safety. His stinger was shot out of his hands twice, but at the end of the day he was still shooting Japs with it. As his mother Rose often said, "He's a tough one, that Tony." On Wednesday evening, D + 2, Tony got hit in the shoulder by shrapnel and was told to hustle himself to the beach for evacuation. He was back in the line by Saturday. On 1 March, D + 10, the 28th was at the other end of the island, on the western side of the fat part. The 1st and 2nd Battalions had taken Hill 362A and were faced with an 80-foot cliff leading into a ravine full of Jap riflemen in tunnels and caves. The only way to the other side was to go around on the shoulders, which were certain to be covered by every sort of fire the Japs had, and crawling with snipers. A Company's Captain Wilkins called for volunteers and Tony Stein responded. . . . Wilkins led a 20-man patrol onto the shoulder to clear out the snipers. Only seven Marines returned, and neither Wilkins nor Stein was among them. . . . Tony Stein was awarded the Congressional Medal of Honor for his conspicuous gallantry on D-Day. D + 10 made it posthumous.[2]

Cpl. Stein had discovered that a "top-down" military organization adapts too slowly to changing circumstances. It depends instead upon abject loyalty to existing procedures. Whatever it produces in writing becomes gospel at all infantry schools. For example, the Marine Corps' new urban warfare manual (MCWP 3-35.3 of 15 April 1998) contains a technique for double-file foot patrolling in the city. Originally developed by the Germans in WWII, this technique allows for each file to cover all windows and rooftops above the other. Marines have always used double files on rural roads to escape ambush more easily. However, such a formation serves no useful purpose in the woods. Should it take fire from either side, half of its weapons would be masked. Still, as of November 2007, East Coast Marine infantry instructors were being told to stick to the double-file method in the woods.[3] Such is too often the nature of doctrine-oriented military "progress."

Headquarters' "Guidelines" More Useful Than Doctrine

The most probable type of future warfare will not be like that of 1945. It won't be waged by "closing with and destroying one's enemy." Proxy fighters are now so easy to acquire that they must be disenfranchised or befriended. All deaths in the Muslim world, however well justified, will create generations of *jihadist* vengeance. It was a Colombian military napalm attack (using U.S. aid) on the breakaway Communist municipality of Marquetalia in 1964 that led to the formation of the FARC. Its aftermath was so grisly that the survivors of that thousand-member collective declared war on Colombia.[4]

Thus, counterinsurgency has more to do with converting one's foes than killing them. The legendary Selous Scouts made a serious attempt to recruit their captives in Rhodesia.[5] The WWII belief that victory is most easily achieved through killing was partially born out of *bushido,* but it came mostly from the tactical superiority of the enemy's squads. The brave GIs who reached the heights above Omaha Beach after a bloodletting so great that the movie footage got lost were in no mood to pick and choose their targets. Had they been able to advance more easily through surprise-oriented maneuver, they could have taken more hostages. The Marines suffered from the same tactical deficiency in the Pacific. (See Figure 12.1.) To

Figure 12.1: Both WWII Foes Had Advanced Tactical Technique
(Source: "Deployment Experiences of Ft. Carson Soliders in Iraq," Powerpoint Briefing, Dept. of Behavior Sciences, U.S. Air Force Academy)

defeat the defensive masterpieces on Pelileu, Iwo Jima, and Okinawa, they had little choice but to stretch the Geneva Conventions with flame weaponry. Thus, the current need to exercise less force on the battlefield can best be accomplished by evolving tactically at the squad level.

America's New Counterinsurgency Manual

Most of the public criticism of FM 3-24 has so far involved its first-chapter paradoxes.[6] While some may confuse the traditionalists, all are reasonable. "Tactical success guarantees nothing" just serves to highlight the other 4GW arenas (political, economic, and psychological). It in no way discourages tactical excellence. "The more you protect yourself, the less secure you are" may address the adverse effect of too much distance from the civilian population. Close-quarters interaction obviously requires caution, but it also takes dispersion. Why on defense, parent units tend to overconsolidate. The Portuguese became so enamored with their perimeters, roads, and vehicles in Mozambique that they effectively sacrificed any chance of defeating the Communist rebels.[7] (See Figure 12.2.)

Thus, FM 3-24 does not remove fighting from the equation. It merely implies that a different kind of fighting will be necessary. In conventional war, U.S. forces have always looked for a 3-to-1 manpower advantage and then assaulted with all guns blazing. Perhaps a 1-to-10 ratio and as little shooting as possible would be more appropriate for counterguerrilla operations. That's what a U.S. squad serving with host-nation police and army squads in a CAP platoon outpost would experience. Near the drug-producing areas of Colombia, most would be under constant threat of attack by several hundred FARC fighters. With a little UW training, those GIs would be at much less risk.

Figure 12.2: Counterinsurgents Can Never Be Road-Bound
(Source: "Deployment Experiences of Ft. Carson Soliders in Iraq," Powerpoint Briefing, Dept. of Behavior Sciences, U.S. Air Force Academy)

Traditionalists worry about the morale problems associated with too little fighting. Yet, enough risk-taking can easily compensate for that. If every GI were routinely to participate in a squad-sized or smaller penetration of enemy territory, he could easily maintain his self esteem without actually having to fight for his life. In the past, he has had more chance to do this in guerrilla wars, but not to the extent that he should have. How many Vietnam veterans can remember a squad-sized maneuver element ever attacking a Viet Cong base camp? Only when those kinds of missions become commonplace will U.S. squad tactics evolve. Troop morale has suffered because of overcontrol by superiors. To be truly content, U.S. soldiers and Marines must be allowed to achieve their full potential as warriors.

What's Really Wrong with FM 3-24

The Army and Marine Corps' new counterinsurgency manual is a good effort by many dedicated people. But it is more of a policy statement than a source of warfighting procedure. Obviously aimed at senior commanders, it contains no illustrations of small-unit maneuvers. Interspersed throughout its 282 pages are one aerial photograph, three map overlay instructions, 26 variable interaction diagrams, 33 tables, too many lists to count, and 21 fairly interesting vignettes.[8]

In other words, a professional military man would find very little in FM 3-24 that he didn't already suspect, and a congressman or lawyer would find few topics missing. In true "top-down-thinker" fashion, its senior architects apparently believe that their subordinates will now work out the functional details. For a number of reasons, that is an unrealistic expectation. The U.S. military has become so driven by "doctrine" and "careerism" that few of its lower ranks are willing to risk expanding upon what their manuals dictate. Those in operational units will try to implement the new policies through existing tactical methods. And those in the educational system will add the manual's main paragraph headings to what their students already memorize. Its ethereal edicts may end up in school curricula all the way down to the squad level, but graduates of those schools will know little more about surviving in combat. More appropriately to react on the streets of Baghdad, riflemen, fire team leaders, and squad leaders will require commensurate techniques. (See Figure 12.3.) The best way to change an enlisted man's perspective is by giving him other procedures to practice.

Figure 12.3: On the Streets of Baghdad
(Source: "Deployment Experiences of Ft. Carson Soliders in Iraq," Powerpoint Briefing, Dept. of Behavior Sciences, U.S. Air Force Academy)

FM 3-24 thankfully asserts that firepower is largely counterproductive against guerrillas. What it fails to mention is that firepower will always be necessary unless supplanted by surprise. More surprise takes better tactical technique. Without experimenting with, and improving upon, squad maneuvers at the company level, GIs will never enjoy good tactical technique. Lower-echelon experimentation is tantamount to the higher echelons relinquishing control, and just as unlikely to happen. The new publications's Appendix E even makes provision for overwhelming firepower. It says that "airpower and spacepower are important force multipliers for U.S., multinational, and host-nation forces fighting an insurgency." One wonders why a free nation would allow parts of that "force multiplier" to be used against discontented segments of its own population. That's like New York's mayor condoning a drone missile strike against a Harlem drug dealer. As for helicopter assaults, how much surprise can one really generate while sitting beneath an internal combustion engine? So, other than satellite surveillance, airpower and spacepower have almost no applicability to counterinsurgency, and those who would claim otherwise are most likely appeasing the Air Force. Counterinsurgency is more about minimal force by collocated ground elements.

What the Counterinsurgency Manual Should Contain

To combat insurrection or 4GW expansion, U.S. troops must be trained as self-sufficient peacekeepers instead of lethal extensions of their commander. That will take considerably more attention to their individual skill, initiative, and tactical-decision-making ability. Business as usual with rewritten manuals will not get the job done. A bureaucratic overhaul would be nice, but neither is that realistic. There is a way—a training method that meshes with the existing schedule without requiring any more time. Only the leaders of most U.S. infantry units are always busy. The troops still suffer from the "hurry up and wait" syndrome. Thus, they have an almost unlimited supply of 15-minute segments in which to teach themselves. This new method will be discussed further in the next section. Part Three also looks like a manual should.

Part Three

4GW Counterinsurgency Techniques

"4GW automatically trumps a 2GW opponent [like the U.S.]."
— William S. Lind, father of 4GW theory

(Source: William S. Lind [writer of adopted 3GW and ignored 4GW handbooks for the U.S. military], in telephone conversation with the author on 7 June 2006)

13 Best 4GW Defense _ Is Locally Tailored

- On what do guerrillas depend most for support?
- How can that source of support be removed?

4GW Activity Draws Popular Support

(Source: DA Pamphlet 550-150 [1990], cover)

4GW Counterinsurgency Will Take a Paradigm Shift

Somewhere within the most recent accomplishments of America's deployed forces lies the secret to 4GW counterinsurgency. That secret must be quickly identified, for it undoubtedly deviates from established (Stateside) procedure. As of mid-March 2008, something in Iraq had changed. In diplomatic circles, it was being called the "Strategy of Patience."[1] To most veterans, it was simply an attempt by U.S. units to reach out to the Iraqi people on a more personal level.

If Maoist guerrillas can swim through a peasant population

like fish through a sea,[2] then the only sure way to stop them is by befriending the population. Yet, Western "liberators" traditionally punish the population. They herd vast segments into "protected zones," detain anyone who looks vaguely suspicious, and counter every lead with maximum force. Such abuses must too easily flow out of the 2GW thought process (kill or be killed). That's why that process has proven so ineffective in countering guerrillas. A more productive way of thinking (4GW counterinsurgency) will require a paradigm shift. To sway peasants, one must think like a peasant. That's quite different from thinking like the leader of a 2GW-trained unit that specializes in standoff obliteration. All the peasant sees is a big hole in the ground and collage of body parts. He usually never realizes that some big guerrilla leader had been the target. Peasants don't see themselves as condoning piranhas, but only as being attacked by them. Pushing those peasants around only serves to increase their terror.

From this perspective, counterinsurgency becomes more like helping a U.S. neighborhood to fend off thugs, or a U.S. school to thwart a deranged killer. In the latter case, which of the following would be more acceptable police procedure: (1) carefully marshalling one's forces outside the school to insure proper coordination between officers; or (2) immediately sending two highly trained officers into the school to confront the killer? For the average American, the second choice is by far the best. He or she figures the officers are being paid to take a risk. He or she considers any delay at a time like this too cautious. And he or she is tired of bureaucratic excuses. Iraqi civilians feel the same way. If they are being asked to risk a beheading, they want to see the one doing the asking standing shoulder to shoulder with them in their neighborhood. If they are poorly armed and outnumbered, they want their American contingent to have the same disadvantages. In other words, they are looking more for local leadership than countrywide "development." Only they, after all, can ultimately remove the menace from their society. If anything at all has become clear from past U.S. combat operations against guerrillas, it is that those operations alone are fruitless.

Thus, GIs can best contribute to 4GW counterinsurgency by setting a good example in as many civilian locales as possible. They must dutifully avoid the stigma of heavy-handed occupier. Dressing more like the locals and operating in squad size has worked well for U.S. Special Forces teams in Afghanistan. Kicking in doors, pointing weapons at women, and quickly acquiring fire superiority may all seem appropriate during Stateside infantry training, but they will do little to befriend a vital constituency. Again, the peasant population is the key to defeating a Maoist or Islamist insurgency. But that population will only help to catch its piranhas, if those piranhas have no way of knowing who told on them. That takes enough day-to-day contact with U.S. troops to allow for hints to be dropped without revealing their source. Very probably, this is how the Marines in Iraq's Anbar Province made such a dramatic turnaround. Instead of believing all the hype about a Sunni insurrection, they mobilized Anbar's predominantly Sunni population to help rid the place of *al-Qaeda*. That *"al-Qaeda* in Iraq" and its affiliate *Ansar al-Sunna* had Iranian Shiite advisers undoubtedly helped with that process.[3]

America's "force protection policy" in Iraq is the equivalent of mustering police in a school yard. It better protects the liberators than those to be liberated. How exactly do motorized patrols keep tipsters or neighborhood council members from getting their heads cut off? And the really sad thing is that a pair of policemen need no additional coordination to save the children in the school. They can instantly enter any building and go right to the killer with almost no chance of fratricide. Then, with the right kind of training, they can even immobilize instead of killing him. Such an approach might appear much less "weak" where the "killer" ended up being a fourteen-year-old with a cap pistol. In essence, the first two policemen on the scene can accomplish the mission better than ten-times their number later. A well-rehearsed SWAT team might also do well, but it again takes a while to get there. Similarly, any terrorist incident is best handled by troops already present. Just describing a unique set of circumstances to a superior means that a few will have changed by the time he makes his decision. The prerequisite, then, to 4GW counterinsurgency is better training all U.S. infantrymen, and then deploying them in tiny, semi-autonomous teams throughout a besieged population. Those teams could not out-muscle their opposition. But, if they were to follow a more Christian methodology, the local population would protect them. Anyone who has traveled the world alone can attest to this most admirable of human impulses.[4] Of course, for the more risky situations, the GIs would need UW training. At least then, throughout the contested peasantry, there would be a someone to counter the Communist or Islamist commissar.

God and one constitute a majority.[5]
— Abraham Lincoln

The Local Political Processes Are of Utmost Importance

U.S. forces now realize how vital neighborhood councils are to the pacification of Iraq. Initially, many units discovered this but couldn't stay long enough to protect the council members who were friendly. Within Latin America, Cuba provides constant political counseling to Hugo Chavez.[6] Similar advice has thus reached the presidents of Ecuador, Bolivia, and Nicaragua, as well as the losers of the Mexican and Peruvian elections.[7] Cuba also provides political instruction to the FARC.[8] And FARC has already helped to finance presidential campaigns in Brazil and Ecuador.[9] In essence, the Communists are trying to win all the elections in Latin America. As most voters live in the countryside, the countryside is where most of the voter-intimidation takes place. At least, that was the case in Rhodesia, where tribesmen became convinced that their local ZANLA (Zimbabwe African National Liberation Army) commissars could find out how they had voted. The following excerpts offer a rare glimpse into the details of Red Guard "politicization." While Latin America's Maoist commissars may not yet be this brutal, FARC's recent interest in children portends future similarities.

> The ZANLA commissars . . . promised the tribesmen, that in return for their support, when ZANLA came to power all the good things belonging to the white men would be theirs. . . .
> The commissars would conclude these meetings by giving clear warnings as to what would happen to the villagers collectively, family units or individual persons, should anyone decide to become a "sellout" by reporting their presence to the authorities. . . .
> The people would then be invited to tell the commissars who the stooges and puppets of the government were. . . . They were also collectively ordered to indicate the families of serving soldiers and policemen. . . .
> Sometimes a man, a wife, a mother or a father, or a whole family would be pushed to the front by the crowd and would be publicly put to death by the commissars. . . . Sometimes

the insurgent commissars, wishing to bind the tribesmen to them by a pact of blood, would order the villagers to kill the sellouts or stooges themselves. . . .

Afterwards . . . the commissars would select and nominate various members of the population . . . to act as contact men and "policemen."

The contact men and policemen played a vital role in the insurgent network and a chain of these men was gradually created until they stretched from inside Mozambique to the farthermost reaches of the operational area. . . .

By order of the insurgents, it became and was the duty of every person in the Tribal Trust Land concerned to pass every scrap of information relating to the security forces to the local contact man. . . .

In addition to collating intelligence, the contact men were responsible for the selection of bases and the collection and provision of food for the insurgents. They were also responsible for the transmission of letters and message between detachments and sections, and arranging and setting up security procedures for meetings between various groups. . . .

The policemen worked with and under the contact men and were responsible for maintaining the insurgents' system of law and order. They could not, however, discipline or punish anyone themselves. Any suspected sellout . . . would be taken by them to the local insurgent leader.

The contact men and policemen were later supplemented, as the war progressed, by the *mujiba* system. . . . Although too young to fight they [the children] could still act as ears and eyes, or as messengers or go-betweens with the civil population. . . .

And so, by these methods, Mao Tse Tung's dictum that to be successful, a guerrilla must move through the population as a fish does through water, was satisfied by ZANLA.[10]

When the "top-down-thinking" British and "overly conciliatory" U.N. stepped in to end the violence in southern Africa through voting, both lacked the insight to make that voting work. Neither realized how much terror Maoist insurgents apply at the community level. The Maoist candidates subsequently won all the elections, and ZANLA's political parent still rules the PRC dependency that is

Zimbabwe today.[11] Because the Chinese/Cuban/Venezuelan/FARC strategy in Latin America is also to win elections, the following little tidbit of "politicization" history takes on added significance.

Some 7,000 guerrillas had gone to ground in the tribal areas on the orders of ZANLA commander, Rex Nhongo. He told them to ignore the cease-fire, hide their weapons, and persuade the people to vote for ZANU P/F (Zimbabwe African National Union Patriotic Front) (Verrier, *The Road to Zimbabwe,* 86). . . .
When ZANLA first infiltrated its political commissars into the Rhodesian tribal areas in 1972, they embraced the . . . methods of the [Communist] Orient to politicise the tribesmen. On entering villages, they selected people for execution. . . . Their objective was to rid communities of their leadership and destroy the *bourgeois.*
Executions were conducted in an exemplary [local] fashion. . . . ZANLA's reign of terror has had few parallels in recent African history.
Not surprisingly, it took little persuasion to get villagers to set up informer networks, report on the activities of the security forces, feed and look after incoming guerrillas, and spy and report on [unseemly] reports of their fellows. . . .
After Lancaster House [the cease-fire conference], . . . [ZANLA] guerrillas were able to live openly amongst the villagers without fear of attack by the Security Forces. . . . [T]he unsophisticated tribesmen took this as a signal the guerrillas had "won." . . .
So when ZANLA guerrillas insisted that ZANU P/F would win the independence election and announced that their first task afterwards would be to open the ballot boxes and identify those who had voted against them with the help of a special machine imported from Romania, the villagers believed them. They also accepted that those who voted against ZANU P/F would afterwards be put up against walls by ZANLA and shot (Sutton-Price, *Zimbabwe,* 63).
. . . Britain's quaint idea of stationing British bobbies in uniform at polling stations to ensure fair play, was at the least naive. . . .
An admission that ZANU P/F used its notorious political commissars to intimidate the indigenous people into voting

for them came during Granada Television's *End of Empire* series when Edison Zvobgo said: "... [W]e had a very large army left (outside the assembly points), who remained as political commissars ... simply to ensure that we would win the election (Flower, *Serving Secretly,* 255-256)." ... So much for the democratic process, African style.[12]
　　—Peter Stiff, renown South African historian

The Role of the Village in 4GW's Economic Arena

Within Colombia and most of the Central American countries, 20% or more of the citizenry depend for their livelihoods on agriculture.[13] That's why coca and poppies are such big parts of the regional puzzle. Within each tiny enclave, the people must be told why some other crop might better serve their interests. Then, some free seed must be offered. And, as was the case with tobacco in North Carolina, so too must government subsidies. A U.S. CAP platoon contingent could make all three of these services available on a regular basis.

If the only industry in an area is its cocaine factory, other small enterprises must be started. Where the jobs of drug runner and coca field guard are among the few available, that of road worker or community watchman might usefully augment the list. As long as there are legitimate ways for residents to support their families, those ways will normally be followed. Thus, from an economic standpoint, counterinsurgency becomes more a matter of providing peaceful alternatives than of blowing something up. The Communist's means of persuasion is no different than that of an Islamist—keeping the people so desperate and destitute that they are unable to say "no." Thus, there are any number of nonmilitary ways to discourage drug trade participation. In concert, they might even force a criminal element to relocate. But they will have much less effect unless individually applied to each village.

Certain Latin Villages Have More Economic Value in 4GW

Several radical Islamic factions have funded Middle Eastern initiatives through Colombian cocaine, but none have fought for Latin America. With the Taliban, things are different. It supports

187

itself through poppies grown in its own theater of operations. It has even consolidated some of its own drug production. As late as December 2007, Coalition forces were still fighting for Musa Qala in Helmand Province. That town had been vacated by the British in October 2006 and then taken over by the Taliban four months later. As a center of heroin production, it became strategically important to both sides.[14]

Unlike the Taliban, the FARC and other Maoist entities treat drug crop tending and processing as a cottage industry. Their fields and laboratories tend to be family owned, much smaller, and well hidden. They are far too numerous to be sufficiently removed through aerial spraying and helicopter assault. That kind of threat takes a tiny U.S. outpost nearby.

> Maoism emphasizes . . . village-level industries independent of the outside world.[15]

Basic Services Must Be Locally Acquired in Rural Areas

As was shown in Chapter 6, FARC has traditionally placed much of its emphasis on discrediting the ruling government's ability to provide basic services to its rural population.

> During the 1970's and 1980's, the FARC established its own schools, judicial system, health care, and agrarian economy, and created its own de facto state in remote regions of southern Colombia.
> . . . [FARC] became known for improving health care, schools, and infrastructure in these remote locations.[16]
> — PBS's Online News Hour, 2003

That is why the U.S. CAP platoon contingent will run a clinic, fix the school roof, and help local authorities to maintain order. How much it physically accomplishes is not nearly as important as the example it sets. Without that example, the people would too easily lose heart. These are not revolutionary ideas, just currently out of vogue. U.S. Army advisers went to Bolivia in 1958. By late 1963, their Civic Action program had the Bolivian army spending 20% of its time in civil works, mostly in the countryside.[17]

Why the "Top-Down" Response Is Now Outdated

Just as a school yard police muster, no on-call maneuver element can adequately respond to a martial incident. Guerrillas are by definition dispersed and opportunistic. Even the drug smugglers have now discovered the advantages of bottom-up organizational structure. America's only way to stop the 4GW onslaught from the south are hundreds of tiny enlisted contingents with enough skill to live among the most terrorized of the peasant populations. While perfectly logical, this is unlikely to happen—not because of any deficiency in America's youth, but because of their leaders desire to remain indispensable.

Meanwhile, drug smugglers and guerilla forces like the FARC work together more easily than states do. The state system is old, creaky, formalistic, and slow. Drug-dealing and guerilla warfare represent a free market, where deals happen fast. Several years ago, a Marine friend went down to Bolivia as part of the U.S. counter-drug effort. He observed that the drug traffickers went through the Boyd [decision] cycle . . . six times in the time it took us to go through it once. When I relayed that to Colonel Boyd, he said, "then we're not even in the game."[18]
                                   —William S. Lind, father of 4GW theory

The Rural Poor Hold the Keys to the Kingdom

The threat to Latin America is no longer the city-oriented Marxist-Leninist revolution of the Soviet era, though Colombia's ELN and Peru's Tupac Amaru still cling to it. It is the rural agenda of the Maoist entities, like FARC and the Shining Path. Whereas the U.S. once helped Latin America's ruling elite to suppress their rural populations, it must now keep that elite from atrocity and re-enfranchise the downtrodden. Just as the Maoists have focused on the agrarian work force, so too must the anti-Maoists. Handouts may keep that force from starving, but only self-confidence will effect the removal of its criminal element. Whether Marxist-Leninist or Maoist, the Communists' traditional rallying cry has been for more equitable land distribution. So, ways must be found for the indigenous resident to own his or her own property—be it a tiny shack on a village lot

189

or a quarter-acre of rural land. To remain close enough to help, the contingents of GIs will need some formidable UW technique. The hinterlands of Colombia are as dangerous as Iraq.

14 __ Deep Interdiction

- Why not secretly occupy the drug-growing areas?
- What new tactical techniques would GIs need?

The Drug Flow Is Most Easily Halted at Its Source

(Source: Courtesy of Sorman Information and Media, from Soldf: Soldaten i falt, @2001 by Forsvarsmakten and Wolfgang Bartsch, Stockholm, p. 431)

FARC Is Not Just A Carry-Over from the Bandit Era

From 1948 to 1957, bandits freely roamed much of Colombia's northern countryside. America's top leaders might think that nation's current troubles to be just a continuation of "La Violencia Period" lawlessness. But Colombia has had to deal with another influence since the mid-1960's. That's when both Maoist and Marxist-Leninist guerrilla factions suddenly appeared.[1] The largest of latter has since been transformed into a full-blown people's army with Maoist tactics. Any U.S. claim that "classic counterinsurgency" has kept the FARC at bay makes an unfounded assumption. The assumption is that the FARC intends to overthrow the Colombian government.[2] What if the FARC just wants the Colombian countryside as a type of haven from which to subvert the rest of Latin America? Then, its limited, yet widespread, success inside its homeland would take on more significance. In a recent periodical published by the U.S. Army's Ft. Leavenworth think tank, there is a telling photograph of a FARC sapper. He is covered in mud and wearing only a loin cloth. The caption reads, "he has been trained by Vietnamese, Cuban, and Salvadorian FMLN contractors." It goes on to say that his organization specializes in infiltration attacks. That same photo shows a diminutive Asian helping that sapper to cover himself with mud.[3] To the younger generation, such things may have little significance. For those who lost 58,000 of their brethren 40 years ago, they are stunning revelations. In one recognized authority's opinion,[4] the Vietnamese War was won by lone saboteurs who crept into U.S. installations, timed charges to look like lucky mortar hits, and then crawled back out. If the FARC has now developed the same capability, then all of Latin America is at risk until its 4GW power base can be more effectively eroded in Colombia. That will take more U.S. troops in that country. But, for them, no glitzy repackaging of the same old 2GW format will be good enough. This chapter provides the martial aspects of a 4GW alternative.

The Center of Focus Must Be the Drug-Producing Areas

For years the Colombian government has concentrated on the majority of its "population . . . [who] lived *outside* the drug-producing zones of the . . . eastern savannah."[5] Elsewhere, it established some 600 platoon-sized "Home Guard" units led by regular army officers.[6] It further created platoon-sized law enforcement contingents that were to operate out of fortified police stations.[7] Though all had ready-reaction forces nearby,[8] few have been able to withstand any serious enemy pressure.[9] Very probably, that's because of infiltration, bribes, and intimidation. Perhaps, as in Iraq, Home Guard and police squads will have to be combined with U.S. infantry squads to form CAP platoons. If such platoons were created in every village along the western boundary of the principal drug-producing area, they might be able to interrupt the flow of refined cocaine into Buenaventura. Within that drug-producing area itself, a much more aggressive scheme will be necessary. There are only enough U.S. special operators to execute part of it. The majority must be done by U.S. infantrymen. But theirs will not be an invasion in the normal sense of the word. Instead, it will be a subtle infiltration of the entire area by hundreds of tiny teams of enlisted GIs.

What Could Have Blocked NVA Infiltration Routes

Any "people's army" suspected of Chinese sponsorship,[10] North Korean methods,[11] and Vietnamese advisers,[12] must be approached as if it were expert at squad tactics. That means doing things differently than in Vietnam in the 1970's, Central America in the 1980's, Iraq in the 1990's, and Afghanistan now. There's an obscure way of fighting that was never tried in Vietnam, but that would have blocked the flow of materiel down the micro-filament ends of the Ho Chi Minh Trail. With a few refinements, that "way" could work well in the FARC's backyard. It involves giving each infantry fire team its own tiny operating area. This area would be otherwise uninhabited and only a few grid squares in size. If clearly separated by linear terrain features, several such sectors in tandem could significantly hamper enemy transit.

In Vietnam, such a scheme would have worked well in the coastal free-fire zones into which the biggest infiltration routes emptied. Every night, those zones were subjected to countless harassing and interdiction fires (U.S. artillery and mortar concentrations). Most were directed at map-recorded trail junctions. Those junctions became part of a target list that was none too long and only occasionally modified. As a result, most of the rounds hit nothing. Yet, they made so much noise that one or more explosions became the most obvious way to deceive the enemy. The Vietnam variant of the fire team sector concept involved the nighttime use of claymores and grenades to mimic bombardment or minefield. With claymore ignition by battery, quick retrieval for wires, and silencing of grenade spoons, enemy soldiers could be easily tricked. What sounded to them like externally launched mortar rounds or inadvertently tripped land mines would actually be an ambush. In effect, the ruse kept the ambushers from being counterattacked. But the situation in Colombia is quite different, so another deception will be needed there.

193

If the GIs in Colombia are also to seem nonexistent, they must damage facilities, transport, and product by "accident." Instead of killing FARC soldiers, they would discreetly sabotage the coca fields, drug factories, and shipping conduits in their respective sectors. Once a target had been identified, its probable operation by kidnapped children would make its destruction by ground explosives or aerial bombardment completely unacceptable. The other disadvantage of too direct a removal strategy is that the field, facility, or route would be subsequently moved and harder to find next time. The constant degradation of stationary resources would be far more useful strategically.

Coca growing might be hard to impede by accident, but cocaine production and shipment aren't. With those, fire, water, and mechanical failure could all come into play. For the same accident to happen more than once, its perpetrators must leave no trace of their visit. (See Figures 14.1 and 14.2.) Most privates first class (PFCs) will only need formal instruction on footprint eradication. All the rest will come naturally. This obscure and hostage-friendly way of fighting will be called the "Fire Team Tactical Area of Operations (TAOR)" technique. (See Map 14.1.)

The "Fire Team TAOR" Method

Only the commissioned veterans of Vietnam, Korea, and WWII are now cringing at the thought of four 18-year-old Americans fending for themselves in enemy country. Those who went to war at 18 better appreciate that age group's potential. If Lt. Terzi and six Marines could single-handedly disrupt the huge force that hit the east end of Guadalcanal's airfield in September 1942,[13] a corporal and three PFCs can sabotage FARC activities in Colombia. While Lt. Terzi may have been exceedingly brave, he most likely had two years in the Corps and little, if any, squad tactics training. That means his subsequent success had more to do with the skill of his enlisted volunteers than his own. All had been armed only with Thompson submachineguns. When the Japanese force bumped into their tiny listening post in the middle of the night, its leaders thought it had mistakenly stumbled into the Marines' front lines. They then deployed their attack units early, and those units were not able to take full advantage of their surprise-oriented assault technique.

Figure 14.1: Expert Saboteurs Leave No Trail
(Source: Courtesy of Sorman Information and Media, from Soldf: Soldaten i falt, @2001 by Forsvarsmakten and Wolfgang Bartsch, Stockholm, p. 430)

Figure 14.2: A Real "Special-Operations-Qualified" Grunt
(Source: Courtesy of Cassell PLC, from Uniforms of Elite Forces, © 1982 by Blandford Press Ltd., No. 2)

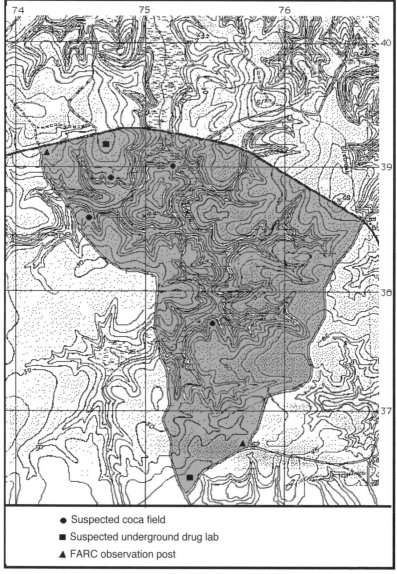

● Suspected coca field

■ Suspected underground drug lab

▲ FARC observation post

Map 14.1: Enemy Targets in a Fire Team TAOR
(Source: U.S. Dept. of Interior, "Jacksonville South Quadrangle," 1:24,000)

Figure 14.3: It's Easy to Live off the Land in Farming Country
(Source: Courtesy of Sorman Information and Media, from Soldf: Soldaten i falt, @2001 by Forsvarsmakten and Wolfgang Bartsch, Stockholm, p. 431)

Only by breathing through hollow reeds in a streambed did the seven Marines survive the encounter,[14] but the precedent had still been set. Similarly, four U.S. volunteers with some unconventional warfare (UW) training could survive a nonconfrontational mission in Colombia. After instruction in mantracking,[15] E & E, and guerrilla warfare,[16] they would no longer need a supporting-arms umbrella, resupply, or rescue. (See Figure 14.3.) Most of their mischief would be done while everyone else was asleep. (See Figure 14.4.) Every three months, they could be relieved in place.

Figure 14.4: This Fire Team Only Musters at Night
(Source: Army/Marine Clipart, Air University, retrieved from www.au.af.mil/au/awc/awcgate/cliparmy.htm)

This would be the first time that the U.S. military has given its junior enlisted personnel either the skill or the authority to fight this way, so it won't be expected. While a single fire team could not significantly erode the Colombian drug mill, 120 fire teams in adjoining TAORs (the equivalent of a widely dispersed U.S. battalion) might. That's the lesson of Vietnam that most U.S. military thinkers have yet to embrace. The Vietnam War was won by thousands of lone sappers who could make sabotage look like misfortune. If the Vietnamese can do it, then so too can FARC and the Pentagon. To believe otherwise is a throw back to America's segregationist past.

Only where all wars are being won does it make sense to overprotect each infantryman. Whenever a conflict is lost, all sacrifice will be for naught. It's now time for America to win another war, and as in WWII, only the junior enlisted can make it happen. With different training, they are more than up to the task.

Fire Team Insertion

This tiny American unit will not be inserted by helicopter like a reconnaissance team would have been. It will enter the Colombian coca-growing region by one of two ways at night: (1) off the back of a truck; or (2) by cross-country walking. Its four members will carry a month's supply of dried food, limited ordnance, cell phones, and not much else. All other essentials will be harvested or stolen. This is possible, because surprise-oriented (3GW) infantry operations require little, if any, firepower.

Once the four have entered their assigned TAOR, they will have two weeks to study and improve its microterrain. (See Map 14.2.) Within that TAOR's natural anomalies, they soon find the following places to hide: (1) a deep gully that runs from GC (grid coordinate) 751382 to GC 752385 but does not show up on any map; (2) a thick stand of adolescent pine trees at GC 755387; (3) a tree with an unusually dense canopy at GC 748387; and (4) a massive bramble bush at GC 755381. From the advice in chapter 19 of *Dragon Days*,[17] they have chosen these natural hides and will soon build others. They also discover how easy it is to get disoriented while crossing the main stream. From either side of its adjoining swamp, the lowland trees make opposite-side ground features almost impossible to distinguish. Here, a diversion could make a pursuer lose sight of his quarry.

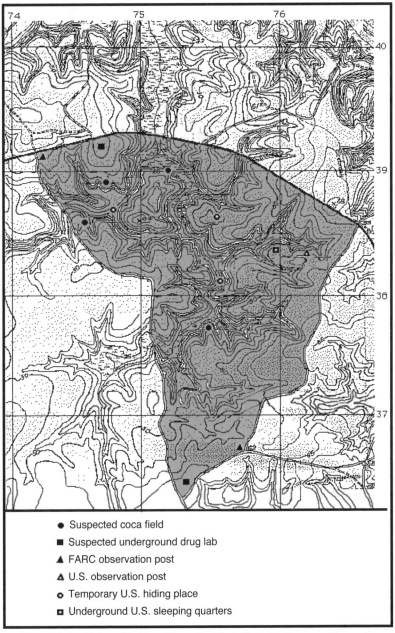

- ● Suspected coca field
- ■ Suspected underground drug lab
- ▲ FARC observation post
- ▲ U.S. observation post
- ○ Temporary U.S. hiding place
- ▫ Underground U.S. sleeping quarters

Map 14.2: Friendly Positions in Relation to Enemy Targets
(Source: U.S. Dept. of Interior, "Jacksonville South Quadrangle," 1:24,000)

Figure 14.5: One-Man Sleeping Quarters
(Source: Courtesy of Sorman Information and Media, from Soldf: Soldaten i falt, @2001 by Forsvarsmakten and Wolfgang Bartsch, Stockholm, p. 81)

Before fully investigating the western part of the TAOR (that believed to contain most enemy facilities), each of the four builds his own underground sleeping quarters. It starts out as a shallow hole the size of a single bed. Then, an entrance is added that can

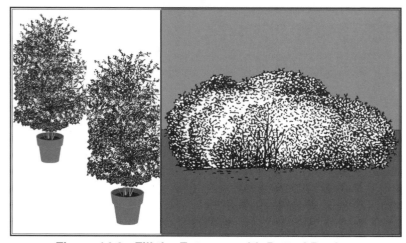

Figure 14.6: Fill the Entrance with Potted Bushes
(Source: Corel Clipart, #35A003; FM 21-76 (1957), pp. 112, 194)

double as a fighting hole. In it, he should be able to sit or kneel with just his head protruding. Next, he places a sod-covered log roof over the sleeping compartment. It must be substantial enough to take a man's weight or an 82-mm mortar impact. Finally, he pots several thick, low-growing shrubs that he knows to be easily transplantable. He will use them to disguise the way into his living compartment. When propped at the entrance sides, they will permit him to see, hear, and smell whatever transpires above his bunker. Then, should an unwelcome visitor become too inquisitive, he can dispatch him through the brush with his silenced rifle. (See Figures 14.5 and 14.6.) Should that GI not want to sleep in his hole every night, he has only to crawl under the thermal blanket he takes on patrol. That will obscure him from the thermal-imaging capabilities of light planes or drones.

The temptation now is to put the four positions into some type of perimeter. This would be a mistake. The fire team does not have enough ammunition for a traditional defense, nor could it hold out for long against a Maoist people's army contingent. Instead, the positions are placed in distant pairs. That way any enemy contingent interested in one pair could be countered by a maneuver element from the other pair. Instead of killing the intruder(s), that maneuver element would remotely trigger a diversion or personally draw the intruders away from the area.

At each pair of bunkers, one man would be on watch all night. Even to a trained sapper, a brush-covered head protruding from an entrance cavity would be indistinguishable from other shadows. The two cavities must be so positioned that the sentry at one has a clear view of the most likely approaches to the other. If he sees someone about to drop a grenade into his partner's hole, he shoots him. Now that all defensive preparations have been made, the GIs can get busy with their primary mission.

Sabotaging Drug Facilities within the TAOR

When it comes to nonconfrontational sabotage, only one or two men are necessary. (See Figure 14.7.) Their stock in trade may be arson, rain damage, and mechanical/electrical failure; but the possibilities are limitless. How much cocaine will be produced from an underground lab the day an immature snake is discovered

Figure 14.7: Self-Contained Wrecking Crew
(Source: Army/Marine Clipart, Air University, retrieved from www.au.af.mil/au/awc/awcgate/clparmy.htm)

in it? Normally, natural combustion, roof leak, or frayed fan belt would be enough to impede progress. As long as less coca and its product leave the majority of TAORs, the grunt battalion will have accomplished its mission. This will insure the special operators of less resistance in selected areas.

The Western Master of Such Things

While the British in Malaysia are often thought to be the best counterinsurgents ever produced by the West, they weren't. The Rhodesian Selous Scouts have a far superior record. From 1973 to 1980, they were credited with 68% of the Communist insurgents killed in Rhodesia while only losing 40 of their own.[18] How they did that contributes to the next set of techniques. To make them viable in Colombia, one has only to replace the destruction of people with that of materiel.

The Selous Scouts started out as mantrackers. After every terrorist incident, a few would track and then ambush its perpetrators. To do so, some went as far as 70 miles into enemy territory. If their quarry joined too many friends, the Scouts called for supporting arms or light infantry. Much of their success was based on recruiting policy. They joined four blacks for every white and tried to convert every captive.[19] This not only provided them with a continuing flow of real-time intelligence, but also kept them from demonizing their opposition.

How the Selous Scouts were trained would work well for "Fire Team TAOR" volunteers. Instead of a Western style "boot camp," the fledgling Scouts had to live off the land for 18 days.[20] Only then were they given the following survival skills: (1) improvising game traps for food; (2) navigation by natural means such as the sun and stars; (3) purifying or filtering stagnant water; (4) building a shelter for protection from the elements; and (5) fire making with a bow and drill. Next they received operational skills: (1) rigging an impromptu antenna; (2) building a boobytrap; and (3) making a "hide" from natural camouflage.[21] Finally, they got formal instruction on foraging, compass-assisted land navigation, personal camouflage, mantracking, and stalking.[22] Everything else was to be learned on the job. Such a regimen would translate into so much daring that disguises became necessary.

Because guerrillas think of themselves as aggressors, they are too complacent in their own rear areas. That's where the Scouts like to strike. They had ways to go after strategic resources and guerrilla resolve at the same time. One was the two-man hunter-killer team. Though similar to a U.S. sniper team, it would go much farther afield to find its quarry and then finish him off from much closer range.[23] It did so not only to prevent mistakes, but also to demoralize defenders.

Another of the Scouts' methods was the long-range, two-man reconnaissance patrol. It would free-fall into a target by parachute at night and then, after looking around, walk out to a helicopter extraction site. Through the diaries, letters, dispatches, and other documents it retrieved, vital "order of battle" information could often be determined.[24] With former guerrillas on the roles, the Selous Scouts could easily interpret such things. (The laptop computer would take their place today, just as the one captured from a FARC commander in Ecuador in March 2008.[25])

The key to the Scouts' success was the extensive reliance

on turned, or "tame" insurgents. A constant inflow of these insurgent recruits kept the intelligence on guerrilla security procedures up-to-date. At its zenith, turned insurgents comprised over 50 percent of the Scouts' fighting force. The rest were the best soldiers, black and white, from various components of the Rhodesian military.

How did they recruit from this pool of seemingly fanatic, dedicated guerillas? Retired Lt. Col. Ron Reid-Daly, a former commander of the Selous Scouts and author of "Pamwe Chete . . . ," put it this way:

"It was simple and direct. He [the terrorist] had the option of being handed over to the police, after which he would be prosecuted for . . . offenses related to terrorism. If found guilty he would be hanged. He could, however, change sides and work with the security forces against his former comrades. After a short period of intensive contemplation, the capture elected to change sides. He was immediately given back his weapon, but unknown to him, its firing pin had been removed. The fact that he had been given a weapon astonished . . . him. [I]t was a shrewdly calculated move designed to sow the seeds of trust. . . .

According to Col. Reid-Daly, despite their vaunted fanaticism, insurgents were relatively easy to turn. They generally lived a tough, hand-to-mouth existence and were acutely aware that while they were putting their lives on the line every day, their leaders were often living in lush accommodations, far removed from any danger, traveling in high diplomatic circles and pilfering the money and supplies intended for them.

Many of the turned insurgents went on to become some of the Scouts' most loyal and decorated soldiers. That the Scouts' formula is an effective counter-insurgency technique is beyond question. Their successes speak for themselves.[26]
— *Defense Watch,* 17 September 2003

Finally, the Selous Scouts became proficient at "pseudo operations"—those in which they pretended to be part of the opposition. These pseudo groups would infiltrate terrorist-infested areas, pass themselves off as terrorists, and then attempt to subvert the terrorist infrastructure.[27] To participate in these fake gangs, the Caucasian Scouts had simply to put on face paint. As long as they stayed away from of other Rhodesian forces, they were relatively safe. It was the very nature of Maoist insurgency that made their pseudo-operations so viable. The various cells knew too little about each other to spot an imposter.

> [M]ost modern guerilla tactics . . . take their inspiration from . . . communist insurgency doctrine. This means a rigorous attention to internal security, with highly compartmentalized, autonomous cell structures, extensive use of codes and signals, and barbaric recruitment and enforcement mechanisms.
>
> As a result, terrorist groups are extremely difficult to crack. No one cell knows what another is doing or even who its members are, and only a few . . . have any contact with any higher authority. Within an area, the terrorists can quickly identify and eliminate potential adversaries while subduing that part of the local population not sympathetic with terror and threats of terror.
>
> The only way to learn anything about these cells . . . is to get inside them. . . .
>
> The Scouts . . . perfected the "pseudo team" counter-insurgency concept. . . . [G]roups of fake or "pseudo" terrorists would enter an area and attempt to gain acceptance within the actual insurgent network.
>
> Having made contact and identified the guerrilla group, the infiltrators would then call in a strike force of . . . Rhodesian Light Infantry. . . . The [Selous] Scouts would . . . arrange to be elsewhere when the attack came. In later meetings with insurgents, they might detail their harrowing escape. . . . Properly conducted, the pseudo team could remain uncompromised.[28]
>
> — *Defense Watch,* 17 September 2003

Of course, the Scouts also liked undercover "sting" operations. On several occasions, black Scout "terrorists" walked right into enemy camps with white Scout "hostages" in tow. Another time, high-ranking Zimbabwe's People's Revolutionary Army (ZIPRA) officers were arrested by Scouts posing as Botswana Defense Force personnel. To increase the level of acceptance, the Scouts would even stage mock attacks against farms and Special Branch informers.[29] There is variation on this theme that might work well in Colombia.

How About a Pseudo-Heist?

A fake gang would be easier to establish in Colombia than Africa. Many U.S. special operators speak Spanish. Their only handicap would be a distaste for child abuse. Any Colombian pseudo-operation must make provision for FARC's underage "enlistees." It cannot—through killing—attempt to spread distrust among guerrilla factions. Instead, it must find some other way to spread distrust throughout the entire criminal network. After all, that network does contain more than just the FARC and ELN. It also has M-19 remnants, the AUC, rogue government security elements, international organized-crime families, several drug cartels, street gangs, and any number of other entrepreneurs. In the world of crime, a dope theft can create far more internal disorder than any amount of killing.

It would be easiest to steal that dope where it is made. Any drug lab that had not already been bombed or assaulted by Colombian forces would be assumed by its operators to be undiscovered. Thus, its security would be somewhat lax. To go after the refined product in any other location would create two irreconcilable problems: (1) a deliberate assault (one with reconnaissance and rehearsal) would be required; and (2) the objective would most likely be transitional. Opposition access to electronic surveillance devices and remotely controlled ordnance that makes the deliberate assault necessary. But, a shifting target cannot always be reconnoitered well enough to permit a thorough rehearsal.

Even if the dope were to stay in one place long enough, U.S. forces generally lack enough assault technique to seize it without casualties. Of course, they could always borrow a technique from the civilian literature. There are doctrinally correct, but surprise-enhanced, infiltration attacks, night attacks, and day attacks in *The Last Hundred Yards.*[30] Instead of the supporting-arms diversion, a "wet-dry" airstrike or grass fire would work nicely. There are more-advanced Eastern assault methods in *One More Bridge to Cross,*[31] *Phantom Soldier,*[32] and *The Tiger's Way.*[33] But even with a state-of-the-art technique, clever disguises and misleading clues will still be necessary. The idea, after all, is to blame the heist on another criminal element so as to create internal dissension in the drug network. Such a thing would most properly be executed by American Rangers or any Marine equivalent. While other parts of the special-operations community may have more equipment and transportation, they generally lack enough state-of-the-art assault experience.

Stealing the contents of a poorly defended drug lab should not be compared with a mock raid at Quantico or Fort Benning. In Caqueta or Putumayo Province, electronics-draped GIs stumbling out of the jungle as if invisible would look and sound like electronics-draped GIs stumbling out of the jungle. An idea from the Mohicans would have a better chance of surprising someone.

The other option is a hasty attack—one that has never been reconnoitered or rehearsed for that kind of terrain. If it were to include the concept of "reconnaissance pull" that was pioneered by the Germans in the latter stages of WWI, it could work. Reconnaissance pull is little more than taking the path of least resistance. It can take two forms: (1) several elements start out on line and then fall in behind the one that encounters a gap in enemy lines; and (2) all elements approach the objective in column and then continue to change course until a gap is found. As the latter is easier to execute, it is the one recommended for the lab. It could be easily conducted on the spur of the moment by any small group of U.S. military or drug enforcement personnel with silenced small arms. It will be called the "Indian-File Night Attack" in honor of the "oneness with nature" that is such an important part of the native-American's heritage. (See Figure 14.8.)

How to Execute an Indian-File Attack

When within a few hundred yards of a known drug factory or its storage facility, the Americans get down on their hands and knees and start crawling toward it in single file. All but the point man have silenced M-4 rifles with back-to-back banana clips slung to their chests. He has a silenced pistol that he normally keeps sheathed in its holster. All are wearing extra-light bullet proof vests and the clothing and insignia of the drug gang to be blamed.

Figure 14.8: The "Indian-File" Night Attack
(Source: MCRP 3-02H [1999], Fig.I-2)

Their only other equipment are pocket flasks of water and empty rucksacks with which to carry their seizure. All have their bare skin blackened and heads bare. They must rely on vegetation and folds in the terrain to obscure them from night vision and thermal-imaging devices. Best to avail themselves of these natural assets, they will stay below the surface of the grass and follow low spots in the ground. (See Figure 14.9.) They will also stay in the shade and away from any light-colored backdrop.

As they near the objective, the Americans pick the side with the most advantageous vegetation and microterrain. Still in column, they veer to that side. (See Figure 14.10.) Their plan is to closely pass by the lab on one side, so that when finally detected they will be already in assault position. (See Figure 14.11.) To execute such a plan, they must not overreact to apparent sentry interest. While less likely in the enemy's backyard, there are several disquieting things that can happen during a night attack. None of the following will fatally compromise the element of surprise: (1) sentries excitedly talking; (2) an ignited trip-flare; (3) a floodlight beam or aerial illumination; or (4) an overhead burst of machinegun fire. Young sentries see things all the time. Rabbits ignite trip flares. Illumination is randomly used. And one of the oldest ways to get suspected night attackers to reveal themselves is to "recon by fire." Thus, the snake keeps crawling as long as it can. If it is still not close enough, it backs up and tries the other side.

With enough perseverance, that snake will eventually get close enough to the lab to take it. Whether directly aligned with the target or not, its segments all assault as soon as the leader is comfortable with the maneuver. (See Figure 14.12.) They will be kept safe by their willingness to crouch while moving forward. Defenders usually shoot high at night, so any bullets should pass harmlessly overhead.

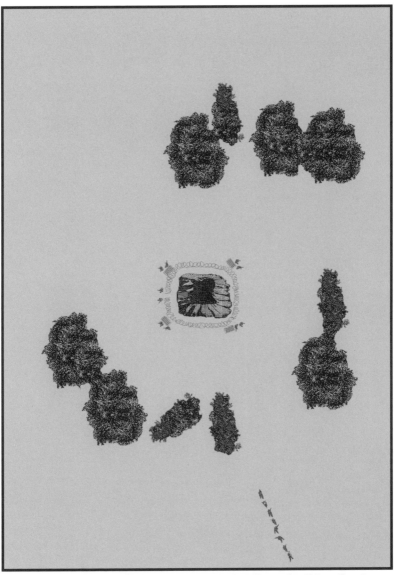

Figure 14.9: Crawling Up on the Lab Like a Stalking Snake
(Source: *The Last Hundred Yards*, Posterity Press, 1997, © 1994, 1995, 1996, 1998 by H.J. Poole, figs. 18.7, 19.3, 20.9)

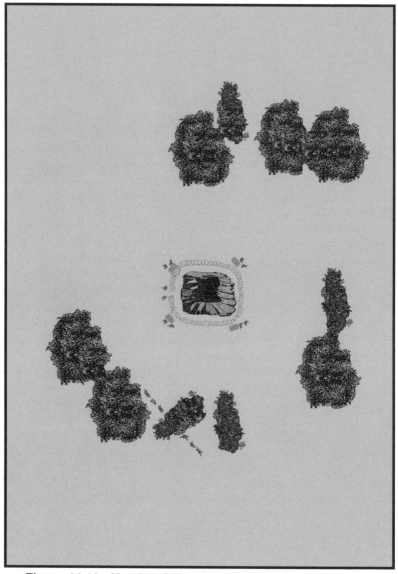

Figure 14.10: Veering Off to the Side with the Most Cover
(Source: *The Last Hundred Yards*, Posterity Press, 1997, © 1994, 1995, 1996, 1998 by H.J. Poole, figs. 18.7, 19.3, 20.9)

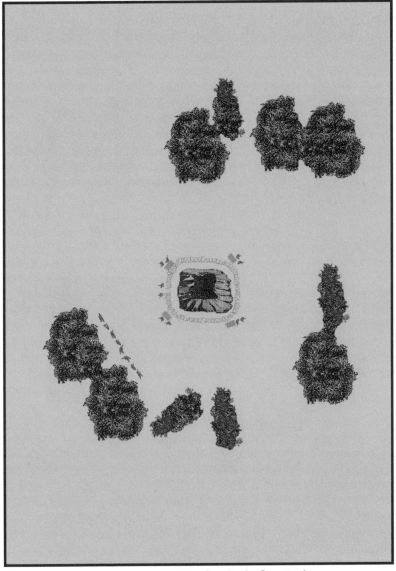

Figure 14.11: The Snake Is Spotted
(Source: *The Last Hundred Yards*, Posterity Press, 1997, © 1994, 1995, 1996, 1998 by H.J. Poole, figs. 18.7, 19.3, 20.9)

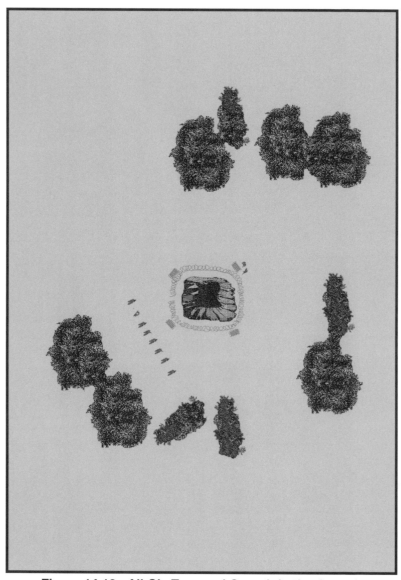

Figure 14.12: All GIs Turn and Crouch in the Assault
(Source: *The Last Hundred Yards*, Posterity Press, 1997, © 1994, 1995, 1996, 1998 by H.J. Poole, figs. 18.7, 19.3, 20.9)

After shooting or capturing the guards (depending on whether they raise their hands), the raiders enter the bunker. They quickly locate the product and load it into their backpacks. After depositing a few clues as to the scapegoat's identity, they leave. Their getaway will be much easier, if every leg has been thoroughly reconnoitered ahead of time.

There is always the chance that the snake will be spotted before getting close enough to assault. Yet, should this happen, all is not lost. One of the strangest paradoxes of night combat is that it can often keep those who have seen it from firing by simply backsliding along the same path.[34] Then, it has only to come back later from a different direction to complete its mission.

If the Americans have done their job well this night, there will be a repercussion so great in Colombia as possibly to start a war between former drug allies. Once those partners in crime have worn each other out a little, they will be a lot easier to handle. U.S. soldiers, Marines, and DEA agents can follow the advice of Sun Tzu too.

15 _____ Buffer Zones

● How might an invisible barrier slow the drug flow?
● What role would villages play in this barrier?

What It Takes to Stop Smugglers

(Source: Courtesy of Sorman Information and Media, from Soldf: Soldaten i fält, @2001 by Forsvarsmakten and Wolfgang Bartsch, Stockholm, p. 431)

A Look to the East for Strategy and Tactics

The U.S. military still practices a "high-tech" version of 2GW, and most U.S. citizens consider shooting to be an absolute prerequisite of war. Thus, the body of knowledge for 4GW counterinsurgency can be most easily derived from outside the American experience. Armies that have, for whatever reason, resisted Westernization would have the best chance of contributing. Their ways of dealing with guerrillas might generate new ways for U.S. troops to operate. As the recognized experts on UW, East Asia's Communist armies would have the greatest predisposition toward 4GW. If the 4GW quagmire of Iraq is any indicator, Iran's Revolutionary Guard *(Sepah)* might also have something to add. In essence, how American soldiers and Marines might more easily combat insurgency in the future will be extracted from what former foes have done to guerrillas in the past. To those who have yet to see the need for imported insight, a few comparisons are offered. The world's most advanced squad techniques logically come from the armies that still operate from the bottom up (frontline scouting drives target choices, maneuver options, and even strategic plans). As most such armies are now within East Asia, East Asian guerrillas are generally thought to be the most proficient. Cambodia is roughly half the size of Iraq and has half as many people. Yet, with the same number of troops the U.S. sent to a guerrilla-free Iraq six years ago, the North Vietnamese were able to contain a former guerrilla army in Cambodia in just two years.[1] And they did so despite Chinese support for their opponent as well as a Chinese invasion of their homeland. Those same Chinese have successfully repressed separatist movements in Tibet and their other western provinces for almost 60 years. And, it was only though North Korean advice that *Sepah's* offspring *(Hezbollah)* has been able to consolidate and hold on to southern Lebanon.[2] Thus—from Vietnam, China, North Korea, and Iran—this chapter will draw most of its ideas for 4GW counterinsurgency technique. For such ideas to be applicable to GIs, one has only to remove all traces of brutality.

How the NVA Handled the Khmer Rouge

With Viet Cong cousins and Chinese arms and training,[3] Cambodia's Khmer Rouge constituted a formidable foe, as well as a genocidal scourge on society, in late December 1978. Yet, in just two weeks,[4] North Vietnamese regulars were able to evict a reconstituted national army with 10,000 Chinese advisers and all other former guerrillas from Phnom Penh.[5] (See Map 15.1.) When China subsequently invaded North Vietnam in mid-February, some of those 180,000 NVA soldiers went home, and others continued to push Pol Pot's forces toward the Cambodian border with Thailand.[6] Only because Vietnamese Home Guard units had been able to single-handedly blunt the fully supported PLA assault on Hanoi, was the

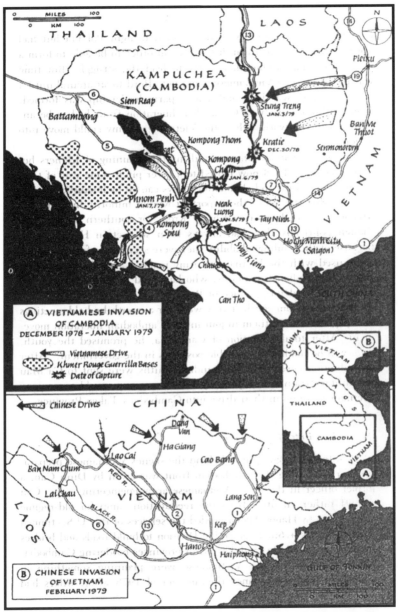

Map 15.1: Prelude to 4GW Counterinsurgency in Cambodia
(Source: Courtesy of The Wylie Agency, from Brother Enemy: The War After the War, © 1986 by Nyan Chanda, p. 337)

NVA's now-depleted expeditionary force still able to accomplish its mission in Cambodia.[7] Once the last of the Khmer Rouge salients had been overrun at the Thai border in November 1979, that force reoccupied Cambodia to limit the amount of civil strife.

The Khmer Rouge had fled into Thailand and could still make short forays across the border. Yet, the North Vietnamese made no attempt to fortify it or to follow them back across it. In effect, they had settled for a localized martial stalemate to achieve a countrywide 4GW victory. With Pol Pot's fighters effectively bottled up at the country's edge, they would concentrate on more important matters—like rebuilding the central government. If the searches during their initial sweep had not been thorough, they could not have made this decision. As that sweep progressed across the Cambodian countryside, the Vietnamese applied an eight point "immediate" program to all "liberated zones." Unfortunately, there is now only limited evidence of what those points might have been.

> Cambodia was to be nominally ruled by the People's Revolutionary Party of Kampuchea, which was hastily organized while the Vietnamese army was marching into Phnom Penh. The party's two hundred members . . . were not up to the job of reviving a nation. . . . Most importantly, they could not hope to defend the new nation against armed opposition from the Khmer Rouge. The [Khmer Rouge] decimation of the Cambodian professional class . . . made the job of rebuilding the country even more difficult.
>
> Thousands of Vietnamese officials and technicians were commandeered to Cambodia to restore the water supply and electricity in Phnom Penh, put the railway line back in service, and reopen rudimentary health clinics with Vietnamese doctors and paramedics. . . . Ministries were set up, with Vietnamese advisers running things behind the scenes. Hundreds of Khmers [Cambodians] were sent to Vietnam to take crash courses in health care, education, banking, foreign trade, and security work.
>
> After a period of a cashless [barter] economy . . . currency was reintroduced. . . . Cambodian children went to school again. . . . Cambodia's revival . . . over a period of six years was a true miracle.[8]

During that "liberation" sweep, the Vietnamese must have left a tiny detachment of troops behind in each good-sized village to replace its Khmer Rouge cadre. They had that capability because all of their infantrymen had been trained in UW. If any of those villages had subsequently come under attack by bypassed Khmer Rouge, its Vietnamese contingent could have then reverted to guerrilla tactics. Because every NVA soldier had spent some time training his own Home Guard, he could also instruct Cambodian villagers on UW. That meant a pro-Vietnamese cadre could be appointed in each village that could also survive on its own. When the Vietnamese army returned from the Thai border 11 months later, the whole region was well on its way toward normalization.

Because of Chinese interest in Cambodia, the Vietnamese knew that their hold on the country was still somewhat fragile. By the end of 1981, squad-sized teams of Chinese re-equipped Khmer Rouge had started to return to Cambodia's interior from the Thai border. Their goal was to start another guerrilla war against the central government.[9] Yet, that was the year North Vietnam offered to withdraw from Cambodia if China agreed to a non-aggression pact. To even make such an offer, Hanoi must have had enough homegrown local security to withstand widespread unrest. It must have further realized that the Cambodian people were so disgusted by the Khmer Rouge genocide, that they would have never supported such a rebellion. As it turned out, China refused the offer to withdraw, and by 1983 the Vietnamese occupation force had only shrunk to 150,000. However, that many soldiers were not needed to prevent a Khmer Rouge resurgence. They were needed to forestall a Chinese invasion.[10]

Finally, in 1991, the Paris Peace Accords mandated democratic elections and a cease fire for Cambodia. Factional fighting in 1997 caused the breakup of the first coalition government, but a subsequent election in 1998 led to a new coalition and more political stability. Remnants of the Khmer Rouge surrendered in 1999, and the last of the NVA occupiers went home shortly thereafter.[11]

The North Vietnamese Defense Matrix

Something momentous had just happened at North Vietnam's border with China. While its seasoned regulars were off fighting in Cambodia,[12] Home Guard units had successfully defended the

219

entirety of its northern border.[13] Its reservists had kept 17 Chinese divisions—backed by tanks, artillery, and a full fifth of the Chinese air force [14]—from penetrating more than 30 miles into the country.[15] When returnees from the Cambodian campaign finally moved toward the last border town in contention, the invaders declared victory and ended the whole operation.[16] By their own estimate, the Chinese had taken 20,000 casualties in 16 days.[17] Including civilians, they guessed that the North Vietnamese had lost only 10,000.[18] Something like their defensive formation might help to stem the flow of drugs and people out of the FARC's now expanded theater of operations. Its beauty must lie in how well it utilizes the local population.

A new concept has been devised to meet this contingency [another Chinese invasion]—called the Military Fortress. While new and innovative, it does have roots in the "combat village" of the Vietnam War and the still earlier "fortified village" of the Viet Minh War.

The Military Fortress concept presently involves some two dozen districts that abut on China—an inaccessible region of mountain, jungle, and Montagnard—that are to be welded into one contiguous defensive structure. Each village of the district is to become a "combat village," linked in tactical planning terms to neighboring villages; the entire district thus becomes a single strategic entity, and all the districts together become a grand Military Fortress. Villagers are armed, and all have combat duties. . . . Each villager spends part of each day training and working on fortifications, for which he gets extra rations. The work includes digging the usual combat trench foxhole, trench, bunker, underground food and weapons storeroom, and the ever-present *"vanish underground" installation,* the hidden tunnel complex [italics added]. These are within the village. Some distance out, usually two to three kilometers, is what is called the "distant fortification," a second string of interlocked trenches, ambush bunkers, manned by well-equipped paramilitary troops serving full time. Several villages (usually about five) are tied together by communication systems and fields of fire into "combat clusters" (about seven per district), and the whole becomes a single strategic entity.[19]

The "Buffer Zone" Strategy

From that just described comes the "buffer zone" strategy for southwestern Colombia, the narrowest part of the Panama, and the Mexican border. Its goal will not be to block invasion or even guerrilla movement. It only discourages the smuggling of certain commodities—namely, narcotics and people. As such, it would be a 4GW strategy in the economic arena, and only loosely based on North Vietnam's 3GW defense matrix.

Towns would be farther apart in a random slice of Latin America than at the Chinese border with Vietnam, so they are no longer the building blocks of the new strategy. It will focus instead on the road and trail network within which towns are only chokepoints. Once authorities have been alerted to the transport of cocaine or illegal immigrants, they can intercept and search as necessary. Some of those searches shall accidently come up with arms and guerrillas. The former can be confiscated and the latter charged. As such, the critical difference between law enforcement and military occupation will be carefully maintained.

While not unlike the "Mesa Redondos" of Peru (where villagers were armed and visited), this buffer zone would more closely follow Vietnam's "defense-in-depth." It does so in three ways. Just as an NVA advisory team was undoubtedly posted to each combat village, a tiny U.S. detachment will live in each Latin American town. Otherwise, local officials will be subjected to bribes or intimidation, and the plan will fail. Next, local citizens will be paid to watch what goes on around them. All towns are connected by road or trail, so a little extra traffic along these lines of communication will seem perfectly normal. Finally, all participants will receive some instruction in UW. Of particular interest to the community watch volunteers shall be the "vanish underground" aspect of E&E.

For each location, there must be a slightly different version of the buffer zone scheme. Within its detail will lie its effectiveness, as with most Asian strategies. Many things have yet to be determined—like how local lookouts will be recruited, asked to operate, and protected while reporting.

The Barrier between Coca Fields and Buenaventura

Within Colombia, most of the dope is being shipped north out

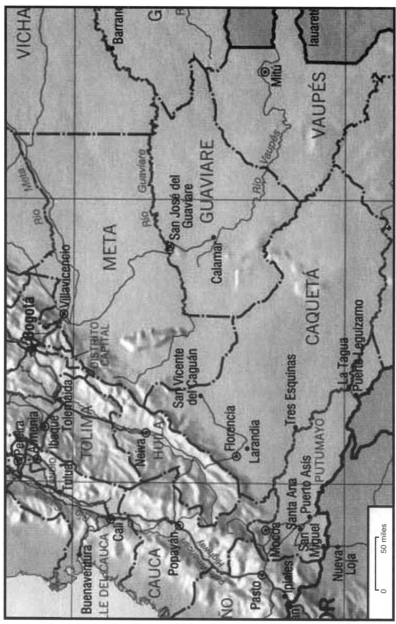

Map 15.2: Strategically Important Part of Colombia
(Source: Courtesy of General Libraries, University of Texas at Austin, from their website for map designator "colombia_rel_2001.pdf")

of the Pacific seaport of Buenaventura. However, some may also be making its way west from Turbo on the Caribbean in the old boats that used to bring contraband coconuts in the opposite direction.[20] Thus, watching the roads that lead north and west from the coca and poppy fields of Caqueta, Putumayu, Huila, Tolima, and Meta Provinces should help to stem the drug flow. And placing tiny U.S. contingents in the towns along those roads would limit the size, number, and provisioning of drug factories. But they must be deployed in such a way as not to look like part an occupying force. (See Figure 15.1.)

Figure 15.1: U.S. Response Team
(Source: Ft. Sill Military Clipart Library, www.hqda.mil/aoguide/clipart, #SOLDRUN.jpg)

Map 15.3: Towns in Colombian Buffer Zone
(Source: Courtesy of General Libraries, University of Texas at Austin, from their website for map designator "colombia_rel_2001.pdf")

As is evident from Maps 6.2 through 6.7, such a deployment would place the GIs just inside FARC territory. They must therefore conduct a "soft defense" to lessen the dope traffic, as opposed to stopping it. (See Map 15.2.) From Chapters 6 and 14, it's clear that Colombia's "Home Guard" and law enforcement outposts have not slowed the flow of refined product into Buenaventura.[21] Though these platoon-sized units had quick-reaction forces nearby,[8] few have been able to withstand any serious FARC pressure.[22] That's largely due to the corrupting influence of their opposition's cash. As in Iraq, Home Guard and police squads will have to be combined with U.S. infantry squads to form CAP platoons. Such a platoon would be appropriate for every town at the west end of Caqueta and Putumayo Provinces—to include Ibague, Tolemaida, Neiva, Popayan, San Vincente de Caguan, Florencia, Larandia, Pasto, Mocoa, Ipiales, San Miquel, Santa Ana, and Porto Asis. (See Map 15.3.) It would also be useful in the villages along the northwestern edge of Meta Province.

Though light-infantry and UW trained, the U.S. squads would do little more than help local counterparts to spot drug-smuggling activity. They would recruit cell-phone-carrying observers who could regularly travel the roads between towns. This will be no small undertaking, because the FARC and local cartel will already have their own intelligence networks in place. Colombian cartels have been known to financially reward any cab driver or bellhop who reports a newcomer's whereabouts. Both criminal factions will also have informants inside the police and Home Guard units. As a result, the road watch part of the plan may have to be known only to the Americans. All phone tips would come directly to them, and those that led to a successful arrest would establish who their true friends were.

The Buffer in Panama

Whatever drugs are not moving west by boat along the Panamanian coast must come overland through the Darien Gap. As shown by Maps 6.2 and 6.3, FARC has always been interested in the Colombian side of that Gap.

Along the north coast of the isthmus is a trail that leads from the tiny settlement of Agandi, Colombia (at the western lip of the

Map 15.4: Town and Patrol Bases in Darien Gap Buffer Zone
(Source: Courtesy of General Libraries, University of Texas atAustin, from their website for map designator "panama_rel_1995.pdf")

Gulf of Turbo), to the equally tiny Porto Obaldia, Panama. From there, trading boats regularly wend their way west through the San Blas Islands to Colon.[23] Any overland shipment from Colon would necessarily have to cross the Bridge of the Americas at Panama City. (Refer back to Map 6.10.)

At the south end of the Darien Gap is where the Cali Cartel's Panamanian drug route was probably pioneered.[24] Its shipments could have crossed the 125-mile-wide Gulf of Panama by large ship. Or, they could have leapfrogged by smaller boat to Jaque, Garachine, La Palma, San Miguel, and anyone of the towns on the western shore of the Gulf of Panama. They may also have gone overland. Porters could have climbed to the headwaters of the Balsas or Tuira Rivers from Riosucio, and then shifted their loads to vehicles at Yaviza. As Map 15.4 clearly demonstrates, there is now a dirt road that runs all the way west from Yaviza to Canita, Chepo, and finally Panama City.

Between Chepo and Canita, the isthmus is only 30 miles wide. Across 10 of those miles, the Rio Chepo forms a natural barrier. In this area, a buffer zone would most logically include two town-based CAP platoons and seven rural patrol bases. (Look more closely at Map 15.4.) Three of these platoon-sized bases would be spaced at five-mile intervals along the western side of the Rio Chepo. The next two would be atop the mountain chain (where there is probably an old path). The final pair would be on the north coast plain. With trained mantrackers in a this lightly populated an area, fire team patrols would have no trouble finding the overland drug route. (See Figure 15.2.) When that route had been located, their job would be to determine its trace and monitor its traffic. After the smugglers' schedule had been established, special operators could be summoned to sabotage their cargo. Any seizure would have to happen much closer to civilization and be part of a routine search. Otherwise, the drug runners could simply change their route.

The Phantom Patrol Base

Drug runners can easily afford drones and thermal imaging, so these patrol bases must be situated beneath double or triple canopy. Their only mission is to map and watch the overland drug route. They can best accomplish that mission by dispatching fire-team-sized

Figure 15.2: Fire-Team-Sized Patrols Can Cover More Ground
(Source: Courtesy of Sorman Information and Media, from Soldf: Soldaten i falt, ©2001 by Forsvarsmakten and Wolfgang Bartsch, Stockholm, p. 225)

patrols. Fire teams are harder to spot than squads and can, through sheer numbers, cover an area three times as large. On the longer routes, those fire teams should have a corpsman or medic attached. They have no intention of making enemy contact, so the fifth man is not for the treatment of gunshot wounds. This part of Panama constitutes one of the most unhealthy environments on earth, so all who serve here must be carefully preconditioned Only a veteran of New Britain in the South Pacific would have experienced anything worse.

Each fire team must have its own trained mantracker and be

Figure 15.3: The Old Way of Moving No Longer Works
(Source: Army/Marine Clipart, Air University, retrieved from www.au.af.mil/au/awc/awcgate/cliparmy.htm)

able to function as a mantracking team. It must further have two specially trained point men.[25] Then, the whole problem boils down to traversing a large unpopulated area without appearing to exist.[26] Movement in the coastal lowlands after dark must generally be confined to the game trails. Any off-trail excursion might result in an unpleasant encounter with an electric eel or night-hunting fer-de-lance.[27] Thus, most travel must be by day and potential drug paths only outposted at night. By restricting most daytime movement to the forest's shadows, the teams can greatly reduce their signature.[28] To disappear, they must crawl across any sunlit area that cannot be bypassed. For such activity, full combat gear would be inappropriate. (See Figures 15.3 and 15.4.) Each patrol member needs only water filter, dried food, limited ordnance, thermal blanket, and miniaturized radio. Should an aircraft appear overhead, he would quickly drape the special blanket over his shoulders.

Figure 15.4: Crawl to Cross an Unavoidable Open Space
(Source: Army/Marine Clipart, Air University, retrieved from www.au.af.mil/au/awc/awcgate/cliparmy.htm)

The Defense at the Mexican Border

Whatever makes it through (or around) the Colombian and Panamanian buffer zones must be blocked (as opposed to slowed) at the Mexican border. That will take a third variant of the buffer zone concept. Of the three, it will most closely resemble that which could stop an invasion. For those who don't think that much defense necessary, some additional statistics are offered. On 22 April 2008, ABC News reported that 2,000 Mexican policemen had been killed over the last two years in fighting with the drug cartels near the U.S. border.[29] Less than two months later, the head of Mexico's federal police force was assassinated.[30]

A huge swath of territory just south of the U.S. border has become an active war zone, and America's security establishment should take note. The U.S.-Mexican border is too porous and long to be blocked by a 2GW defense, no matter how "high-tech" it might be. As the Marines found out on Guadalcanal,[31] such a defense offers little resistance to anyone with world-class assault technique who can get within 60 yards of it unobserved. Any post-Vietnam veteran may have trouble even imaging a procedure that good. It follows logically that the Japanese could also prevent someone from getting within 60 yards. Whatever the Nipponese could do was soon apparent on the Mainland. So, Japanese methods can be added to the research.

At the University of Texas' Perry Castaneda Library website exists a complete set of detailed maps (from satellite imagery) of the Mexican border. Most come from the U.S. Geological Survey and are 1:25,000 in scale vice the usual 1:50,000. Such a map of a rare north-south section of that border will be used to demonstrate this buffer zone variant. (See Map 15.5.)

A New Role for the Towns

In this buffer zone, there is already a man-made barrier—namely, the fencing and electronic surveillance devices along the U.S. side of the Rio Grande. What to do on the Mexican side will be patterned after what the Japanese did in front of their lines during WWII. It will include the Eastern techniques of "hidden picket post,"[32] "roving sentry,"[33] and "non-apparent ambush."[34] Together, they will provide two absolute prerequisites for a state-of-the-art defense: (1) direct frontline intelligence; and (2) attack force interruption.

Any drug penetration—whether by backpacker, tunnel, or hang glider—must be partially obstructed before it can be fully launched. Simply alerting the U.S. Border Patrol or National Guard to its impending arrival won't be enough. In this particular sector, the hamlets are tiny and seldom more than a mile apart. Other than offering a place at which a tunnel might be built, backpackers hidden, or illicit cargo unloaded, they are less important to the scheme than in Colombia or Panama. There, the towns were at least chokepoints in road and trail network. At this part of the Mexican border, any

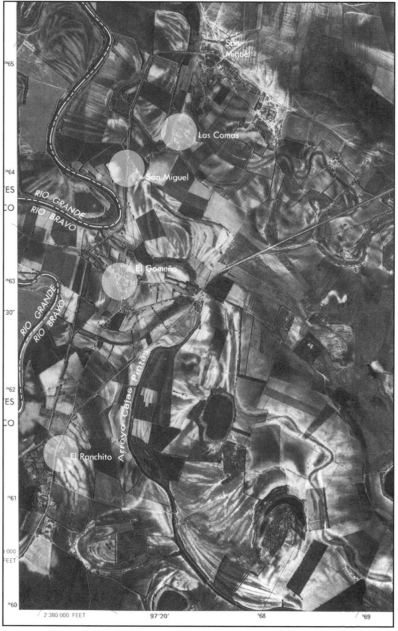

Map 15.5: Towns in Mexican Border Buffer Zone

(Source: U.S. Geological Survey map "Palmito Hill Texas-Tamaulipas 1983," 1:25,000. U.S.-Mexico border series, from Univ. of Texas Castaneda Library website)

Figure 15.5: This Last Worked in 1902 (on Boer Guerrillas)
(Source: FM 5-103 [1985], p. 4-1)

crossing attempt could be more easily launched between the hamlets. Thus, most will not need CAP platoons, or even resident policemen. And the idea of fortifying them against attack would make defending the border more difficult. Not since the British used barbed-wire-enclosed blockhouses against the Boers in South Africa, has such a strategy succeeded. (See Figure 15.5.) It would further limit all resident travel at night. As the best source of resistance against the smugglers, those residents must be free to leave their homes and settlements at any hour. The hamlets will most usefully function as "hidden picket posts." That means their physical appearance must not be altered in any way.

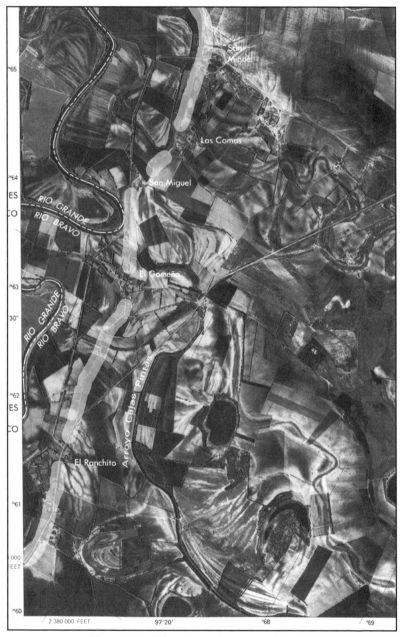

Map 15.6: The Areas between Towns

(Source: U.S. Geological Survey map "Palmito Hill Texas-Tamaulipas 1983," 1:25,000. U.S.-Mexico border series, from Univ. of Texas Castaneda LIbrary website)

Instead of soldiers or policemen, these hamlets will have armed community watch personnel. But, unlike the ones in Iraq, all will know of the "disappear underground" aspect of UW. They will have cell phones, and their commander will be in continuous and direct contact with his U.S. counterpart (as opposed to haphazard contact with that person's boss). Still, those in the hamlet can make little difference alone. The real contribution with come from between and behind the towns.

The 4GW Equivalent to a Roving Sentry

Between these tiny Mexican border hamlets will be residents who while returning home or visiting friends can function as roving sentries. (See Map 15.6.) While each will carry a cell phone, it should only be used for emergencies. Anything the sentries notice out of the ordinary should be discreetly reported to the community watch commander at their destination. Otherwise, a village informant or advance element from the cartel may guess their role in the defense.

The 4GW Equivalent of a Non-Apparent Ambush

In the Eastern version of conventional battle, claymore ambushes are made to look like minefield intrusions or mortar barrages, and tanks mysteriously break a track. Both will erode the momentum of an enemy attack force. And in both, the victim never suspects a nearby enemy soldier.

On any road into these border hamlets from Mexico's interior will be a pair of civilian buddy teams. One will act as the lookout to warn the town and its counterpart of the smugglers' approach, and the other will be more pro-active. Once the second team has heard over its cell phone that a smuggler convoy is approaching, it will arrange for a slight impediment in the roadway. Its goal will not be to preclude the border penetration attempt, but only to interrupt its timing. Anywhere in Mexico, that impediment could take the form of farm animals that have strayed, a car that has broken down, or rocks that have slid. None of the three would give the smugglers any indication that they had just entered a forward defense zone.

235

The End Result

In tandem, the hidden picket posts, roving sentries between them, and non-apparent ambushes behind them, constitute a formidable forward defense zone. All will be armed. Should any of the sentries or ambushers come under attack, they have only to ask for assistance from the hamlets. Should any of the hamlets come under attack, their male residents have only to hide their families in the "disappear underground facilities" and assist each other. After encountering so disruptive a picket formation on the Mexican side of the border, the best planned cartel penetration will have little chance of surprising anyone on the U.S. side. Its timing will be off, and so too will any prearranged support. That's all the edge a good Texas, Arizona, New Mexico, or California security detachment needs.

16 Working a Heavily Populated Area

- How is urban counterinsurgency different from rural?
- Is jailing a large number of suspects productive?

All Detainees Afforded Legal Protection in 4GW

(Source: Courtesy of Sorman Information and Media, from Soldf: Soldaten i falt, ©2001 by Forsvarsmakten and Wolfgang Bartsch, Stockholm, p. 431)

Cities Can No Longer Be Pacified As Before

From the multi-dimensional Islamist assault has come a new paradigm for U.S. soldiers and Marines. To achieve long-tern success over an insurgency (whether Muslim or Maoist), those GIs must now be as good at waging peace as they are at waging war. The contested areas are no longer awash with mortal foes and dastardly sympathizers, but only have occasional criminals that prey on friendly populations. As such, the most densely inhabited can be compared to a troubled American neighborhood. Whatever U.S. police would not do in such a neighborhood should also be avoided by GIs overseas. That means military commanders abandoning their time-honored tradition of "maximum force to save U.S. lives." It means adversaries being more often arrested than killed. And finally, it means working harder to remove the underlying reasons for dissatisfaction. Anything less may create the initial illusion of victory, but as has happened throughout Central America, that illusion will eventually fall away.

Within Every Guerrilla Method Lies Its Own Antidote

Many a guerrilla technique may also be useful to counterinsurgency. For example, a pro-government cell in a guerrilla area could serve as a valuable bridgehead.

When Iran's Revolutionary Guard *(Sepah)* was born in 1979, "[it] was a diverse group of guerrillas who [had] initially fought against the Shah's regime but then joined . . . the successful insurrection of 11-12 February."[1] Then, for three years, *Sepah* consolidated control over other guerrilla factions in Iran. In 1982, it sent a contingent to Lebanon to see what could be done about the Israeli invasion. That contingent's offspring—*Hezbollah*—subsequently brought most of the Lebanese factions into alignment (to include Communist, Socialist, Shiite, Sunni, and Palestinian militias).[2] From the *Sepah* and *Hezbollah* methodologies might come some new counterinsurgency techniques to use against the *Hezbollah*-like Mahdi Army in Iraq or 4GW-proficient FARC in Latin America.

How *Sepah* Handled the Iranian Competition

Ayatollah Khomeini had designated *Sepah* as the "guardians of the Revolution,"[3] with an overall mission of preserving the new State. In essence, *Sepah* had been directed to use its guerrilla abilities to control any external or internal resistance to the fledgling government.

Besides waging war with Iraq, Sepah's role included the following: (1) dislodging other guerrilla factions and restoring order to the cities; (2) suppressing ethnic uprisings in the countryside; and (3) providing internal security to expand the Ayatollah's control.[4] To accomplish those things, it would need to develop its own "human intelligence."

For neutralizing the anti-Khomeini underground forces, *Sepah* relied on meticulous information gathering and occasional infiltration.[5] To keep an eye on the Iranian armed forces, it became an integral part of those forces.[6] To counter both threats at once, *Sepah's* personnel were widely dispersed, and then each tiny contingent given considerable authority.

> In rural regions . . . [Iranian] Guard bases [are] located in individual small towns. In more urbanized areas . . . a subordinate headquarters, which may even be a storefront or large house, overseas further subdivisions of the city ("Duties, Aims, Policies of Guard," *Tehran Kayhan,* 14 February 1984, 167). The intention and result is that the Guard achieves maximum penetration of the civilian population *(Defense and Foreign Affairs Handbook,* 1989, 514).[7]

In effect, every Iranian town and neighborhood would have its own *Sepah* detachment. From deep inside the society, those detachments were to enforce Islamic law, collect intelligence, quell anti-government sentiment, and recruit/train soldiers for an Iranian "people's army." That's not too different from squads of UW-trained GIs helping to man Colombian police and army outposts, so as simultaneously to discourage FARC attacks and government atrocities.

Hezbollah's Solution to Competing Resistance Groups

The people in Shiite *Hezbollah's* Iranian nucleus wanted not personally to fight the Israelis but rather to prepare locals (most notably the Sunni Palestinians) to do it.[8] They have since relied on Sunni *Hamas* to do most of the fighting in the Occupied Territories.[9] But, right after inception, *Hezbollah's* principal competition came not from the Palestinian Liberation Organization (PLO), but rather from *Amal.* Though also Shiite, *Amal* was only interested in security for southern Lebanon, whereas *Hezbollah* wanted to project the struggle into Israel itself.[10] *Amal* desired no armed Palestinian presence in Lebanon and a greater role for Shiites in a secular government. *Hezbollah* wanted armed Palestinian help in expelling the Israelis from an Islamic Republic.[11] *Hezbollah's* founders had more tactical experience and finally resolved their differences with *Amal* through active combat.[12]

239

All the while, *Hezbollah* was endearing itself to the local population and, in effect, capturing its loyalty. It provided social services to the poorest elements of Lebanese society, thereby creating a quasi-state in the midst of chaos. In southern Lebanon, it provided education, loans, grants, health care, and security to those in most need of help.[13]

Hezbollah concurrently established a vast neighborhood watch network. As such, it received more of its real-time intelligence from the population than from long-range observation.[14] U.S. veterans of Iraq will be quick to attest to the power of such an arrangement.

For GIs to Do What *Sepah* and *Hezbollah* Had Done

A beleaguered society needs an alternative to the Islamist, Maoist, or drug commissar who inhabits every village or neighborhood. Local officials are often corrupt, so the most productive alternative to that commissar is a few resident GIs. By copying some of the commissar's least objectionable methods, those GIs could more easily survive, as well as beat him at his own game.

Fully to emulate the Iranian version of 4th-generation counterinsurgency, each tiny U.S. contingent would have to do the following: (1) be a part of the local security establishment; (2) live off the local economy; (3) be proficient at UW; (4) provide basic services; (5) have its own intelligence and community watch networks; and (6) be able to train local militiamen for any contingency. The only thing not already a part of the CAP plan is the fifth. These Americans will not have airstrikes and a relief force, should they get into trouble. If too big an enemy force comes after them, they and the rest of their CAP platoon will have to temporarily fade away (resort to E&E). Without a sophisticated early warning apparatus, they will have no way of knowing when to do that. This chapter will provide the techniques for such an apparatus.

In a CAP platoon setting, a squad of visiting Americans cannot hope to enjoy the societal leeway of a more culturally consistent group. But, for safety, it must have an intelligence-gathering and community watch network of which its host-nation counterparts are unaware. As do embassy guards, it would also need a strict code of behavior—to include a deep commitment to minimal force, interrogation etiquette, and civilian judicial process. It would have its own chain of command and be required to report immediately any evidence of a host-nation excess. And finally, it would need special training in how to combine intelligence gathering, defensive maneuver, and law enforcement.

How the Three Factors Interrelate

Criminal investigators depend for early leads on informants. Some of these informants do what they do as a service to the community, both most are being paid or working off some favor. The GIs will need civilian informants to counteract the local commissar, but they will also need lookouts.

A lookout is easier to recruit than an informant. His role will be ostensibly defensive in nature, so much less risky. Still, he may be subjected to bribes, threats, or death during an enemy attack. Some may be far enough from the GI headquarters to make valuable intelligence sightings. That means all lookouts must be carefully hidden. It is from *Sepah* and *Hezbollah* procedure that one can learn how best to hide them.

Nothing Must Be Obviously Altered in the Neighborhood

Throughout the Eastern world, the principal axiom of urban defense is in no way to alter the appearance of the area to be defended. Among other things, that means lookouts able to sound an alarm discreetly. Muslims are better at the first than the second, so their ways to hide a lookout will be more closely explored than their reporting procedures.

The Corner Lookout

Both *Sepah* and *Hezbollah* employ street corner lookouts who can see for blocks in several directions.[15] These are people who normally work there (like a news stand operator) and have been paid to watch for suspicious activity. Or they are people who temporarily inhabit that location, like a public-service repair man, street vendor, or beggar. (See Figure 16.1.) To make such a posting less obvious, the latter can be randomly rotated.

Each of the U.S.-employed lookouts should have his or her own

Figure 16.1: The Corner Lookout
(Source: *DA PAM 550-65* [January, 1986], p. 139)

communication device, but be told to carefully hide any transmission. To all passersby, the moving lips of an obviously normal person can only mean one thing.

The Building Watcher

In Manila near the end of WWII and again in Seoul in the early 1950's, U.S. troops encountered lone enemy sentries inside of buildings.[16] This would be preferable to the fully silhouetted rooftop sentry that U.S. troops have come to expect in Iraq. From a building's upper-story windows, a lone sentry could scan a wide area—and peer into otherwise defiladed spaces—without doing anything out

Figure 16.2: The Building Guard
(Source: *FM 90-10-1* [1982], p. B-29; *FM 3-4* [1985], p. 3-5)

A JUNKED CAR COULD BE DRAGGED OVER A MANHOLE TO FUNCTION BOTH AS A SENTRY POST AND A POSITION FROM WHICH TO AMBUSH ENEMY FORCES MASSING FOR AN ATTACK. AUTOMATIC-WEAPONS FIRE FROM THE REAR CAN BE VERY DISCONCERTING TO AN ATTACKER.

Figure 16.3: The Invisible Outpost
(Source: TC 90-1 [1986], p. 3-23; FM 90-10-1 [1982], pp. 3-35, 5-7; FM 22-100 [1973], p. 2-4)

of the ordinary. Because of the canalizing effect of city walls, some of those areas (like a segment of alleyway) might reveal as a much enemy intention as a much broader view. (See Figure 16.2.)

The Invisible Outpost

In WWII, not only the Japanese, but also the Russians had many ways of hiding permanent sentry posts in a rural setting. The latter ranged from fake hay piles, to prefabricated tree stumps, mounds, and rocks.[17] The same idea could easily be applied to a city. From an open manhole cover beneath a wrecked car, a lone sentry could secretly watch an intersection and all streets leading into it. He could secretly move into position and then be periodically relieved through the sewer. Basement windows and gutter openings might also offer covert access, but not as good a view. (See Figure 16.3.)

The Roving Sentry

Finally, both Japanese and German armies regularly employed two-man "reconnaissance and visiting" patrols within their string of picket posts. Those patrols consisted only of buddy teams. Their mission was to observe the intervening areas and perform liaison.[18] If performed by a single civilian, the same concept would work in the city. On every street and in most buildings, there is pedestrian traffic. As long as all pedestrians alter their times, paces, and routes, none will seem artificially imposed. (See Figure 16.4.)

With all the above methods, the U.S. CAP platoon contingent should be able to develop enough of a community watch network

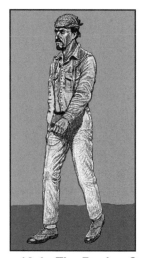

Figure 16.4: The Roving Sentry
(Source: Courtesy of Orion Books, from *World Army Uniforms since 1939*, © 1975, 1980, 1981, 1983 by Blanford Press Ltd., Part II, Plate 124)

around their headquarters to be forewarned of any concerted attack. To monitor all activity around an opponent's facility, they have only to establish another series of outposts. In law enforcement lingo, all lookouts now become part of a "stake-out." But, fully to control that opponent, they will need a more pervasive form of human intelligence.

Public-Intelligence Harvesting

Electronic surveillance can locate unusual activity and intercept suspect communications, but it can't positively identify all participants, their motives, or their movement plans. As a result, it often leads to the wrong people getting hurt. In a struggle for hearts and minds of a population, one can more productively act on what its members already know. That the U.S. military has traditionally put such a low priority on learning this type of information may help to explain why it has had so much trouble beating guerrillas. One of the biggest strengths of the CAP concept is that it facilitates the collection of public intelligence.

The most useful public intelligence does not come from detainees. It comes from paid informants and the civilian population as a whole. As a detainee's level of discomfort grows, so too will his imagination. That's the least obvious of all 4GW reasons to treat him humanely. The most obvious is that he and his extended circle will be voters. Of course, some member of the commissar's personal entourage would make the best informant, but he is also the hardest to acquire. The only real chance to do so is right after he has been captured. In exchange for immunity to prosecution, he may give up his boss. (See Figure 16.5.) The Selous Scouts took this idea one step further. After handing a guerrilla captive an ostensibly loaded pistol, they would give him the choice between civilian prosecution or joining their organization. In compliance with local culture, the captive then felt obligated to the organization that had just spared his life. The erstwhile foes could more easily interpret leads (many from captured diaries and letters) and soon became some of the Scouts most dedicated and decorated warriors.[19]

Figure 16.5: The Paid Informant
(Source: *DA PAM 550-25* [December, 1988], chapt. 4)

Much less difficult to mine for information are the taxi drivers and bellhops. In several Colombian and Lebanese cities, they routinely sell the whereabouts or destination of strangers to the local drug cartel and *Hezbollah*. In Beirut, even the shop owners know what telephone number to call to report any suspicious Western activity.[20] CAP platoon GIs could also make known their dedicated phone number and how much various types of information might be worth.

In every locale, there will be families loyal to the host government. With a little encouragement, they will name others of similar persuasion. When all have been mapped, opportunities arise. The most obvious is the cell multiplication method of the Communists. It would work just as well for Americans.

Similarly, the public can be of great help in locating the Maoist, Islamist, or narcotics representative in their midst. Normally, such an investigation starts out with a list of suspects. By determining who works for whom, the top man eventually becomes apparent. But such information will only begin to flow after the GIs have earned the trust of local residents. That's the reason for the community service projects, soccer leagues, and entrepreneurial loans. Only through the population itself, does 4th generation counterinsurgency succeed

How All Techniques Could be Combined in Latin America

In the southeastern provinces of Colombia, every U.S. squad with an isolated CAP platoon will need its own early warning and intelligence gathering system. (See Maps 16.1.) Wherever drugs are prevalent, so too will be corruption. Many of the government outposts in those provinces have already come under attack. In every town, FARC and one of the cartels will have a similar system around their facilities.

Every avenue of approach to the GIs' headquarters will be under continual observation by civilian "volunteers." During the day, building guards look through binoculars for trouble approaching from long range, while corner lookouts scan the streets for two blocks in every direction around the CAP headquarters. At night, invisible outposts watch the sewers and alleyways leading to the headquarters, while building guards scan with night vision equip-

Map 16.1: Latin American Town to Be Protected
(Source: Courtesy of General Libraries, University of Texas at Austin, from their website for map designator "cali.jpg")

ment all rooftops and breezeways near it. If an attack is expected, roving outposts perform liaison between those that are static. (See Map 16.2.)

Short of vehicle barriers and an E&E route, there is little more that the GIs can do to actively defend themselves. As world travel-

▨	CAP platoon headquarters
△	Lone building sentry
■	Street corner lookout
●	Covered manhole observer
★	Roving one-man outpost

Map 16.2: GI's Civilian Lookout Network on Full Alert
(Source: Courtesy of General Libraries, University of Texas at Austin, from their website for map designator "cali.jpg")

Figure 16.6: CAP Members May Look Like Traditional GIs
(Source: Army/Marine Clipart, Air University, retrieved from www.au.af.mil/au/awc/awcgate/cliparmy.htm)

ers have done for years, they must largely depend for protection on the inherent humanity of the local community. That humanity will become more evident as the GIs embrace their new role of peace-maker (vice war-maker). (See Figures 16.6 and 16.7.)

Figure 16.7: But Their Job Is No Longer to Kill Enemy Soldiers
(Source: Army/Marine Clipart, Air University, retrieved from www.au.af.mil/au/awc/awcgate/cliparmy.htm)

Figure 16.8: The "Now Handsome" American
(Source: Ft. Sill Military Clipart Library, www.hqda.mil/aoguide/clipart, #SOLDWALK.jpg)

Throughout the indigenous peoples of Latin America, this new breed of U.S. soldier and Marine will be remembered as their northern cousin who personally cared enough to rescue them from their darkest hour. (See Figure 16.8.)

Afterword

Impressions of Other Peoples Now More Important Than Ever

Americans often wonder why their fine nation is not more widely revered around the world. Has it not greatly sacrificed for other people's freedoms? The answer is quite simple really. The rest of the world does not object as much to America's intentions as to its methods. U.S. forces have traditionally relied more on bombardment than maneuver and still draw too little distinction between hostage and sympathizer. Though difficult to substantiate, the number of French civilians killed during the pre-invasion bombing of Normandy was almost certainly in the thousands. During the initial stages of the U.S. deployments to Afghanistan and Iraq, there was more inadvertent bombing of innocent bystanders. Just as ants near a heavy boot, beleaguered societies eventually come to resent American military help. In a globally fought 4th-generation war, such resentment could tip the scales in favor of a less well intended, but more clever opponent. Whether the Communists and Islamists take over the world by force or election, the end result will be the same. Thus, the Pentagon now has little choice but to change. Its infantry leaders must come to realize that enough small-unit tactical proficiency to overcome guerrillas will also permit fewer casualties at short range in conventional battle. With a slightly different way of training and utilizing infantry squads, they could replace much of their firepower with surprise, and thus keep from alienating foreign populations.

In recent years, this need for tactical transformation has been far more evident to progressive military thinkers than its precise formula. They finally allowed enough of the CAP platoon and community watch concepts into Baghdad to lower that city's level of violence. But, most are still unaware that their assault and defense techniques (like football plays) are still some 90 years behind the state of the art. The U.S. Army's new counterinsurgency manual

(FM 3-24) is more of an expanded policy statement than an explanation of small-unit procedure. Senior officers tend to believe that all good ideas can be executed. As trained, U.S. troops cannot do much of what FM 3-24 proposes. Their gear load alone (now some 75 pounds) would preclude it. By openly marketing this manual over the internet, its signers have created the impression that their service branches are keeping pace with tactical evolution. They have additionally diverted attention from more-procedure-oriented "manual supplements." Little do most know that this "bottom-echelon" deficiency has existed since 1917 (with the advent of German Stormtrooper tactics). Nor do they realize that it has already been addressed by a president (Franklin D. Roosevelt with the Carlson's Raider initiative) and service branch head (Marine Gen. Al Gray with maneuver war doctrine). Unfortunately, both tactical reform attempts failed. The Marine Raider concept was scrapped in February 1944, and maneuver doctrine has yet to be applied to anything smaller than a company. The very nature of Western bureaucracy is, of course, the problem. Because it is so decidedly "top-down," it first resists delegating sufficient authority to its lowest echelons, and then ignores their recommendations.

America's infantry branches will now have to improve tactically at the small-unit level, or things will continue to deteriorate around the world. Such an improvement will take a nontraditional "bottom-up" way of training. Only then, can three very important qualities be developed at the rifleman-through-squad level: (1) less predictability and better maneuvers; (2) tactical-decision making; and (3) more initiative. Among the new individual skills must be those for unconventional warfare and criminal investigation. They will permit tiny contingents of U.S. soldiers or Marines to anchor Combined Action Platoons in some of the most isolated places on earth. America's enemies have now managed to perfect a 4GW upgrade to Mao's 3GW method. According to William S. Lind (father of 4GW theory), any manifestation of 4GW will automatically trump a "high-tech" 2GW format.[1]

Clearly, the next attempt at peace in Latin America must be specifically tailored to region, as opposed to some rerun of "standard operating procedure" from Iraq or Afghanistan. It must concurrently address the political process, guerrilla activity, and drug trafficking. All the while, it cannot stray too far from the Ten Commandments.

Islamists Are Not to Blame for the Turmoil in Latin America

Much of the Islamic unrest in the world is only symptomatic of a bigger problem. That problem is twofold and so entrenched and controversial as to defy solution: (1) PRC-encouraged chaos (through drugs, revolution, U.N. protection, and disinformation); and (2) America's bombardment-heavy way of war. Until every U.S. commander comes to see his mission differently, long-term victory will be elusive. That mission must be perceived as more of a police effort against a radical fringe (wherein bystanders are protected) than a war against an entire sect (wherein bystanders are expendable). Most U.S. leaders are still more focused on *al-Qaeda,* than its affiliates and manipulators. One cannot help but wonder why bin Laden felt it necessary in late 2007 to announce that he was the only one responsible for 9/11.[2] As Latin America is predominantly Catholic, it only has a token *al-Qaeda* presence. Most of that region's Islamic "terrorists" are from *Hezbollah* and only interested in money making. Its ongoing Communist revolution is more obvious. For plausible deniability, the new overseer of this revolution has established a proxy string: Cuba—Venezuela—FARC. Operatives of the latter have been spotted in Venezuela, Panama, Ecuador, Brazil, Paraguay, Bolivia, Nicaragua, Honduras, and Mexico. FARC's drug involvement appears aimed at acquiring enough political influence to pursue the politicization phase of Mao's method. That method involves armed rebellion only where the democratic processes cannot be manipulated.

At Fault Are Crime Families, FARC, and Any Mutual Mentor

Trading in illicit drugs produces great sums of money. That money can be used for more than just sophisticated weaponry; it can buy advanced tactical instruction. The best small-unit assault and defense techniques now reside in East Asian armies. Should any of those techniques ever make it to Colombia, American leaders might wish they hadn't. For a military in which schedules and lanes still force the rushing of machineguns, a people's army with sophisticated arms and next generation of Maoist tactics could pose quite a challenge.

253

As previously mentioned, the FARC already has people in Mexico,[3] and in no fewer than seven other Latin American nations. Recently released videotapes reveal a more-self-assured infantry force than ever before.

More Contras Are Not the Answer

After the International Court of Justice and U.N. General Assembly forced the United States to stop supporting the Contras, Mr. Daniel Ortega has once again been elected the president of Nicaragua.

For a while, the AUC was the fastest-growing vigilante organization in Latin America. However, many of its members were former policemen and soldiers who had been discharged for human rights abuses.[4] Still others got lured into the drug trade. This is not the kind of assistance U.S. forces will need to restore peace to Colombia.

Counterinsurgency Is Not the Answer

At one time or other, almost every Latin American nation has applied force to what it perceived to be a Communist insurgency. Despite the deaths of hundreds of thousands of peasants, most of those countries now have left-leaning presidents. And the four who are Marxist have clearly been helped to manipulate their country's democratic processes. So what long-term good did all of those counterguerrilla operations really do?

It might be more appropriate to disrupt the drug money and political advice that has helped the leftists to win their elections. Without drug proceeds, the most troublesome of guerrilla factions—like the FARC and Shining Path—could no longer expand. That would mean their eventual demise without more bloodshed.

Not Even Martial Law Is the Answer

The leader who first tried to suppress Peru's guerrillas through martial law is now in jail. Military dictatorships in Argentina,

Uruguay, Chile, Guatemala, Peru, Honduras, and El Salvador were responsible for even more loss of life after too little civilian adjudication. In the first four, left-leaning candidates have since won the elections. In Central America, the *maras* were initially formed by disenfranchised fighters from both sides. So, more militarization will do little to alleviate their discontent.

The Solution Is a New Type of Peacekeeper

Recent tragedies on another continent point to a cure for Latin America. In Africa, the Chinese have been heavily investing in Sudan and Zimbabwe. While both countries sport terrible human-rights records, only the first has any natural resources. And, only the first has hosted U.N. peacekeepers from the PRC. They have been stationed just southeast of Darfur since 2005.[5]

In Zimbabwe, the illusion created by China's ongoing "trade, charm, and foreign-aid campaign" has begun to fade. The same West that so naively helped Robert Mugabe to gain power has finally acknowledged some of his more brutal excesses. Even *Time* magazine now asserts that his "special forces" massacred some 20,000 Ndebele "tribespeople" in the early 1980's for simply supporting a rival.[6] So, when Mugabe lost the April 2008 election, his response was sadly predictable. First, he cried foul and then for a runoff election. Soon, Mugabe's thugs were beating up his opponent and as many opposition supporters as they could find. To save the hard-pressed Zimbabwean people from another bloodbath, Morgan Tsvangirai then wisely conceded the race. As of the end of June, Mugabe's bully boys had shifted their attention to anyone who could not prove they had voted for him.[7] It's no secret that Zimbabwe came into existence through a PRC-supported rebel invasion and has since become a Chinese satellite. At the height of the election crisis, a Chinese ship attempted to unload arms for Zimbabwe,[8] and PRC military personnel showed up in Mutare to provide "advice." Some reports even had them helping to patrol the streets.

> The Chinese, together with about 70 Zimbabwean senior army officers are staying at the Holiday Inn, in the city's central business district.

255

There are about 10 Chinese soldiers. "We were shocked to see Chinese soldiers in their full military regalia and armed with pistols checking at the hotel," said one worker.[9]

It is thus not unreasonable to conclude that the PRC's U.N. peacekeepers in Sudan and Lebanon may be doing more than just separating the warring factions. Within Haiti, the Chinese now have a military police contingent that operates under U.N. auspices. The U.S. would do well to follow suit with its own more comprehensive form of "peacekeeper."

Specially trained U.S. squads could also provide local law enforcement assistance throughout Latin America. (See Figure A.1.) In the process, they could discourage both drug trafficking and host-nation excesses. The American generals who "won't want to risk that many young lives" must come to realize how survivable UW-trained squads really are. The vast quantities of cocaine that are still reaching America's streets are not doing other young lives much good either. The jails are filling up so fast that programs of rehabilitation are no longer feasible. In effect, Americas prisons have become a breeding ground for sociopaths. Thus, the U.S. military must step forward in an unfamiliar role to protect America from this new threat.

Finding the Proper Mix between Military and Police Activity

Cops on the beat work in pairs but get little training in how to surprise or even "fire and move" toward a suspect. Soldiers in an urban 4GW environment should work in pairs and be instructed on how to weed out the most likely suspect. Through real-world parallels, a U.S. soldier or Marine might more easily discover this interface. But there is no official publication on the subject, because those in charge no longer think at that level. Many have so little personal experience with combat that they deal only in esoterics.

U.S. Infantrymen Must Be Differently Prepared for this Role

Tall "top-down" organizations—like those in the U.S. military—tend to be least proficient at their lowest echelons. Their junior ranks get too little chance to exercise initiative, make tactical decisions, and develop tactical techniques (their own individual, fire team, and squad maneuvers). As a result, their parent units underperform at short range in both conventional or unconventional combat. Both U.S. infantry services have long sought some way to correct this problem—somehow to harness their NCOs' collective experience so as to help each individual to reach his or her full potential. That

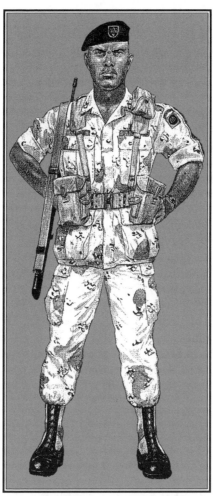

Figure A.1: Some PFCs Don't Need Much Supervision
(Source: Courtesy of Cassell PLC, from *Uniforms of Elite Forces,* © 1982 by Blandford Press Ltd., No. 8)

way has now been found. It has already been adopted (during a single CO's tenure) by three Marine battalions.[10] By now showing it to all junior officers, both infantry services could reap its benefits. Designed for use at the company level, this method accomplishes several things at once. Among its most intriguing are the following: (1) better tactical technique (through experimentation); (2) less predictability (no two companies' procedures exactly alike); (3) a more compelling learning dynamic (competition between units); and (4) better morale, initiative, and tactical-decision making at the lowest echelons (every NCO a trainer).

When allowed to train this way, each company's squad leaders develop three or more "numbered" maneuvers for each of the most probable combat scenarios (e.g., counterambushing). They practice those maneuvers daily with their subordinates (at boots-and-rifles physical training [PT]). Then, when the foe shows up, the squad leader has only to ask his deployed fire team leaders which number they advise. By so doing, he makes possible a "deliberate attack" (one that has already been reconnoitered and rehearsed). Trying to carry a "prepared enemy position" with anything less will result in too many friendly casualties. That the squad leader can decide upon a deliberate attack so quickly makes possible the "Holy Grail" of short-range combat—momentum. Such was the German Storm-troopers' secret to success in the spring offensives of 1918. Americans can do this too. (Refer back to Figure A.1.)

American soldiers and Marines already have squad and platoon drills they occasionally practice. However, no platoon drill contributes much to momentum. To adapt to a fluid situation, anything more than 14 people will still need to be "managed" by a leader. The 14 members of a squad, on the other hand, can readily adjust to changing circumstances without the help of a "coordinator." All they need is a little practice on what approximately to do. Then, when the time comes, each can exercise sufficient initiative without undermining the overall team effort. That's why football teams are the size they are.

The problem with the existing squad drills is in who designs them and whether they have enough flexibility. In the new way of training in the Appendix, the NCOs of each company collectively design/modify their own drills through continual experimentation. In the existing arrangement, higher headquarters infrequently designs some drills that are much too likely to be used under all circumstances.

Though the higher ranks may have trouble seeing this Appendix as the solution to chronic military ineptitude, it nevertheless is. It will not only allow American forces finally to evolve tactically, but also end the age-old rift between officers and enlisted men. As currently trained and utilized, U.S. squads have neither the ability nor the self-confidence safely to outpost a volatile region. That's the same as saying they can't beat a 4GW warrior or Maoist insurgent. This method would also permit American advisers finally to show indigenous soldiers how to refine their own ways of fighting. It should be of great interest to anyone wishing to avoid a replay of what happened in Vietnam in the 1970's or Central America in the 1980's.

U.S. infantry branches perpetuate their short-range combat ineptitude by under-employing junior enlisted personnel, too quickly promoting them, and then complaining about how little they know. The more senior or otherwise qualified one is, the easier it is to fall into this trap. The method in the Appendix does not follow the individual advice of NCOs; it captures their collective advice. Even underused squad and fire team leaders are smarter collectively on the subject of short-range combat than the best officer or staff non-commissioned officer. To test this theory, try asking for a show of hands from 20 or more combat-seasoned NCOs. If 15 out of 20 can agree on a short-range tactical maneuver, their combined opinion will be better than anything one can find in an official manual. That does not alleviate the need to "field-test" this opinion through simulated casualty assessment. Fewer friendly casualties will mean better tactical technique.

The bottom line is that tactical experimentation at the company level will produce far better results than headquarters or its commander telling everyone what to practice. By training that way at Camp Lejeune's Platoon Sergeant School in the late 1980's, one instructor came up with a Stormtrooper-like night attack without ever reading a history book.[11] Until U.S. infantry organizations come to realize that the problem is in how they train at the squad level, they will continue to struggle at short range. To do better, they must exercise more respect for the collective opinions of their NCOs. They are the ones with the most experience at short range (or alternatively the ones with the most to lose at short range). Collective-decision making is an Asian concept that predates Communism by thousands of years. Unfortunately, it makes little sense to the "top-down-thinking" Western military officer. As a result, U.S. squads may continue to be tactically outclassed wherever they encounter an Asian influence.

Appendix:
Bottom-Up Training

1. In 4GW, GIs will always be outnumbered.

2. For enough skill to operate alone, they will need "bottom-up" training.

    a. There can be no true maneuver warfare capability without decentralization of control and troop initiative.

    b. Each company must learn to operate as nine semi-independent maneuver squads.

        (1) Squads can fight like football teams.

            (a) If they've practiced and numbered several plays for each category of enemy contact.

            (b) If the squad leader asks his fire team leaders (by hand-and-arm signal) which play to run before picking.

            (c) If that play need not be run just as rehearsed (so individuals can react to unforeseen events).

        (2) The squad leader will have adequate control if all plays practiced in varied terrain beforehand.

        (3) Training for squad combat is like football too.

            (a) Individual, buddy team, fire team, and squad drills are followed by force-on-force scrimmage.

            (b) Instead of daily physical training (PT), squads do battledrills on cross-country runs with boots and rifles.

    c. Training must give every squad member initiative, tactical-decision-making practice, and nonpredictability.

(1) Best way is to let the troops in each company collectively identify and fix their own deficiencies.

(2) Companies no longer need identical methods.

(3) Only through experimentation can the lowest echelons of a "top-down" organization gain "world class" tactical proficiency.

   d. Officers must control "bottom-up" training indirectly.

     (1) By providing solutions from history.
     (2) By choosing situations to be solved.
     (3) By monitoring improvement in surprise generated and simulated casualties suffered.

2. Planning Phase

   a. CO and platoon leaders publish "mission-type" training order to Gy.Sgt.—a short list of squad combat situations to be solved.

     (1) E.g. security patrol, counterambush, ambush, chance contact, defense, day attack, night attack, short-range infiltration attack, urban attack, urban defense.

     (2) Best are those involving large numbers of enemy soldiers because they will require total surprise.

   b. Gy.Sgt. convenes NCO conference to record needs on blackboard.

     (1) Group arrives at prerequisite skills for each situation—what squads, fire teams, buddy teams, and individuals must do.

     (2) More than elementary "basics" will be required.

       (a) Must covertly shoot, move, and communicate.
       (b) Must also have microterrain appreciation, harnessing senses, night skills, deception, decision making.

     (3) Gy.Sgt. schedules instruction for progressively larger elements (individuals first).

       (a) Weapons training can have one of two formats.

         1 Explain, demonstrate, imitate, practice, test.

2 Create situation for students to solve (more retention and applicable to enemy weapons).

(b) Teach established tactical maneuvers thru battledrills.

1 Attention gainer and lecture.
2 Demonstration and practical application.

a Outdoors.
b Blackboard or overhead projector.
c Sand table with miniatures.

3 Practical application testing (e.g., count U.S. losses).

(c) Teach new tactical maneuvers thru "situation stations."

(4) NCO assigned to each period of instruction.

(a) Leaders of next-higher echelon will do the teaching.
(b) Situation station "experiments" given to NCOs with "by-the-book" mentalities.

(5) Instructors refer to *Last Hundred Yards* and *Tiger's Way*.

(a) Fully tested maneuver warfare methods.
(b) All methods have sources fully identified.

(6) All instruction takes place near the unit's headquarters or barracks with rubber rifles and makeshift training aids.

3. Execution Phase

a. Training is conducted for whole company at once.

(1) Either sequentially or in round-robin format.
(2) Normally in 20-minute sessions for 12-man "sticks."
(3) Assigned instructor can ask any number of peers to help.
(4) Most training consists of technique rehearsal.

(a) Success measured through surprise (speed, stealth, deception) or simulated casualties.

(b) Individuals and subunits are asked to compete or to improve themselves on successive tries.

(5) Instructors statistically track how well techniques
have been working and constantly try to improve them.

b. Next comes the Tactical Demonstration.

(1) Officers arrange training support and recreate situations
(2) Squads run through situations under simulated fire.

(a) Machinegun and artillery simulators add realism
(b) Surprise indicators and friendly casualties measured.

(3) Only recourse for dissatisfied officers is to change
situations or pick another group facilitator.

c. Then comes Free Play — force-on-force exercise in which the
side with the fewest losses wins.

(1) Sides required to solve twice each situation for which
technique taught (e.g., two assaults on foe's camp).

(a) One side reverses its shirts.
(b) Sides given command posts (CP's) not too far apart.
(c) One third of each force defends own CP with no outposts.
(d) Two thirds of each force needed to assault enemy CP.
(e) Each man records any 3-second sight picture of upright
foe or flour grenade hit within 10 feet of himself.
(f) Casualties reenter problem via own CP after short delay.
(g) Secretly seizing the enemy's flag nets bonus points.
(h) Umpires assess demerits for any bodily contact
or not doing required events.

(2) At end of the event, sides are moved beyond earshot of
each other while all counts are made.

d. Finally, a Lessons-Learned Field Day is held.

(1) All enlisted personnel assembled.
(2) Privates given chance to demonstrate better ways.
(3) Gy.Sgt. gauges worth of each way through a show of hands.

4. All squads expected to practice the new techniques daily during PT.

a. First some combat warm-ups.

(1) Crawling races.

(2) Duck walking like in some types of urban terrain.
(3) Window entry practice.

  b. Then each squad takes its own combat run with boots and rifles.

(1) Move in Indian file through all types of terrain.
(2) Periodically stop to practice a squad maneuver.
(3) Make mental note of terrain limitations to that maneuver.

5. Gy.Sgt. reconvenes all NCOs quarterly.

  a. Results of last training session rehashed.
  b. Techniques modified as necessary.
  c. Next training session planned.

6. Evolution is continually repeated whether in garrison or deployed.

Notes

SOURCE NOTES

Illustrations:

Maps on pages 5, 23, 29, 35, 39, 41, 45, 47, 49, 53, 54, 61, 65, 76, 77, 82, 87, 91, 95, 97, 107, 109, 132, 222, 224, 226, 232, 234, 247, and 248 reprinted after written assurance from GENERAL LIBRARIES OF THE UNIVERSITY OF TEXAS AT AUSTIN that they are in public domain.

Maps on pages 67, 68, and 70 reproduced under the GNU Free Documentation License, from *WIKIPEDIA ENCYCLOPEDIA,* s.v. "FARC" and "ELN." Copyright © n.d. by Juan Jose Araujo. All rights reserved.

Map on page 81 reproduced after asking permission of *NATIONAL GEOGRAPHIC MAGAZINE.* It appeared in the article, "An Illegal Cash Crop Sustains . . . 40-Year-Old Guerrilla Movement in Southern Colombia." Copyright © July 2004. All rights reserved.

Pictures on pages 36, 88, and 244 reproduced after written assurance from Orion Books, London, that the copyright holders for *WORLD ARMY UNIFORMS SINCE 1939,* text by Andrew Mollo and Digby Smith, color plates by Malcolm McGregor and Michael Chappell, can no longer be contacted. They are from Part II (plates 101, 103, and 124, respectively) of the Orion publication. Copyrights © 1975, 1980, 1981, and 1983 by Blandford Books Ltd. All rights reserved.

Pictures on pages 37, 89, 195, and 257 reprinted after written assurance from Cassell PLC, London, that the copyright holders for *UNIFORMS OF THE ELITE FORCES,* text by Leroy Thompson, color plates by Michael Chappell, can no longer be contacted. The illustrations are from Illustration Numbers 90, 91, 2, and 8 of the Cassell publication, respectively. Copyright © 1982 by Blandford Press Ltd. All rights reserved.

Pictures on pages 159, 191, 195, 197, 200, 215, 228, and 237 reproduced with permisson of the Swedish Armed Forces and written assurance from Sorman Information/Media that the illustrator can no longer be contacted, from *SOLDF: SOLDATEN I FALT,* by Forsvarsmakten, with illustrations by Wolfgang Bartsch. These pictures appear on pages 81, 225, 394, 430, and 431 of the Swedish publication. Copyrights © 2001 by Forsvarsmakten and Wolfgang Bartsch. All rights reserved.

Picture on page 217 reproduced with permission of The Wylie Agency, Inc., New York, NY, from *BROTHER ENEMY: THE WAR AFTER THE WAR,* by Nayan Chanda. The illustration is from page 337 of the Collier Books publication. Copyright © 1986 by Nyan Chanda. All rights reserved.

Text:

Reprinted after asking permission of *BRITISH BROADCASTING CORPORATION ONLINE NEWS,* London, UK, from the following article(s): (1) "BBC Country Profile: Uruguay"; (2) "BBC Country Profile: Argentina"; "BBC Country Profile: Bolivia"; "BBC Country Profile: Chile"; "BBC Country Profile: Costa Rica"; "Columbia's Most Powerful Rebels, 19 September 2003; and "Defying Silence in Honduras," 4 July 2007. Copyrights © 2003, 2007, and 2008 by BBC. All rights reserved.

Reprinted with permission of *UNITED PRESS INTERNATIONAL,* from the following article(s): (1) "Analysis: Chinese Arms and African Oil," by Andrei Chang, 5 November 2007. Copyright © 2007 by UPI. All rights reserved.

Reprinted with permission of C. Hurst & Co., Ltd., London, UK, from *INSIDE AL-QAEDA: GLOBAL NETWORK OF TERROR,* by Rohan Gunaratna. Copyright © 2002 by Rohan Gunaratna. All rights reserved.

Reprinted with permission of the Jamestown Foundation, Washington, D.C., from the following chapters in *UNMASKING TERROR*: (1) "Al-Qaeda's Unlikely Allies in Central America," by Pineda Cruz, vol. II; (2) "Terrorism and Human Smuggling Rings in South and Central America," by Thomas Davidson, vol. III. Copyrights © 2005 and 2007 by Jamestown Foundation. All rights reserved.

Reprinted with permission of *THE WASHINGTON TIMES*, from the following article(s): (1) "Chinese Military Trains in West," by Bill Gertz, 15 March 2006; and (2) "Who Needs the Panama Canal," by Robert Morton, Nat. Weekly Ed., 1-8 March 1999. Copyrights © 1999 and 2006 by The Washington Times LLC. All rights reserved.

Reprinted with permission of East-West Services, Springfield, VA, publishers of *WORLD TRIBUNE* and *GEOSTRATEGY-DIRECT*, from the following article(s): (1) "Intel. Report: Venezuela Training Ecuador Rebels," 25 October 2005; and (2) "Iran's Improved Fajr-5 Rockets Can Be Fired Remotely," 31 May 2006. Copyrights © 2005 and 2006 by East-West Services. All rights reserved.

Reprinted after being unable to contact *AHN NEWS* (Ecuador), from the following article(s): (1) "Ecuador Offers Concession Of Manta Air Base To China, Declines To Renew Contract With U.S.," by Vittorio Hernandez, 26 November 2007. Copyright © 2007 by AHN News. All rights reserved.

Reprinted with permission of William S. Lind, c/o The Free Congress Research and Education Foundation, Alexandria, VA, contributor to *ANTI-WAR.COM*, from the following article(s): (1) "More on Gangs and Guerrillas vs. the State," 29 April 2005. Copyright © 2005 by William S. Lind. All rights reserved.

Reprinted with permission of the Marine Corps Association, Quantico, VA, publisher of the *MARINE CORPS GAZETTE*, from the following article(s): (1) "The Hezbollah Model: Using Terror and Creating a Quasi-State in Lebanon," by Lt.Cdr. Youssef H. Aboul-Enein USN, June 2003. Copyright © 2003 by MCA. All rights reserved.

Reprinted after asking permission of the Federation of American Scientists, Washington, D.C., manager of *FAS.ORG*, from the following article(s): (1) "FARC Weapons Supplies Revealed," 6 September 1999. Copyright © 1999 by FAS. All rights reserved.

Reprinted after asking permission of Lt.Col. Reid-Daly, c/o Covos-Day Books, Weltevreden Park, South Africa, from *PAMWE CHETE: THE LEGEND OF THE SELOUS SCOUTS*. Copyright © 1999 by Lt.Col. R.F. Reid-Daly. All rights reserved.

Reprinted with permission of the Naval Order of the United States, Merrifield, VA, publisher of the *MISSION: HISTORY,* from the following article(s): (1) "1945: Marine Corps Fights Its Most 'Savage' Battle Ever," vol. 3, no. 2, 5 February 2001. Copyright © 2001 by the Naval Order of the U.S. All rights reserved.

Reprinted after asking permission of Peter Stiff, c/o Galago Publishing, Alberton, South Africa, from *THE SILENT WAR: SOUTH AFRICAN RECCE OPERATIONS, 1969-1994.* Copyright © 1999 by Peter Stiff. All rights reserved.

Reprinted after asking permission of Dr. Kenneth Katzman, from *WARRIORS OF ISLAM: IRAN'S REVOLUTIONARY GUARD.* Copyright © 1993 by Kenneth Katzman. All rights reserved.

Reprinted after asking permission of the *ARMED FORCES JOURNAL,* Springfield, VA, from the following article(s): (1) "Venezuelan Vagaries," by Peter Brookes, July 2007; and 2) "Infantry and National Priorities," by Maj.Gen. Robert H. Scales U.S. Army (Ret.), December 2007. Copyright © 2007 by Armed Forces Journal. All rights reserved.

Reprinted after asking permission of *THE POWER AND INTEREST NEWS REPORT,* Chicago, IL from the following article(s): (1) "Mexico's Internal Drug War," by Sam Logan, 14 August 2006 . Copyright © 2006 by PINR. All rights reserved.

Reprinted after asking permission of the Center for International Development and Conflict Management, College Park, MD, manager of *CIDCM.UMD.EDU,* from the following article(s): (1) "China's Influence on Africa," by Ernest J. Wilson III, 28 July 2005. Copyright © 2005 by CIDCM. All rights reserved.

Reprinted with permission of The Wylie Agency, Inc., New York, NY, from *BROTHER ENEMY: THE WAR AFTER THE WAR,* by Nayan Chanda. Copyright © 1986 by Nyan Chanda. All rights reserved.

Reprinted after asking permission Jack Sweeney and *THE WASHINGTON TIMES,* from "DEA Boosts Its Role in Paraguay," 21 August 2001. Copyright © 2001 by Jack Sweeney. All rights reserved.

Reprinted with permission of *NATIONAL PUBLIC RADIO,* from
the following article(s): (1) "Calderon Fights Mexico's Gangs with
Little Success," by Lourdes Garcia-Navarro, *All Things Considered,*
16 May 2007; (2) "Drug Violence Rampant in Mexico," by Lourdes
Garcia-Navarro, *Morning Edition,* 18 May 2007; and (3) "Smuggled
Chinese Travel Circuitously," by Irene Jay Liu, *Morning Edition,*
20 November 2007. Copyright © 2007 by NPR.
All rights reserved.

Reprinted with permission of the Memorial Institute for the
Prevention of Terrorism, Oklahoma City, OK, manager of *MIPT.ORG,*
from the following article(s): (1) "FARC." Copyright © 2008 by MIPT.
All rights reserved.

Reprinted with permission of Random House, from *PAVN: PEOPLE'S
ARMY OF VIETNAM.* Copyright © 1986 by Douglas Pike. All rights
reserved.

ENDNOTES

Preface

1. "Analysts Debate al-Qaeda's Strength," by Tom Gjelten, NPR's "Morning Edition" News, 10 March 2008.
2. "Latin America: Terrorism Issues," by Mark P. Sullivan, Congressional Research Service (CRS) Report for Congress, Order Code RS21049 (Washington, D.C.: Library of Congress, 22 January 2007), p. 2. [This work will henceforth be cited as "Latin America: Terrorism Issues," by CRS.]
3. Bruce I. Gudmundsson, *Stormtroop Tactics — Innovation in the German Army 1914-1918* (New York: Praeger, 1989), pp. 146-149.
4. H. John Poole, *The Tiger's Way: A U.S. Private's Best Chance of Survival* (Emerald Isle, NC: Posterity Press, 2003).
5. "Latin America: Terrorism Issues," by CRS.
6. Nayan Chanda, *Brother Enemy: The War after the War* (New York: Collier Books, 1986), chapt. 10.
7. H. John Poole, *Terrorist Trail: Backtracking the Foreign Fighter* (Emerald Isle, NC: Posterity Press, 2006), chapts. 9 and 10.
8. Constantine Menges, *China: The Gathering Threat* (Nashville, TN: Nelson Current, 2005), p. 328; *Wikipedia Encyclopedia*, s.v. "People's Liberation Army"; *Chinese Defense Today* (www.sinodefence.com), s.v. "Home Ground Forces Order of Battle."
9. Joseph S. Bermudez, Jr., *North Korean Special Forces* (Annapolis: Naval Inst. Press, 1998), p. 147.
10. Robert Burns, AP, "Special Forces Feeling the Strain of War," *Jacksonville Daily News* (NC), 6 May 2006, p. 4A.
11. H. John Poole, *Militant Tricks: Battlefield Ruses of the Islamic Insurgent* (Emerald Isle, NC: Posterity Press, 2005), chapt. 13.
12. Erin McClam, AP, "Americans See No End to Iraq War," *Jacksonville Daily News* (NC), 16 September 2007, pp. 1A, 2A.
13. H. John Poole, *Dragon Days: Time for "Unconventional" Tactics* (Emerald Isle, NC: Posterity Press, 2007), part three.
14. *Fourth Generation War*, FMFM 1-A (Draft Copy), by William S. Lind (Washington, D.C., 2005).
15. "The Gift of Ourselves," *Columbia*, October 2007, pp. 38-40; "Saints of Service," *Columbia*, November 2007, pp. 10, 11.
16. *The Columbia Encyclopedia*, sixth ed., 2001-07, s.v. "Garrido Canabal, Tomas."

Introduction

1. Chris Zambalis, "Al-Qaeda's Inroads in the Caribbean," in *Unmasking Terror: A Global Review of Terrorist Activities,* vol. III, ed. Jonathan D. Hutzley (Washington, D.C: Jamestown Foundation, 2007), p. 476 [the source document will henceforth be cited as *Unmasking Terror,* vol. III].

2. *Tehran's War of Terror and Its Nuclear Delivery Capability,* by Stephen E. Hughes (Victoria, Canada: Trafford Publishing, 2007), p. 152. [This work will henceforth be cited as *Tehran's War of Terror,* by Hughes]

3. Michael Melia, "Fourth JFK Terror Suspect Surrenders," *Jacksonville Daily News* (NC), 6 June 2007, p. 5A; Chris Zambelis, "The Threat of Religious Radicalism in Guyana," in *Unmasking Terror,* vol. III, p. 488.

4. Rick Bayless, PBS's "Mexico: One Plate at a Time," NC Public TV, 3 June 2007.

5. *Tehran's War of Terror,* by Hughes, pp. 149, 169.

6. Melia, "Fourth JFK Terror Suspect Surrenders," p. 5A.

7. Ibid.

8. Rohan Gunaratna, *Inside al-Qaeda: Global Network of Terror* (Lahore: Vanguard, 2002, p. 165; Aaron Mannes, *Profiles in Terror: The Guide to Middle East Terrorist Organizations* (Oxford: Rowman & Littlefield, 2004), p. 152.

9. *Tehran's War of Terror,* by Hughes, pp. 147, 158.

10. Ibid., p. 158.

11. "Paraguay: Court Investigates Hizballah Base Photos," ABC Color (Paraguay), as translated for FBIS, in *Tehran's Wars of Terror,* by Hughes, p. 157.

12. "Latin America: Terrorism Issues," by CRS

13. *Tehran's Wars of Terror,* by Hughes, p. 146.

14. Ibid., pp. 147, 152.

15. Lt.Col. Patrick Myers and Patrick Poole, "Hezbollah, Illegal Immigration, and the Next 9/11," *Front Page Magazine,* 28 April 2006; Neamatollah Nojumi, *The Rise of the Taliban in Afghanistan: Mass Mobilization, Civil War, and the Future of the Region* (New York: Palgrave, 2002), pp. 135, 136.

16. Aaron Mannes, *Profiles in Terror: The Guide to Middle East Terrorist Organizations* (Oxford: Rowman & Littlefield, 2004), p. 168; Chris Zambelis, "Radical Islam in Latin America," in *Unmasking Terror,* vol. III, p. 484; Chris Zambelis, "Al-Qaida in the Andes: Spotlight on Colombia," in *Unmasking Terror,* vol. III, p. 496.

17. Mike Boettcher and Ingrid Arnesen, "South America's 'Tri-Border' Back on Terrorism Radar," CNN, 8 November 2002, in *Tehran's Wars of Terror,* by Hughes, p. 161.
18. Gunaratna, *Inside al-Qaeda,* pp. 164, 165.
19. Harris Whitbeck and Ingrid Arneson, "Terrorists Find Haven in South America," CNN, 8 November 2001, in *Tehran's Wars of Terror,* by Hughes, p. 150.
20. Antonio Garrastazu and Jerry Haar, "International Terrorism: The Western Hemisphere Connection," OAS, *America's Forum North-South Center Update,* 2001; Sara Miller Llana, "Nicaragua Plans a Big Dig to Rival Panama Canal," *Christian Science Monitor,* 1 December 2006, pp. 1, 5.
21. *CIA—The World Factbook,* s.v. "Venezuela"; *Tehran's Wars of Terror,* by Hughes, pp. 145-149.
22. Marcio Aith, "Argentine Intelligence Chief Says Terrorism Seeking New 'Tri-Border' Area," *Folha de Sao Paulo,* 8 November 2002, as translated for FBIS, in *Tehran's Wars of Terror,* by Hughes, p. 169.
23. *Tehran's Wars of Terror,* by Hughes, p. 169.
24. Ibid., p. 151.
25. Ibid., p. 148.
26. "Drug Trafficking and North Korea: Issues for U.S. Policy," by Ralph F. Perl, Congressional Research Service Report RL32167, last in a series of updates, 27 November 2006). [This work will henceforth be cited as "Drug Trafficking and North Korea," by CRS, appropriate date.]
27. *CIA—The World Factbook* s.v. "China."
28. Bill Gertz and Rowan Scarborough, "China-Trained Taliban," Inside the Ring, *Washington Times,* 21 June 2002, unedited version, from www.gertzfile.com; Bill Gertz, "China-Made Artillery Seized in Afghanistan," *Washington Times,* 12 April 2002; Abdel Bari Atwan, *The Secret History of Al-Qa'ida* (London: Abacus, an imprint of Little, Brown Book Group, 2006), p. 122.
29. *Tehran's Wars of Terror,* by Hughes, p. 171.
30. Tripartite Command of the Three Borders, "Regional Strategic Security Database in 2000," in *Tehran's Wars of Terror,* by Hughes, p. 173.
31. "Strong Ties Seen between Hong Kong Mafia, Tri-Border Based Hizballah," ABC Color (Paraguay), 22 November 2002, as translated for FBIS, in *Tehran's Wars of Terror,* by Hughes, p. 166.
32. Bill Powell and Adam Zagorin, "The Sopranos State," *Time,* 23 July 2007.
33. "Latin America: Terrorism Issues," by CRS; "Country Reports on Terrorism 2005: Supplement," U.S. State Dept., Office for the Coordinator of Counterterrorism, April, 2006.

34. "Nicaragua Corredor de Armas," by Elizabeth Romero, *La Prensa,* 17 April 2005; "Colombia Says FARC Rebels Operating in Bolivia, Paraguay," Xinhua, *People's Daily on Line* (Beijing), 23 June 2006; Thomas Davidson, "Terrorism and Human Smuggling Rings in South and Central America," in *Unmasking Terror,* vol. III, p. 500; "Terrorist and Organized Crime Groups in the Tri-Border Area," by Rex Hudson, Fed. Research Div., Library of Congress, July 2003; Fed. of American Scientists (www.fas.org), s.v. "FARC"; *Wikipedia Encyclopedia,* s.v. "Revolutionary Armed Forces of Colombia."

35. "Brazilian President Party Received Money from FARC, Say Documents," *Wikinews.org,* 15 March 2005; "Denuncian que Farc habrian ofrecido cinco millones de dolares a campaia electoral del PT, de Brasil," *El Tiempo,* 13 March 2005, in "Brazilian President Party Received."

36. *Wikipedia Encyclopedia,* s.v. "Che Guevara."

37. BBC *Country Profile,* s.v. "Chile."

38. *Terrorist Group Profiles* (U.S. Naval Postgraduate School), s.v. "Revolutionary Armed Forces of Colombia (FARC)."

39. "Latin America: Terrorism Issues," by CRS.

40. *Terrorist Group Profiles* (U.S. Naval Postgraduate School), s.v. "Revolutionary Armed Forces of Colombia (FARC)."

41. Ibid.

42. *Wikipedia Encyclopedia,* s.v. "Ejercito de Liberacion Nacional (ELN)."

43. *Terrorist Group Profiles* (U.S. Naval Postgraduate School), s.v. "Ejercito de Liberacion Nacional (ELN)"; "Latin America: Terrorism Issues," by CRS.

44. *Wikipedia Encyclopedia,* s.v. "Argentina" and "Dirty War"; NPR's "Morning Edition" News, 13 November 2007.

45. *Wikipedia Encyclopedia,* s.v. "Shining Path" and "Internal Conflict in Peru."

46. "Latin America: Terrorism Issues," by CRS.

47. Menges, *China: The Gathering Threat,* p. xi; *Wikipedia Encyclopedia,* s.v. "Grenada."

48. "Cuba and the State Sponsors of Terrorism List," by Mark P. Sullivan, Congressional Research Service (CRS) Report for Congress, Order Code RL32251 (Washington, D.C.: Library of Congress, 13 May 2005). [This work will henceforth be cited as "Cuba and the State Sponsors of Terrorism List," by CRS.]

49. *Wikipedia Encyclopedia,* s.v. "M-19."

50. *Wikipedia Encyclopedia,* s.v. "Nicaragua" and "Sandinista National Liberation Front."

51. Maryknoll Brother Martin Shea, as quoted in "The Virgin of the Massacres," by Lynn F. Monahan, *Maryknoll Magazine,* April 2007, pp. 31-34.

52. Former resident of Panama (daughter of Panamanian college professor), in conversation with the author on 9 December 2007.
53. E-5 Marine veteran of the Panama invasion, in conversation with the author around 1990; E-7 Marine veteran of the Panama invasion, in conversation with the author around 1990.
54. *Wikipedia Encyclopedia,* s.v. "Panama."
55. BBC *Country Profile,* s.v. "Timeline: El Salvador" and "Timeline: Guatemala."
56. "China's Growing Interest in Latin America," by Kerry Dumbaugh and Mark P. Sullivan, Congressional Research Service (CRS) Report for Congress, Order Code RS22119 (Washington, D.C.: Library of Congress, 20 April 2005). [This work will henceforth be cited as "China's Growing Interest in Latin America," by CRS.]
57. "China-U.S. Relations: Current Issues and Implications for U.S. Policy," by Kerry Dumbaugh, Congressional Research Service (CRS) Report for Congress, Order Code RL33877 (Washington, D.C.: Library of Congress, 1 October 2007). [This work will henceforth be cited as "China-U.S. Relations," by CRS.]; *Wikipedia Encyclopedia,* s.v. "Haiti."
58. *Wikipedia Encyclopedia,* s.v. "Maras (gangs)."
59. *Wikipedia Encyclopedia,* s.v. "Tupac Amaru Revolutionary Movement (MRTA)," "Japanese Embassy Hostage Crisis," and "Internal Conflict in Peru."
60. Menges, *China: The Gathering Threat,* p. 393.
61. Simon Romero and Juan Forero, "Bolivia's Energy Takeover: Populism Rules the Andes," *New York Times,* 3 May 2006.
62. ABC's Nightly News, 1 March 2007.
63. Menges, *China: The Gathering Threat,* p. xi.
64. *Wikipedia Encyclopedia,* s.v. "Luiz Inacio Lula da Silva."
65. 'Kirschner dejo un fuerte apoyo a Chavez y se llevo un gesto por Malvinas," *La Nacion,* 5 July 2006, in *Wikipedia Encyclopedia,* s.v. "Nestor Kirschner."
66. Bill Gertz, *The China Threat* (Washington, D.C.: Regnery Publishing, 2002), p. 82; "Country Profile: Venezuela," Library of Congress, Fed. Research Div., March 2005.
67. Embassy Information (www.embassyinformation.com). s.v. "Embassies of North Korea; "Venezuela's Chavez Planning Arms-for-Oil Trip to N. Korea," East-Asia-Intel., *World Tribune,* 5 July 2006.
68. Probable CIA official (McClean address and too much knowledge), in phone call to author around the middle of October 2006.
69. Bill Gertz, "Chinese Military Trains in West," *Washington Times,* 15 March 2006.
70. Menges, *China,* p. 428.
71. Ibid.
72. *Wikipedia Encyclopedia,* s.v. "Non-Aligned Movement."

73. "U.S. Hopes China Will Help Moderate Havana Meeting," *China Confidential,* 11 September 2006.
74. Anthony Boadle, "Absent Castro Overshadows Non-Aligned Summit," Reuters, 14 September 2006.
75. Jim Avila, "Dream Team of U.S. Bashers Gathers in Cuba," *New York Times,* 11 September 2006; Scott MacLeod, "A Date with a Dangerous Mind," *Time,* 25 September 2006, pp. 34.
76. Daniel Schearf, "China-North Korea Relations Tested as Reports Say Kim Jong Il to Visit Beijing," *VOA,* 24 August 2006; "Chavez's Whistlestop World Tour," BBC News, 1 September 2006.
77. Alejandro Kirk and Dalia Acosta, "Non-Aligned Summit Opens amidst Suspense over Castro," Inter-Press-Service News Agency, 21 September 2006; Ardeshir Ommani, "The Non-Aligned Movement Has Been an Organization of, More or Less, Deprived Nations of the Planet," *Iran Heritage,* 18 September 2006.
78. Sara Miller Llana, "Nicaragua Plans a Big Dig to Rival Panama Canal," *Christian Science Monitor,* 15 November 2006, pp. 1, 12.
79. Mark Anderson, "China's Massive Port Grab," *American Free Press* (Washington, D.C.), issue 3, 15 January 2007.
80. "Truth Be Tolled," by William H. Molina, Storm Pictures LLC, 2006, 99 minutes, dvd # 7-44773-0162-6.
81. Leslie Miller, "Cross-Border Trucking Plan Draws Criticism," AP, 24 February 2007.

Chapter 1: Drug Dealers, Gangs, Islamists, or Maoists?

1. Lisa Hoffman, Scripps Howard, "Cocaine Use Is on the Rise in the U.S.," *Jacksonville Daily News* (NC), 1 November 2007, p. 4A; ABC's Nightly News, 5 July 2008.
2. "Drug Trafficking and North Korea," by CRS, 27 November 2006; *CIA—The World Factbook* s.v. "China."
3. NPR's "Morning Edition" News, 22 October 2007.
4. Ibid.
5. Lourdes Garcia-Navarro, "Calderon Fights Mexico's Gangs with Little Success," NPR's *All Things Considered,* 16 May 2007.
6. Lourdes Garcia-Navarro, "Drug Violence Rampant in Mexico," NPR's "Morning Edition" News, 18 May 2007.
7. *Wikipedia Encyclopedia,* s.v. "Maras (gangs)" and "Mara Salvatrucha."
8. "The Maras: A Menace to the Americas," by Frederico Breve (former Minister of Defense of Honduras), *Military Review,* July/August 2007.
9. "Cuba and the State Sponsors of Terrorism List," by CRS.
10. Mario Daniel Montoya, "War on Terrorism Reaches Paraguay's Triple Border," *Jane's Intell. Review,* December 2001, p. 12, in *Inside al-Qaeda,* by Gunaratna, p. 165.

11. Gunaratna, *Inside al-Qaeda,* p. 165; Mannes, *Profiles in Terror,* p. 152.

12. "Terrorist and Organized Crime Groups in the Tri-Border Area," by Rex Hudson, Fed. Research Div., Library of Congress, July 2003.

13. *Tehran's War of Terror,* by Hughes, p. 200.

14. James S. Milford (former Deputy Administrator of the DEA), in *Tehran's Wars of Terror,* by Hughes, p. 200.

15. *Tehran's War of Terror,* by Hughes, p. 200.

16. *CIA—The World Factbook* s.v. "Venezuela."

17. Gen. Chi Haotian (Chinese Defense Minister), as quoted in *The China Threat,* by Gertz, p. 96.

18. Report by Congressional Aides Santoli and Doran, as quoted in *The China Threat,* by Gertz, p. 93.

19. U.S. Customs Service Report, as quoted in *The China Threat,* by Gertz, pp. 90, 91.

20. Menges, *China,* pp. 395, 398; Gertz, *The China Threat,* pp. 82, 94.

21. Al Santoli, "The Panama Canal in Transition," American Foreign Policy Council Investigative Report, 23 June 1999.

22. Gertz, *The China Threat,* pp. 94, 95.

23. Menges, *China,* pp. 393; Adm. Alejandro Kenny, "China's Presence in Latin America: A View on Security from the Southern Cone," *Military Review,* September/October 2006.

24. *Prensa Latina* (Havana), as quoted in "Chinese, Venezuelan Oil Majors Start Joint Venture," from China National News and Indo-Asian News Service (IANS), 6 April 2008.

25. "China's Growing Interest in Latin America," by CRS.

26. Menges, *China,* pp. 395.

27. Chris Zambelis, "Al-Qaeda's Inroads into the Caribbean," in *Unmasking Terror,* vol. III, p. 477.

28. "China's Growing Interest in Latin America," by CRS.

29. Juan Forero, "China's Oil Diplomacy in Latin America," *New York Times,* 1 March 2005, in "China's Growing Interest in Latin America," by CRS.

30. Gertz, "Chinese Military Trains in West."

31. Ibid.

32. Anderson, "China's Massive Port Grab"; Hutchison Whampoa website, s.v. "International Operations."

33. "China's Growing Interest in Latin America," by CRS.

34. "China's Presence in Latin America," by Kenny.

35. Poole, *Dragon Days,* Part One.

36. "3 members of China's Politburo visited Mexico in 2005," East-Asia-Intel., *World Tribune,* 10 March 2006.

37. Energy Information Agency website (www.eia.doe.gov), s.v. "Country Energy Profiles."

38. Hutchison Whampoa website, s.v. "International Operations."

39. Menges, *China,* p. 393.
40. Poole, *Terrorist Trail,* p. 237.
41. Ibid.
42. Peter Brookes, "Venezuelan Vagaries," *Armed Forces Journal,* July 2007, p. 44.
43. "Latin America: Terrorism Issues," by CRS.
44. "Cuba and the State Sponsors of Terrorism List," by CRS.
45. "Country Reports on Terrorism 2005: Supplement," U.S. State Dept., Office for the Coordinator of Counterterrorism, April 2006.
46. "Chinese Criminal Enterprises," by Ning-Ning Mahlmann, FBI, n.d., as retrieved from U.S. Dept. of State website (usinfo.state.gov); "China's Presence in Latin America," by Kenny.
47. "Transnational Activities of Chinese Crime Organizations," by Glenn E. Curtis, Seth L. Elan, Rexford A. Hudson, and Nina A. Koll, Federal Research Division, Library of Congress, April 2003; Mario Daniel Montoya, "War on Terrorism Reaches Paraguay's Triple Border," p. 14, from *Inside al-Qaeda,* by Gunaratna, p. 166.
48. Guillermo R. Delamer, Lyle J. Goldstein, Jorge Eduardo Malena, and Gabriela E. Pom, "Chinese Interests in Latin America," *The Newport Papers* (2004), p. 91, in "China's Presence in Latin America," by Kenny; "Chinese Criminal Enterprises," by Mahlmann.
49. "Asian Triads," by Wade O. Koromantee, from *Into The Abyss: A Personal Journey into the World of Street Gangs,* by Mike Carlie, as extracted from faculty.missouristate.edu; "Chinese Triads," as extracted from www.geocities.com; "Chinese Criminal Enterprises," by Mahlmann; *Wikipedia Encyclopedia,* s.v. "List of Triad Societies."
50. Ed Blanche, "The Latin American Connection," BNet Business Network (a CBS company), May 2003; Sebastian Rotella, "Jungle Hub for World's Outlaws," *Los Angles Times,* 24 August 1998.
51. "Chinese Criminal Enterprises," by Mahlmann.
52. "Attorney General's Report to Congress on the Growth of Violent Street Gangs in Suburban Areas," Nat. Drug Intell. Ctr., April 2008; *Wikipedia Encyclopedia,* s.v. "Triads"; "Transnational Activities of Chinese Crime Organizations," by Curtis et al; "Partners in Crime," Parts I & II, by Fredric Dannen, *The New Republic,* 14 and 27 July 1997.
53. Gen. Bantz J. Craddock (head of U.S. Southern Command), as quoted in "Chinese Military Trains in West," by Gertz.
54. Gertz, "Chinese Military Trains in West."
55. Larry Wortzel (former Pentagon intelligence official), as quoted in "Chinese Military Trains in West," by Gertz.
56. *Wikipedia Encyclopedia,* s.v. "People's Liberation Army Second Artillery Corps."
57. "Who Needs the Panama Canal," by Robert Morton, *Washington Times,* Nat. Weekly Ed., 1-8 March 1999, as reprinted in *World Tribune,* 4 March 1999; "China's Presence in Latin America," by Kenny.

58. LaVerle Berry, Glenn E. Curtis, John N. Gibbs, Rex A. Hudson, Tara Karacan, Nina Kollars, and Ramon Miro, "Nations Hospitable to Organized Crime and Terrorism," Fed. Research Div., Library of Congress, October 2003, p. 160. [This work with henceforth be cited as "Nations Hospitable . . . to Terrorism," by Berry et al.]
59. "Terrorist and Organized Crime Groups in the Tri-Border Area," by Hudson.
60. "Chinese Criminal Enterprises," by Mahlmann; *Wikipedia Encyclopedia*, s.v. "List of Triad Societies.
61. Santoli, "The Panama Canal in Transition."

Chapter 2: Cuba, the Caribbean, and Venezuela

1. Fred Bridgland, *War for Africa* (Gibraltar: Ashanti, 1991), p. 17, and Helmoed-Romer Heitman, *War in Angola — The Final South African Phase* (Gibraltar: Ashanti, 1990), pp. 15-16, in *The Silent War: South African Recce Operations, 1969-1994,* by Peter Stiff (Alberton, South Africa: Galago Publishing, 1999), p. 533.
2. *Wikipedia Encyclopedia,* s.v. "MPLA."
3. *CIA — The World Factbook,* s.v. "Angola."
4. Ibid.
5. "China's Influence on Africa," by Ernest J. Wilson III, Internat. Develop. and Conflict Management, Univ. of Maryland, in testimony before Congress on 28 July 2005.
6. "China in Angola: An Emerging Energy Partnership," by Paul Hare, Jamestown Foundation, *China Brief,* vol. 6, issue 22, 8 November 2006; "China and Angola Strengthen Bilateral Relationship," by Loro Horta, *Power and Interest News Report,* 23 June 2006.
7. Ibid.
8. "China in Angola," by Paul Hare.
9. "Analysis: Chinese Arms and African Oil," by Andrei Chang UPI (Hong Kong), 5 November 2007.
10. *Wikipedia Encyclopedia,* s.v. "Bolivarian Alternative for the People of Our America."
11. Gertz, "Chinese Military Trains in West"; Gertz, *The China Threat,* p. 97.
12. "Chinese Regime Eyes Texas Port Facilities," *American Free Press* (Washington, D.C.), issue 33, 14 August 2006.
13. Brookes, "Venezuelan Vagaries," p. 14.
14. *Wikipedia Encyclopedia,* s.v. "Bahamas."
15. "Caribbean Region: Issues in U.S. Relations," by Mark P. Sullivan, Congressional Research Service (CRS) Report for Congress, Order Code RL32160 (Washington, D.C.: Library of Congress, 25 May 2005). [This work will henceforth be cited as "Caribbean Region," by CRS.]

16. "U.S. Hires Foreign Firm to Help Detect Nuclear Materials at Bahamas Port," AP, 24 March 2006.
17. "Haiti: Developments and U.S. Policy Since 1991 and Current Congressional Concerns," by Maureen Taft-Morales and Clare M. Ribando, Congressional Research Service (CRS) Report for Congress, Order Code RL32294 (Washington, D.C.: Library of Congress, 21 June 2007). [This work will henceforth be cited as "Haiti," by CRS.]
18. Ibid.
19. "Caribbean Region," by CRS.
20. "Dominican Republic: Political and Economic Conditions and Relations with the United States," by Clare M. Ribando, Congressional Research Service (CRS) Report for Congress, Order Code RS21718 (Washington, D.C.: Library of Congress, 8 March 2005. [This work will henceforth be cited as "Dominican Republic," by CRS.]
21. "Country Profile: Venezuela," Library of Congress, Fed. Research Div., March 2005.
22. Brookes, "Venezuelan Vagaries," pp. 12, 13.
23. Ibid.
24. "Four Spies for the U.S. Have Been Caught by Venezuelan Security," World News in Brief, *Christian Science Monitor,* 21 August 2006, p. 7.
25. "Venezuela's Chavez Planning Arms-for-Oil Trip to N. Korea," East-Asia-Intel., *World Tribune,* 5 July 2006.
26. Brookes, "Venezuelan Vagaries," p. 14.
27. Ibid.; Simon Romero, "Files Released by Colombia Point to Venezuelan Bid to Arm Rebels," *New York Times,* 30 March 2008, p. 1.
28. "Intel. Report: Venezuela Training Ecuador Rebels," *World Tribune,* 25 October 2005; John Moore (former DOD counter-terrorism analyst), in testimony before Congress on 14 September 2001, from "The Emergence of the Terrorist International," by Orlando Gutierrez-Boronat, UPI, 14 September 2001.
29. *Venezuela* (N.p.: Lonely Planet Publications, 2007), p. 29.
30. "Country Profile: Venezuela," Library of Congress, Fed. Research Div., March 2005.
31. Tyler Bridges and Casto Ocando, McClatchy Newspapers, "Vote Today Decides Chavez's Power," *The News and Observer* (Raleigh, NC), 2 December 2007, p. 19A.
32. NPR's "Morning Edition" News, 3 December 2007.
33. Sara Miller Llana, "Chavez Plan Stirs a Rising Backlash," *Christian Science Monitor,* 28 November 2007, pp. 1, 12;
34. "Chavez Says No Oil if U.S. Hurts Vote," World Briefs Wire Reports (AP), *Jacksonville Daily News* (NC), 1 December 2007, p. 6A.

35. NPR's "Morning Edition" News, 3 December 2007.
36. Ibid.
37. Ibid; Daniel Cancel, "Venezuela's Chavez Presses on Undaunted," *Christian Science Monitor,* 6 December 2007, pp. 1, 10.
38. "Chavez Accepts Defeat in Venezuelan Referendum," by AP, *Jacksonville Daily News* (NC), 4 December 2007, p. 5A.
39. NPR's "Morning Edition" News, 3 December 2007.
40. "Country Profile: Venezuela," Library of Congress, Fed. Research Div., March 2005; Brookes, "Venezuelan Vagaries," pp. 12-14.

Chapter 3: The Guianas, Brazil, and Paraguay

1. Chris Zambelis, "The Threat of Religious Radicalism in Guyana," in *Unmasking Terror,* vol. III, p. 487; *Wikipedia Encyclopedia,* s.v. "Organization of Islamic Conference" and "Arab League."
2. "Soldiers and Police Began a Manhunt along the Border," World News in Brief, *Christian Science Monitor,* 20 February 2008.
3. BBC *Country Profile,* s.v. "Brazil."
4. Energy Information Agency website (www.eia.doe.gov), s.v. "Country Energy Profiles"; *CIA—The World Factbook,* s.v. "Brazil."
5. BBC *Country Profile,* s.v. "Brazil."
6. *Wikipedia Encyclopedia,* s.v. "Luiz Inacio Lula da Silva."
7. "Brazil," *Library of Congress Country Studies,* April 1997.
8. ABC's Morning News, 16 January 2008; *Wikipedia Encyclopedia,* s.v. "Luiz Inacio Lula da Silva."
9. Robert B. Asprey, *War in the Shadows: The Guerrilla in History,* vol. II (Garden City, NY: Doubleday, 1975), p. 974.
10. *Wikipedia Encyclopedia,* s.v. "Land Reform in Zimbabwe."
11. "A 'Huge' New Discovery of Natural Gas," World News in Brief, *Christian Science Monitor,* 23 January 2008, p. 7.
12. Andrew Downie, "Is Latin America Heading for an Arms Race," *Christian Science Monitor,* 16 January 2008, p. 7.
13. "Paraguay: Court Investigates Hizballah Base Photos," ABC Color (Paraguay), in *Tehran's Wars of Terror,* by Hughes, p. 157.
14. "Chinese Criminal Enterprises," by Mahlmann.
15. BBC *Country Profile,* s.v. "Paraguay."
16. "Country Profile: Paraguay," Library of Congress, Fed. Research Div., October 2005.
17. Ibid.
18. Ibid.
19. Andrea Machain, "This Is Oviedo's Third Coup Attempt in Seven Years," BBC News, 19 May 2000.

20. Pedro Servin, "Kidnapped Daughter of Ex-President Killed," *The Independent* (London), 18 February 2005; BBC *Country Profiles,* s.v. "Timeline: Paraguay."
21. William S. Lind, "More on Gangs and Guerrillas vs. the State," Anti-war.com, 29 April 2005.
22. "Brazilian President Party Received Money from FARC, Say Documents."
23. "Former Roman Catholic Bishop Fernando Lugo Won the Presidency . . . ," World News in Brief, *Christian Science Monitor,* 22 April 2008, p. 7.

Chapter 4: Uruguay, Argentina, and Bolivia

1. BBC *Country Profiles,* s.v. "Timeline: Uruguay."
2. BBC *Country Profile,* s.v. "Uruguay."
3. BBC *Country Profiles,* s.v. "Timeline: Uruguay."
4. BBC *Country Profiles,* s.v. "Timeline: Argentina."
5. Ibid.
6. *Wikipedia Encyclopedia,* s.v. "Nestor Kirschner."
7. BBC *Country Profile,* s.v. "Argentina."
8. NPR's "Morning Edition" News, 14 December 2007.
9. Thomas Davidson, "Terrorism and Human Smuggling Rings in South and Central America," in *Unmasking Terror,* vol. III, p. 502; *Wikipedia Encyclopedia,* s.v. "Tablighi Jamaat and Allegations of Terrorism."
10. Simon Romero, "Files Released by Colombia Point to Venezuelan Bid to Arm Rebels," *New York Times,* 30 March 2008, p. 1.
11. BBC *Country Profile,* s.v. "Bolivia."
12. Ibid.
13. Ibid.
14. BBC *Country Profiles,* s.v. "Timeline: Bolivia."
15. Jaime Daremblum, "Bolivia on the Brink," *New York Sun,* 8 April 2008.

Chapter 5: Chile, Peru, and Ecuador

1. BBC *Country Profile,* s.v. "Chile."
2. Ibid.
3. BBC *Country Profiles,* s.v. "Timeline: Chile"; *Patterns of Global Terrorism: 1990* (Washington, D.C.: U.S. Dept. of State, 1991), as retrieved from www.fas.org; *Terrorism Chronology*, U.S. Dept. of State, from its website, usinfo.state.gov; Council on Foreign Relations (cfr.org), s.v. "Shining Path, Tupac Amaru (Peru, leftists)."
4. BBC *Country Profile,* s.v. "Chile."

5. BBC *Country Profiles,* s.v. "Timeline: Chile."
6. BBC *Country Profile,* s.v. "Peru."
7. *Wikipedia Encyclopedia,* s.v. "Alan Garcia."
8. BBC *Country Profiles,* s.v. "Timeline: Peru"; Council on Foreign Relations (cfr.org), s.v. "Shining Path, Tupac Amaru (Peru, leftists)."
9. Ibid.
10. Ibid., *Wikipedia Encyclopedia,* s.v. "Alan Garcia" and "Ollanta Humala"; Council on Foreign Relations (cfr.org), s.v. "Shining Path, Tupac Amaru (Peru, leftists)."
11. BBC *Country Profile,* s.v. "Peru."
12. *Wikipedia Encyclopedia,* s.v. "Tupac Amaru"; *CIA — The World Factbook,* s.v. "Peru."
13. Council on Foreign Relations (cfr.org), s.v. "Shining Path, Tupac Amaru (Peru, leftists)."
14. Mark Sexton (GI formerly deployed to Peru), in telephone conversation with the author on 27 December 2007.
15. *Wikipedia Encyclopedia,* s.v. "Abimael Guzman."
16. Sexton phonecall, 27 December 2007.
17. Ibid.
18. *Wikipedia Encyclopedia,* s.v. "Seventh Guerrilla Conference of the FARC-EP" and "Socio-Economic Structure of the FARC-EP."
19. "Latin America: Terrorism Issues," by CRS.
20. *Wikipedia Encyclopedia,* s.v. "Shining Path."
21. *Terrorist Group Profiles* (U.S. Naval Postgraduate School), s.v. "Shining Path."
22. BBC *Country Profile,* s.v. "Peru."
23. Lucien Chauvin, "Peru See Shadowy Hand of Chavez," *Christian Science Monitor,* 3 April 2008, p. 4.
24. Council on Foreign Relations (cfr.org), s.v. "Shining Path, Tupac Amaru (Peru, leftists)"; "Latin America: Terrorism Issues," by CRS.
25. "Intel. Report: Venezuela Training Ecuador Rebels."
26. BBC *Country Profiles,* s.v. "Timeline: Ecuador."
27. BBC *Country Profile,* s.v. "Ecuador."
28. Romero, "Files Released by Colombia Point to Venezuelan Bid to Arm Rebels"; NPR's "Morning Edition" News, 4 March 2008; ABC's Nightly News, 8 March 2008.
29. "Ecuador Offers Concession Of Manta Air Base To China, Declines To Renew Contract With U.S.," by Vittorio Hernandez, AHN News (Ecuador), 26 November 2007.
30. BBC *Country Profiles,* s.v. "Timeline: Ecuador."

Chapter 6: Colombia and Panama

1. "Latin America: Terrorism Issues," by CRS.

2. *Terrorist Group Profiles* (U.S. Naval Postgraduate School), s.v. "AUC."
3. Ibid.
4. Ibid.
5. Memorandum for the record by H.J. Poole.
6. "Cuba and the State Sponsors of Terrorism List," by CRS; *Wikipedia Encyclopedia*, s.v. "M-19."
7. "Cuba and the State Sponsors of Terrorism List," by CRS.
8. "China," "India," and "Colombia," *World History of Organized Crime*, History Channel, n.d., DVD, disk 2, vol. 2, in *Wikipedia Encyclopedia*, s.v. "Palace of Justice Siege."
9. Jeremy McDermott, Colombia's Rebel Kidnappers," BBC News, 7 January 2002; *Terrorist Group Profiles* (U.S. Naval Postgraduate School), s.v. "ELN."
10. Ibid.
11. Fed. of American Scientists (www.fas.org), s.v. "FARC."
12. GlobalSecurity.org, s.v. "FARC."
13. *Wikipedia Encyclopedia*, s.v. "Maoism."
14. Fed. of American Scientists (www.fas.org), s.v. "FARC."
15. Gertz, *The China Threat*, p. 85.
16. Andy Webb-Vidal, "Farc Guerrillas Kill 29 Colombian Soldiers," *Financial Times* (London), 28 December 2005.
17. *Wikipedia Encyclopedia*, s.v. "Socio-Economic Structure of the FARC-EP."
18. Ibid., "Seventh Guerrilla Conference of the FARC-EP."
19. Ibid., s.v. "Jacobo Arenas."
20. Ibid., s.v. "Revolutionary Armed Forces of Colombia."
21. Ibid.
22. "FARC guerrillas in the street in San Vicentedel Caguan, Caqueta," photo, by Ariana Cubillos, as extracted from www.colombiajournal.org; memorandum for the record by H.J. Poole.
23. *Wikipedia Encyclopedia*, s.v. "Seventh Guerrilla Conference of the FARC-EP."
24. "Colombia's Most Powerful Rebels," BBC News, 19 September 2003.
25. "Colombia's Civil War," PBS's Online News Hour, 2003.
26. The Memorial Institute for the Prevention of Terrorism (MIPT) Knowledge Base, s.v. "FARC." [This source will henceforth be cited as MIPT Knowledge Base.]
27. "Colombia's Most Powerful Rebels"; "Colombian Leader Ends FARC Talks," BBC News, 20 October 2006.
28. *Wikipedia Encyclopedia*, s.v. "Maoism."
29. Ibid., s.v. "Revolutionary Armed Forces of Colombia."
30. Chris Zambelis, "Al-Qaeda in the Andes: Spotlight on Colombia," in "*Unmasking Terror*, vol. III, p. 492.
31. GlobalSecurity.org, s.v. "FARC."

32. "Colombia's Civil War."
33. *Wikipedia Encyclopedia,* s.v. "Jacobo Arenas."
34. "Colombia's Civil War."
35. FOX's Morning News, 20 October 2006; "Drug Trafficking and North Korea," by CRS, 27 November 2006.
36. U.S. Dept. of State, International Narcotics Control Strategy Report [INCSR], March 2003, p. VIII-43, in "Drug Trafficking and North Korea," by CRS, 4 March 2005, p. 8; Powell and Zagorin, "The Sopranos State."
37. Keith Bradsher, "North Korean Ploy Masks Ships Under Other Flags," *New York Times,* 20 October 2006.
38. "Colombia's Civil War."
39. *Wikipedia Encyclopedia,* s.v. "Military History of the FARC-EP."
40. Ibid.; "GlobalSecurity.org., s.v. "Revolutionary Armed Forces of Colombia"; "Colombia's Civil War."
41. *Wikipedia Encyclopedia,* s.v. "List of FARC attacks in 2005."
42. "Colombia's Civil War."
43. Fed. of American Scientists (www.fas.org), s.v. "FARC."
44. GlobalSecurity.org, s.v. "FARC."
45. "Colombia's Civil War."
46. Ibid.
47. MIPT Knowledge Base, s.v. "FARC."
48. Ibid.
49. "Nicaragua Corredor de Armas"; "Colombia Says FARC Rebels Operating in Bolivia, Paraguay," Xinhua, *People's Daily on Line* (Beijing), 23 June 2006; Davidson, "Terrorism and Human Smuggling Rings . . . ," in *Unmasking Terror,* vol. III, p. 500; "Terrorist and Organized Crime Groups in the Tri-Border Area"; Fed. of American Scientists (www.fas.org), s.v. "FARC"; *Wikipedia Encyclopedia,* s.v. "Revolutionary Armed Forces of Colombia."
50. NPR's "Morning Edition" News, 16 May 2008.
51. *Wikipedia Encyclopedia,* s.v. "Revolutionary Armed Forces of Colombia"; "Nicaragua Corredor de Armas."
52. "DEA Boosts Its Role in Paraguay," by Jack Sweeney, *Washington Times,* 21 August 2001.
53. "Terrorist and Organized Crime Groups in the Tri-Border Area."
54. "DEA Boosts Its Role in Paraguay."
55. NPR's "Morning Edition" News, 17 December 2007.
56. Fed. of American Scientists (www.fas.org), s.v. "FARC."
57. "Colombia's Most Powerful Rebels."
58. *Wikipedia Encyclopedia,* s.v. "ELN."
59. China's State Commission of Science, Technology and Industry for National Defense, as quoted in "Chinese Military to Make Billions through Capitalism," *Geostrategy Direct,* 16 January 2008.
60. Gertz, *The China Threat,* pp. 76, 78, 80, 91, 92.

61. BBC *Country Profile,* s.v. "Panama."
62. *CIA – The World Factbook,* s.v. "Panama."
63. "Background Note: Panama," U.S. Dept. of State, November 2007.
64. Fed. of American Scientists (www.fas.org), s.v. "FARC."
65. "Nicaragua Corredor de Armas."
66. *CIA – The World Factbook,* s.v. "Panama."
67. *Wikipedia Encyclopedia,* s.v. "Panama."
68. *CIA – The World Factbook,* s.v. "Panama."
69. *Wikipedia Encyclopedia,* s.v. "Panama."
70. U.S. Customs Service Report, as quoted in *The China Threat,* by Gertz, pp. 90, 91.
71. Gunaratna, *Inside al-Qaeda,* pp. 164, 165; *Tehran's Wars of Terror,* by Hughes, p. 148.
72. *Wikipedia Encyclopedia,* s.v. "Panama."

Chapter 7: Costa Rica, Nicaragua, and Honduras

1. *Catechism of the Catholic Church* (New York: Doubleday, 1995), par. 2309.
2. BBC *Country Profile,* s.v. "Costa Rica."
3. "Profile: Oscar Arias," BBC News, 3 February 2006.
4. *CIA – The World Factbook,* s.v. "Costa Rica."
5. BBC *Country Profile,* s.v. "Costa Rica."
6. BBC *Country Profile,* s.v. "Timeline: Costa Rica."
7. BBC *Country Profile,* s.v. "Nicaragua"; *CIA – The World Factbook,* s.v. "Nicaragua."
8. *CIA – The World Factbook,* s.v. "Nicaragua."
9. BBC *Country Profile,* s.v. "Nicaragua" and "Timeline: Nicaragua."
10. *CIA – The World Factbook,* s.v. "Nicaragua."
11. BBC *Country Profile,* s.v. "Nicaragua."
12. *CIA – The World Factbook,* s.v. "Nicaragua."
13. BBC *Country Profile,* s.v. "Timeline: Honduras"; Carlos Mauricio Pineda Cruz, "Al-Qaeda's Unlikely Allies in Central America," in *Unmasking Terror: A Global Review of Terrorist Activities,* vol. II, ed. Christopher Heffelfinger (Washington, D.C: Jamestown Foundation, 2005), p. 458 [the source document will henceforth be cited as *Unmasking Terror,* vol. II].
14. BBC *Country Profile,* s.v. "Honduras."
15. "Concession Brings Honduras Result," BBC, 8 December 2005.
16. *CIA – The World Factbook,* s.v. "Honduras."
17. BBC *Country Profile,* s.v. "Honduras."
18. *Honduras: A Country Study,* DA Pamphlet 550-151, Area Handbook Series [Washington, D.C.: Dept. of the Army, 1984], p. xxxi; BBC *Country Profile,* s.v. "Timeline: Honduras."

19. Ibid.
20. Ibid.
21. Ibid.
22. Fergal Keane, "Honduras's Child Killings," BBC News, 5 October 2002.
23. "Honduras Acts over Child Killings," BBC News, 14 March 2003; BBC *Country Profile,* s.v. "Timeline: Honduras."
24. BBC *Country Profile,* s.v. "Timeline: Honduras."
25. "Defying Silence in Honduras," BBC News, 4 July 2007.
26. *CIA — The World Factbook,* s.v. "Honduras."
27. *Wikipedia Encyclopedia,* s.v. "Honduras."
28. "Nicaragua Corredor de Armas."
29. Davidson, "Terrorism and Human Smuggling Rings . . . ," *Unmasking Terror,* vol. III, p. 502.
30. "FARC Weapons Supplies Revealed," *Santa Fe de Bogota Semana* (on-line edition), 6 September 1999, FBIS trans., as retrieved from www.fas.org.
31. Larry Rohter, "Fighting in Panama: Panama's Military; Changing an Army Poses a Challenge," *New York Times,* 23 December 1989.
32. An American Special Forces official, as quoted in "Fighting in Panama," by Rohter.
33. U.S. Customs Service Report, as quoted in *The China Threat,* by Gertz, pp. 90, 91.
34. "Mexico's Internal Drug War."

Chapter 8: El Salvador, Belize, Guatemala, Mexico

1. *Mexico* (N.p.: Lonely Planet Publications, 2007), history section; *CIA — The World Factbook,* s.v. "Mexico."
2. Memo for the record from H.J. Poole.
3. *CIA — The World Factbook,* s.v. "Mexico," "Guatemala," "Belize," "El Salvador," "Honduras," "Nicaragua," "Costa Rica," and "Panama."
4. Mark Anderson, "China's Massive Port Grab," *American Free Press* (Washington, D.C.), issue 3, 15 January 2007; "Chinese Regime Eyes Texas Port Facilities."; William H. Molina (author and producer of "Truth Be Tolled), in telephone conversation with the author in November 2006.
5. Davidson, "Terrorism and Human Smuggling Rings . . . ," *Unmasking Terror,* vol. III, p. 502; Pineda Cruz, "Al-Qaeda's Unlikely Allies in Central America," *Unmasking Terror,* vol. II, p. 459.
6. "Country Profile: Mexico," Library of Congress, Fed. Research Div., July 2006.

7. "Chinese Regime Eyes Texas Port Facilities."
8. "Drug Trafficking and North Korea," by CRS, 5 December 2003; Powell and Zagorin, "The Sopranos State."
9. BBC *Country Profile,* s.v. "El Salvador."
10. Ibid.
11. "Guerrilla Wars," *People's Century,* BBC in conjunction with WGBH (Boston), as aired on NC Public TV, 29 June 1999.
12. BBC *Country Profile,* s.v. ""Timeline: El Salvador"; *Wikipedia Encyclopedia,* s.v. "Jose Napoleon Duarte."
13. *Wikipedia Encyclopedia,* s.v. "Oscar Romero."
14. Ibid., s.v. "Carlos Humberto Romero."
15. BBC *Country Profile,* s.v. "Timeline: El Salvador."
16. *Wikipedia Encyclopedia,* s.v. "Jose Napoleon Duarte."
17. BBC *Country Profile,* s.v. ""Timeline: El Salvador."
18. Ibid.
19. "The Maras," by Breve.
20. *Wikipedia Encyclopedia,* s.v. "Mara 18."
21. "The Maras," by Breve.
22. Ibid.
23. Claire Marshall, "Combatting El Salvador's Gangs," BBC News, 20 March 2004.
24. Ricardo Pollack, "Gang Life Tempts Salvador Teens," BBC News, 24 January 2005.
25. Ibid.
26. *CIA—The World Factbook,* s.v. "El Salvador."
27. Ibid.
28. Tom Gibb, "El Salvador Buries Revolutionary," BBC News, 30 January 2006.
29. *El Salvador: A Country Study,* DA Pamphlet 550-150, Area Handbook Series [Washington, D.C.: Dept. of the Army, 1990], p. 43; Council on Foreign Relations (cfr.org), s.v. "Shining Path, Tupac Amaru (Peru, leftists)."
30. *Wikipedia Encyclopedia,* s.v. "Nicaragua."
31. MIPT Knowledge Base, s.v. "FMLN."
32. *Wikipedia Encyclopedia,* s.v. "FMLN."
33. Fed. of American Scientists (www.fas.org), s.v. "FMLN."
34. Ibid.
35. *Wikipedia Encyclopedia,* s.v. "FMLN."
36. Ibid.
37. Fed. of American Scientists (www.fas.org), s.v. "FMLN."
38. "Left Claims El Salvador Victory," BBC News, 17 March 2003.
39. "Central America's Street Gangs Are Drawn into the World of Geopolitics," *Power and Interest News Report (PINR),* 26 August 2005.

40. "At Least 31 killed in Guatemala Prison Gang War," MSNBC, 15 August 2005.
41. Pineda Cruz, "Al-Qaeda's Unlikely Allies in Central America," *Unmasking Terror,* vol. II, p. 459.
42. BBC *Country Profile,* s.v. "Guatemala."
43. Frank LaRue (of the Presidential Human Rights Commission), as quoted in "Crime Dominates Guatemala Campaign," by James Painter, BBC News, 10 May 2007.
44. James Painter, "Crime Dominates Guatemala Campaign," BBC News, 10 May 2007.
45. Adam Blenford, "Guatemala's Epidemic of Killing," BBC News, 9 June 2005.
46. President Oscar Berger, as quoted in "Guatemala's Epidemic of Killing," by Blenford.
47. *CIA — The World Factbook,* s.v. "Guatemala."
48. Ibid.; BBC *Country Profile,* s.v. "Guatemala."
49. *CIA — The World Factbook,* s.v. "Guatemala."
50. Ibid.
51. Ibid.
52. *Guatemala* (N.p.: Lonely Planet Publications, 2007), history section.
53. Simon Watts, "Guatemala Secret Files Uncovered," BBC News, 5 December 2005.
54. *Wikipedia Encyclopedia,* s.v. "Che Guevara."
55. *Encyclopedia Britannica Online,* s.v. "Guatemala: Civil War Years."
56. BBC *Country Profile,* s.v. "Timeline: Guatemala."
57. *Guatemala: A Country Study,* DA Pamphlet 550-78, Area Handbook Series [Washington, D.C.: Dept. of the Army, 1984], p. 34.
58. Ibid., *Guatemala* (N.p.: Lonely Planet Publications, 2007), history section.
59. Ibid.
60. Ibid.
61. Ibid.
62. Ibid.
63. BBC *Country Profile,* s.v. "Belize."
64. *CIA — The World Factbook,* s.v. "Belize."
65. BBC *Country Profile,* s.v. "Timeline: Belize."
66. Ibid.
67. *CIA — The World Factbook,* s.v. "Belize."
68. BBC *Country Profile,* s.v. "Belize."
69. *CIA — The World Factbook,* s.v. "Belize."
70. Sara Miller Llana, "Mexico, U.S. Step Up Drug Cooperation," *Christian Science Monitor,* 23 January 2008.
71. BBC *Country Profile,* s.v. "Mexico."

72. *CIA — The World Factbook,* s.v. "Mexico."
73. Ibid.
74. Ibid.
75. Howard Lafranchi, "Free Trade Accords Face Rocky Road," *Christian Science Monitor,* 7 February 2008, p. 2.
76. Charles Hurt, "Senate Denies Funds for New Border Fence," *Washington Times,* 14 July 2006; S.A. Miller and Stephen Dinan, "Spending Bill Shrinks Border Fence," *Washington Times,* 18 December 2007; Daniel B. Wood, "Where the Border Fence Is Tall, It Works," *Christian Science Monitor,* 1 April 2008, pp. 1, 12, 13.
77. Mexican Secretary of Governance (Interior), as quoted in "Terrorism and Human Smuggling Rings . . . ," by Davidson, *Unmasking Terror,* vol. III, p. 500.
78. Zambelis, "Al-Qaida in the Andes," *Unmasking Terror,* vol. III, p. 492.
79. "Nations Hospitable . . . to Terrorism," by Berry et al.
80. Davidson, "Terrorism and Human Smuggling Rings . . . ," *Unmasking Terror,* vol. III, p. 502.
81. Pineda Cruz, "Al-Qaeda's Unlikely Allies in Central America," *Unmasking Terror,* vol. II, p. 459.
82. Davidson, "Terrorism and Human Smuggling Rings . . . ," *Unmasking Terror,* vol. III, p. 501.
83. *Tehran's War of Terror,* by Hughes, pp. 147, 158.
84. Davidson, "Terrorism and Human Smuggling Rings . . . ," *Unmasking Terror,* vol. III, p. 502.
85. Ibid., pp. 497-502.
86. Ibid., p. 499.
87. BBC *Country Profile,* s.v. "Mexico."
88. *CIA — The World Factbook,* s.v. "Mexico."
89. BBC *Country Profile,* s.v. "Mexico."
90. *CIA — The World Factbook,* s.v. "Mexico."
91. BBC *Country Profile,* s.v. "Mexico."
92. *Wikipedia Encyclopedia,* s.v. "Andres Manuel Lopez Obrador"; *Venezuela* (N.p.: Lonely Planet Publications, 2007), p. 29.
93. Ibid., s.v. "Che Guevara."
94. Ibid., s.v. "Tlatelolco Massacre"; BBC *Country Profile,* s.v. "Timeline: Mexico."
95. BBC *Country Profile,* s.v. "Timeline: Mexico."
96. Ibid.
97. *Wikipedia Encyclopedia,* s.v. "Zapatista Army of National Liberation."
98. BBC *Country Profile,* s.v. "Timeline: Mexico."
99. Ibid.

100. *Mexico* (N.p.: Lonely Planet Publications, 2007), history section; "Mexico's Internal Drug War," by Sam Logan, *Power and Interest News Report (PINR)*, 14 August 2006.

101. BBC *Country Profile*, s.v. "Timeline: Mexico."

102. *Wikipedia Encyclopedia*, s.v. "Popular Revolutionary Army."

103. Ibid.

104. MIPT Knowledge Base, s.v. "EPR."

105. "Mexico's Internal Drug War."

106. *Timelines of History* (timelines.ws/countries), s.v. "Timeline El Salvador."

107. Davidson, "Terrorism and Human Smuggling Rings . . . ," *Unmasking Terror*, vol. III, p. 501.

108. Jim Kouri, "Threat from Violent MS-13 Gang Continues to Escalate," *Family Security Matters,* 19 January 2008.

109. "Gang-Related Gun Battle Kills Three in Southern Mexico," from AP, 23 September 2004.

110. Pineda Cruz, "Al-Qaeda's Unlikely Allies in Central America," *Unmasking Terror*, vol. II, p. 459.

111. Chris Zambelis, "Radical Islam in Latin America," *Unmasking Terror,* vol. III, p. 484.

112. Davidson, "Terrorism and Human Smuggling Rings . . . ," *Unmasking Terror,* vol. III, p. 500.

113. Mark Mosher (special-operations-qualified veteran of Iraqi War), in e-mail to author on 23 January 2008.

114. "[The] 3 members of China's Politburo Visited Mexico in 2005," *World Tribune,* 10 March 2006.

115. *Wikipedia Encyclopedia,* s.v. "snakehead (gang)."

116. "Smuggled Chinese Travel Circuitously," by Irene Jay Liu, NPR's "Morning Edition" News, 20 November 2007.

117. Garcia-Navarro, "Drug Violence Rampant in Mexico."

118. Davidson, "Terrorism and Human Smuggling Rings . . . ," *Unmasking Terror,* vol. III, p. 500.

119. "Chinese Regime Eyes Texas Port Facilities."

120. Gertz, "Chinese Military Trains in West."

121. Professional military historian, in telephone conversation with the author during January 2008.

122. "Venezuela - Chavez's Bolivarian Military Machine: A Cuban Model for Internal Repression," by John Sweeney, as extracted from vcrisis.com on 14 February 2008.

123. Gertz, *The China Threat,* p. 94.

124. Peter Stiff, *The Silent War: South African Recce Operations, 1969-1994* (Alberton, South Africa: Galago Publishing, 1999), p. 46; Greig, *The Communist Challenge to Africa,* p. 103, in *The Silent War,* by Stiff, p. 47; Hutchison Whampoa website, www.hutchison-whampoa.com.

125. Hutchison Whampoa website, www.hutchison-whampoa.com.
126. "Who Needs the Panama Canal."
127. "Police Chief from Mexican Border Town Seeks Asylum," World Briefs Wire Reports (AP), *Jacksonville Daily News* (NC), 23 March 2008, p. 5A.
128. Garcia-Navarro, "Drug Violence Rampant in Mexico."
129. "Chinese Regime Eyes Texas Port Facilities."
130. Sibylla Brodzinsky, "FARC Acquired Uranium, Says Colombia," *Christian Science Monitor,* 28 March 2008, p. 7; "In Another Blow to Colombia's Largest Left-Wing Rebel Force," World News in Brief, *Christian Science Monitor,* 28 March 2008, p. 7.
131. Joby Warrick and Carrie Johnson, "Chinese Spy 'Slept' in U.S. for 2 Decades: Espionage Network Said to Be Growing," *Washington Post,* 3 April 2008, p. A01.
132. "Hizbullah Infiltrates Israeli Military," by Geostrategy-Direct, *Middle East Report,* 9 April 2008.

Chapter 9: The 4GW Difference in Latin America

1. *Wikipedia Encyclopedia,* s.v. "Adolph Hitler."
2. Tony Perry, "U.S. 'Micro-Loan' Effort Yields Big Results In Iraqi Province," *Los Angeles Times,* 22 February 2008.
3. *Wikipedia Encyclopedia,* s.v. "Civilian Conservation Corps."
4. NPR's "Morning Edition" News, 16 January 2008.
5. Gordon Lubold, "In Iraq, More Detainees Released," *Christian Science Monitor,* 22 February 2008.
6. NPR's "Morning Edition" News, 20 March 2008.
7. William Wood (ambassador to Afghanistan), in interview on NPR's "Morning Edition" News, 31 December 2007; Anne Gearan, AP, "Drugs Grim Side of Afghanistan," *Jacksonville Daily News* (NC), 1 March 2008, p. 1A.
8. "NATO and Afghan Troops Searched for Remaining Taliban," World News in Brief, *Christian Science Monitor,* 12 December 2007, p. 12.
9. Mark Sexton (multi-tour veteran of Afghanistan), in telephone conversations with author between 26 September 2006 and 1 February 2007.
10. John Moore (former DOD counter-terrorism analyst), in testimony before Congress on 14 September 2001, from "The Emergence of the Terrorist International," by Orlando Gutierrez-Boronat, UPI, 14 September 2001.
11. Wife of Marine deployed to Argentina, in conversation with the author in December 2007.

12. "U.S. Nun Killed In Brazil," from AP, 12 February 2005.
13. Juan Forero, "Colombian Army Units Accused of Killing Peasants," NPR's "Morning Edition" News, 14 April 2008.
14. "The Maras," by Breve.
15. Rory Stewart, "How to Save Afghanistan," *Time,* 28 July 2008, p. 31.

Chapter 10: Undermining the Proxy Coalition

1. *Unrestricted Warfare,* by Qiao Liang and Wang Xiangsui (Beijing: PLA Literature and Arts Publishing House, February 1999), FBIS trans.
2. Hugo Chavez, as quoted in "Chavez, China Share Oil But Not Goals," by Sara Miller Llana and Peter Ford, *Christian Science Monitor,* 3 January 2008, p. 6.
3. "Drug Trafficking and North Korea," by CRS, 4 March 2005; Powell and Zagorin, "The Sopranos State."
4. Attributed to Winston Churchill.
5. NPR's "Morning Edition" News, 18 April 2008
6. *Wikipedia Encyclopedia,* s.v. "Medellin Cartel" and "Pablo Escobar."
7. Ibid., s.v. "North Coast Cartel" and "Norte del Valle Cartel."
8. Ibid., s.v. "Norte del Valle Cartel."
9. Ibid., s.v. "Cali Cartel."
10. "Chinese Criminal Enterprises," by Mahlmann.
11. *Wikipedia Encyclopedia,* s.v. "14K Triad."
12. Santoli, "The Panama Canal in Transition."
13. Ibid.
14. Roger Faligot, Le Mafia Chinoise en Europe (Paris: Calmann-Levy, 2001), pp. 142-143, in "Transnational Activities of Chinese Crime Organizations," by Curtis et al.
15. Santoli, "The Panama Canal in Transition."
16. "Chinese Criminal Enterprises," by Mahlmann.

Chapter 11: A Quasi-Military Solution

1. Memorandum for the record by H.J. Poole.
2. The author's sister (a long-time resident of, and frequent traveler to, Mexico), in telephone conversations.
3. Maj.Gen. Robert H. Scales, U.S. Army (Ret.), "Infantry and National Priorities," *Armed Forces Journal,* December 2007, pp. 14-17, 45.
4. "North Koreans Assisted Hezbollah with Tunnel Construction," Jamestown Foundation, *Terrorism Focus,* vol. III, issue 30, August 2006; ABC's Nightly News, 28 July 2006; Embassy World, s.v. "Embassy Listings for North Korea"; Poole, *Terrorist Trail,* pp. 35-38; Poole, *Dragon Days,* pp. 5, 6.

5. Scales, "Infantry and National Priorities," pp. 14-17, 45.

6. "North Koreans Assisted Hezbollah with Tunnel Construction," Jamestown Foundation.

7. Edward Cody and Molly Moore, "Analysts Attribute Hezbollah's Resilience to Zeal, Secrecy and Iranian Funding," *Washington Post,* 14 August 2006.

8. "Iran's Improved Fajr-5 Rockets Can Be Fired Remotely," *Geostrategy-Direct,* 31 May 2006.

9. Thomas Pakenham, *The Boer War* (New York: Avon Books, 1979), pp. 522-532.

10. *Wikipedia Encyclopedia,* s.v. "Malayan Emergency."

11. Simon Montlake, "Pro-Muslim Tilt in Malaysia's Courts," *Christian Science Monitor,* 29 January 2008, p. 6.

12. Simon Montlake, "Tension Grows between Thai Security Forces and Muslim Locals," *Christian Science Monitor,* 12 July 2005, pp. 7, 10; Carl Hammer, *Tide of Terror* (Boulder, CO: Paladin Press, 2003), p. 507; "The Emir" and "Gauging Jemaah Islamiyah's Threat in Southeast Asia," by Sharif Shuja, in *Unmasking Terror,* vol. II, ed. Heffelfinger, pp. 402, 403, 421.

13. "Zimbabwe: No Money to Print Currency," from IRIN (Harare), as reprinted in *Khartoum Monitor,* 31 May 2006, p. 10; "China Winning Resources and Loyalties of Africa," *The Financial Times* (UK), 28 February 2006.

14. "Analysis," by Chang.

15. Robin Wright and Peter Baker, "Iraq, Jordan, See Threat to Election from Iran," *Washington Post,* 8 December 2004, pp. 1A, 2A.

16. Sam Dagher, "Baghdad Safer, But It's a Life behind Walls," *Christian Science Monitor,* 10 December 2007, pp. 1, 11.

17. Sam Dagher, "Baghdad Strategy: 'Preserve Gains'," *Christian Science Monitor,* 30 January 2008, p. 6.

18. Robert H. Reid, AP, "U.S. Steps Deeper into Iraqi Fights," *Jacksonville Daily News* (NC), 29 March 2008, p. 1A.

19. Robert H. Reid, AP, "U.S. Jets Targeting Rebel Force," *Jacksonville Daily News* (NC), 30 March 2008.

20. Sam Dagher, "Anger Follows Fight with Sadr Army," *Christian Science Monitor,* 1 April 2008, p. 6.

21. Sam Dagher, "The Shiite Militia Front Reopens," *Christian Science Monitor,* 26 March 2008, pp. 1, 11; Sam Dagher, "Sadr Sends Mixed Signals," *Christian Science Monitor,* 31 March 2008, pp. 1, 11.

22. Kim Gamel, AP, "Iraqi Cleric Orders His Forces off the Streets," *Jacksonville Daily News* (NC), 31 March 2008, pp. 1A, 6A; NPR's "Morning Edition" News, 31 March 2008.

23. Robert H. Reid and Qassim Abdul-Zahra, AP, "Iraq's Prime Minister Orders Freeze in Raids Versus Militants," *Jacksonville Daily News* (NC), 5 April 2008. p. 4A; NPR's "Morning Edition" News, 7 April 2008.

24. ABC's Nightly News, 12 April 2008; CBS's "60 Minutes" News Program, 13 April 2008.
25. Lt.Cdr. Youssef H. Aboul-Enein USN, "The Hezbollah Model: Using Terror and Creating a Quasi-State in Lebanon," *Marine Corps Gazette,* June 2003, p. 35.
26. Muqtada al-Sadr, in interview with Scott Johnson, from " 'I Demand a Timetable'," *Newsweek,* 8 May 2006, p. 41.
27. Aboul-Enein, "The Hezbollah Model," pp. 34, 35; ABC's Nightly News, 26 March 2006; Rod Nordland, "Al-Sadr Strikes," *Newsweek,* 10 April 2006, pp. 45-47; Charles Levinson, "Ballot-Box Win Boosts Iraqi Radical," *Christian Science Monitor,* 30 January 2006, pp. 1, 11; Dan Murphy, "A Militia Tightens Grip on Healthcare," *Christian Science Monitor,* 25 May 2006, pp. 1, 12.
28. Aboul-Enein, "The Hezbollah Model," p. 35.
29. "North Koreans Assisted Hezbollah with Tunnel Construction," Jamestown Foundation.
30. Ramit Plushnick-Masti, AP, "Militant Groups Join Forces, Get Hezbollah Help," *Jacksonville Daily News* (NC), 28 October 2003, p. 1A; "Strong Chinese-Hamas Intelligence Connection," *DEBKAfile* (Israel), 19 June 2006.
31. BBC *Country Profiles,* s.v. "Bolivia" and "Timeline: Bolivia."
32. Prof. Robert Smith, *Road to War* (South Carolina, n.d.), as remembered by a professional military historian, in a telephone conversation with the author during January 2008.

Chapter 12: What's Not in the U.S. Manuals

1. Gudmundsson, *Stormtroop Tactics,* pp. 146-149.
2. "1945: Marine Corps Fights Its Most 'Savage' Battle Ever," *Mission: History,* vol. 3, no. 2 (San Francisco: Naval Order of the United States, 5 February 2001).
3. Infantry school instructor, in conversation with the author in November 2007.
4. "Colombia's Civil War."
5. Jim Simpson, "Scouts to the Rescue," *Defense Watch,* 17 September 2003.
6. Lt.Col. Gian P. Gentile, "Eating Soup with a Knife: Missing from the New COIN Manual's Pages Is the Imperative to Fight," Armed Forces Journal, September 2007, pp. 30-47.
7. Stiff, *The Silent War,* pp. 85, 86.
8. *Counterinsurgency,* FM 3-24 (Washington, D.C: Hdqts., Dept. of the Army, December 2006).

Chapter 13: Best 4GW Defense Is Locally Tailored

1. ABC's Morning News, 15 March 2008.
2. *Wikipedia Encyclopedia,* s.v. "Maoism."
3. "Profile: Tawhid and Jihad Group," BBC News, 8 October 2004, and C.J. Chivers, "Threats and Responses . . . ," *New York Times,* 13 January 2003, and "Here Is the Kurdish Al-Qaeda," *Financial Times Information,* 7 January 2003, in "Iraqi Wahabbi Factions Affiliated with Abu Musaab al Zarqawi," by Deanna Linder, Rachael Levy, and Yael Shahar, Internat. Policy Inst. for Counter-Terrorism, November 2004; Lafranchi, "Anti-Iran Sentiment Hardening Fast," *Christian Science Monitor,* 22 July 2002, pp. 1, 10; Michael Rubin, "Ansar al-Sunna: Iraq's New Terrorist Threat," *Middle East Intelligence Bulletin,* vol. 6, no. 5, May 2004; "Translation of Ansar al-Sunna Army's 'Banners of Truth' Video," TIDES World Press Reports, in "Ansar al-Sunna," by Rubin; "Hizbullah Suspected of Joining Sunni Insurgents," *Iraqi News,* 17 February 2005, from www.iraqinews.com.
4. Memorandum for the record by H.J. Poole.
5. Attributed to Abraham Lincoln.
6. Gertz, *The China Threat,* p. 94.
7. Brookes, "Venezuelan Vagaries," p. 44.
8. Fed. of American Scientists (www.fas.org), s.v. "FARC."
9. "Brazilian President Party Received Money from FARC, Say Documents"; Romero, "Files Released by Colombia Point to Venezuelan Bid to Arm Rebels."
10. Lt.Col. R.F. Reid-Daly, *Pamwe Chete: The Legend of the Selous Scouts* (Weltevreden Park, South Africa: Covos-Day Books, 1999), pp. 71-73.
11. "China Winning Resources and Loyalties of Africa."
12. Stiff, *The Silent War,* pp. 289, 290.
13. *CIA – The World Factbook,* s.v. "Colombia," "Panama," "Costa Rica," "Nicaragua," "Honduras," "El Salvador," "Guatemala," and "Mexico."
14. "Afghan Government Troops Reached the Center of Musa Qala," World News in Brief, *Christian Science Monitor,* 11 December 2007, p. 7.
15. *Wikipedia Encyclopedia,* s.v. "Maoism."
16. "Colombia's Civil War."
17. Asprey, *War in the Shadows,* vol. II, p. 975.
18. William S. Lind, "More on Gangs and Guerrillas vs. the State," anti-war.com, 29 April 2005.

Chapter 14: Deep Interdiction

1. BBC *Country Profile,* s.v. "Timeline: Colombia; "*Wikipedia Encyclopedia,* s.v. "Colombia."

2. Thomas A. Marks, "A Model Counterinsurgency: Uribe's Colombia (2002-2006)," *Military Review,* March-April 2007, p. 41.

3. Photograph, in "A Model Counterinsurgency," by Marks, p. 42.

4. Poole, *Dragon Days,* p. 23.

5. Marks, "A Model Counterinsurgency," p. 43.

6. Ibid., pp. 44, 48.

7. Ibid., p. 49.

8. Ibid., pp. 48, 49.

9. Ibid., p. 54.

10. *Wikipedia Encyclopedia,* s.v. "Socio-Economic Structure of the FARC-EP."

11. *Wikipedia Encyclopedia,* s.v. "Jacobo Arenas."

12. Photograph, in "A Model Counterinsurgency," by Marks, p. 42.

13. William H. Bartsch, "Crucial Battle Ignored," *Marine Corps Gazette,* September 1997, pp. 82-84.

14. Ibid.

15. Poole, *The Tiger's Way,* chapt. 16; Poole, *Terrorist Trail,* chapt. 14,

16. Poole, *Dragon Days,* Part Three.

17. Ibid., chapter 19.

18. Reid-Daly, *Pamwe Chete,* p. ii.

19. Chris Vermaak, "Rhodesia's Selous Scouts," *Armed Forces (Journal),* May 1977; Leroy Thompson, *Dirty Wars: Elite Forces vs. the Guerrillas* (Devon, England: David & Charles, 1991).

20. David Scott-Donelan (former member of Selous Scouts and SA Recce), in telephone conversation with the author on June 2004; Vermaak, "Rhodesia's Selous Scouts."

21. "Bushcraft," *Selous Scouts* website.

22. Ibid.

23. Reid-Daly, *Pamwe Chete,* pp. 182, 183.

24. Ibid., p. 342; Thompson, *Dirty Wars.*

25. *Brodzinsky,* "FARC Acquired Uranium, Says Colombia."

26. Jim Simpson, "Scouts to the Rescue," *Defense Watch,* 17 September 2003.

27. Thompson, *Dirty Wars.*

28. Simpson, "Scouts to the Rescue."

29. Thompson, *Dirty Wars.*

30. H.J. Poole, *The Last Hundred Yards: The NCO's Contribution to Warfare* (Emerald Isle, NC: Posterity Press, 1997), chapts. 17-20 and 24.

31. H. John Poole, *One More Bridge to Cross: Lowering the Cost of War* (Emerald Isle, NC: Posterity Press, 1999), chapt. 11.

32. H. John Poole, *Phantom Soldier: The Enemy's Answer to U.S. Firepower* (Emerald Isle, NC: Posterity Press, 2001), chapts. 7, 10, and 11.

33. Poole, *The Tiger's Way,* chapts. 19 and 20.
34. Memorandum for the record from H.J. Poole.

Chapter 15: Buffer Zones

1. Grant Evans and Kelvin Rowley, *Red Brotherhood at War* (London: Verso, 1984), p. 123; Chanda, *Brother Enemy,* p. 213.
2. "North Koreans Assisted Hezbollah with Tunnel Construction"; ABC's Nightly News, 28 July 2006; Embassy World, s.v. "Embassy Listings for North Korea."
3. Ibid., pp. 17, 18, 339.
4. Chanda, *Brother Enemy,* p. 318.
5. Ibid., pp. 334, 337.
6. Evans and Rowley, *Red Brotherhood at War,* p. 208.
7. Ibid., chapt. 7.
8. Chanda, *Brother Enemy,* pp. 371, 372.
9. Ibid., p. 382.
10. Ibid., p. 346; Evans and Rowley, *Red Brotherhood at War,* pp. 210, 213-215, 228.
11. *CIA — The World Factbook* s.v. "Cambodia."
12. Evans and Rowley, *Red Brotherhood at War,* p. 161.
13. Chanda, *Brother Enemy,* p. 361.
14. Ibid., p. 350.
15. Nguyen Khac Can and Pham Viet Thuc, *The War 1858 - 1975 in Vietnam* (Hanoi: Nha Xuat Ban Van Hoa Dan Toc, n.d.), fig. 754; Andrew Mollo and Digby Smith, *World Army Uniforms Since 1939,* part 2 (Poole, England: Blandford Press, 1981), pp. 18, 19.
16. Chanda, *Brother Enemy,* p. 360.
17. Lin Man Kin, *Sino-Vietnamese War* (Hong Kong: Kingsway Internat. Publications, 1981), p. 60, from Chanda, *Brother Enemy,* p. 361.
18. Foreign Broadcast Information Service — Asia Pacific, 22 March 1979, L-1, from Chanda, *Brother Enemy,* p. 361.
19. Douglas Pike, *PAVN: People's Army of Vietnam* (Novato, CA: Presidio Press, 1986), p. 268.
20. Plushnick-Masti, "Militant Groups Join Forces, Get Hezbollah Help," p. 1A; memorandum for the record by H.J. Poole.
21. Marks, "A Model Counterinsurgency," pp. 44, 48, 49.
22. Ibid., pp. 48, 49.
23. Memorandum for the record by H.J. Poole.
24. *Wikipedia Encyclopedia,* s.v. "Cali Cartel."
25. Poole, *The Tiger's Way,* chapts. 15 and 16.
26. Ibid., chapt. 7.

27. *Wikipedia Encyclopedia,* s.v. "electric eel"; www.ypte.org.uk, s.v. "fer-de-lance."
28. Poole, *One More Bridge to Cross,* chapt. 11.
29. ABC's Nightly News, 22 April 2008.
30. "Acting Chief of Mexico's Federal Police Shot Dead," World Briefs Wire Reports, *Jacksonville Daily News* (NC), 9 May 2008, p. 6A.
31. Poole, *One More Bridge to Cross,* chapt. 6.
32. *Night Movements,* trans. and preface by C. Burnett (Tokyo: Imperial Japanese Army, 1913; reprint Port Townsend, WA: Loompanics Unlimited, n.d.), pp. 62-69; Poole, *The Tiger's Way,* pp. 178, 179.
33. Ibid.
34. Poole, *The Tiger's Way,* pp. 173-175.

Chapter 16: Working a Heavily Populated Area

1. Sepehr Zabih, *The Iranian Military in Revolution and War* (London: Routledge, 1988), p. 14.
2. Aboul-Enein, "The Hezbollah Model," p. 34.
3. *Iran: A Country Study,* DA Pamphlet 550-68, Area Handbook Series (Washington, D.C.: Dept. of the Army, 1989), p. 267.
4. Zabih, *The Iranian Military,* pp. 210-212.
5. Ibid., p. 211.
6. Ibid., p. 14.
7. Kenneth Katzman, *Warriors of Islam: Iran's Revolutionary Guard* (Boulder, CO: Westview Press, 1993), pp. 82-84.
8. Wright, *Sacred Rage,* pp. 33-35, as quoted in *Warriors of Islam,* by Katzman, p. 71.
9. Plushnick-Masti, "Militant Groups Join Forces, Get Hezbollah Help," p. 1A.
10. *Warfare in Lebanon,* ed. Kenneth J. Alnwick and Thomas A. Fabyanic (Washington, D.C.: Nat. Defense Univ., 1988), pp. 71, 72.
11. Ibid., p. 71.
12. Ibid., p. 54; Lawrence Pintak, *Seeds of Hate: How America's Flawed Middle East Policy Ignited the Jihad* (London: Pluto Press, 2003), pp. 313-314.
13. Aboul-Enein, "The Hezbollah Model," pp. 34, 35.
14. Lt.Col. (Ret., IDF) David Eshel, "Counterguerrilla Warfare in South Lebanon," *Marine Corps Gazette,* July 1997, p. 42.
15. Memorandum for the record by H.J. Poole.
16. S.Sgt. Lee Bergee and PFC Fred Davidson, as quoted in *The Korean War: Pusan to Chosin, An Oral History,* by Donald Knox (San Diego: Harcourt Brace Jovanovich, 1985), pp. 289-291; Poole, *The Tiger's Way,* p. 291.

17. A.E. Taras and F.D. Zaruz, *Podgotovka Razvegchika: Sistema Spetsnaza GRU [Training of Agents: Special Forces of the GRU]* (Minsk, Belarus: AST Publishing, 2002), pp. 374, 375.
18. *The German Squad in Combat*, trans. and ed. U.S. Mil. Intell. Service from a German manual (n.p., 1943); republished as *German Squad Tactics in WWII*, by Matthew Gajkowski (West Chester, OH: Nafziger, 1995), p. 42; *Night Movements*, pp. 72, 73.
19. Stiff, *The Silent War*, p. 192, pp. 208-215.
20. Memorandum for the record by H.J. Poole.

Afterword

1. William S. Lind (writer of adopted 3GW and ignored 4GW handbooks for the U.S. military), in telephone conversation with the author on 7 June 2006.
2. Osama bin Laden, in videotaped statement on ABC's Nightly News, late 2007.
3. "Nations Hospitable . . . to Terrorism," by Berry et al, p. 171.
4. Ibid.
5. *Wikipedia Encyclopedia,* s.v. "United Nations Mission in Sudan."
6. "A Brief History of Robert Mugabe," *Time,* 7 July 2008, p. 14.
7. ABC's Morning News, 30 June 2008.
8. "South African Union Refuses to Unload Chinese Arms Destined for Zimbabwe," Reuters, 18 April 2008.
9. David Baxter, "Armed Chinese Soldiers Police Mutare Streets," Assoc. of Zimbabwe Journalists, 15 April 2008.
10. Memorandum for the record by H.J. Poole.
11. Ibid.

Glossary

AK-47	Russian and Chinese weapon designator	Eastern-bloc assault rifle
ALBA	Bolivarian Alternative for the People of Our America	Alliance of nations started by Chavez
ANECFM/LN	Former Fighters of the Farabundo Marti National Liberation Front	Group of erstwhile Salvadorian rebels
ARENA	National Republican Alliance	Rightist Salvadorian political party
AUC	Autodefensas Unidas de Colombia	Colombia's rightist paramilitaries
BBC	British Broadcasting Corporation	English radio and TV network
C-5A	U.S. aircraft designator	American cargo jet
CAFTA	Central American Free Trade Agreement	Economic pact between nations in the Americas
CAP	Combined Action Platoon	Consists of one squad each of U.S. troops, host-nation police, & and host-nation army
CCC	Civil Conservation Corps	New Deal project
CIA	Central Intelligence Agency	U.S. spy organization
CLC	Concerned Local Citizens	Community watch arrangement in Iraq

COSCO	China Ocean Shipping Company	PLA's civilian fleet
CP	Command Post	Unit headquarters
DEA	Drug Enforcement Administration	U.S. narcotics police
DIM	Direccion de Inteligencia Militar	The military intelligence agency of Venezuela
DMZ	Demilitarized Zone	Buffer area between two combatants
DOD	Department of Defense	U.S. military
DPO	Drug Prosecutor's Office	Panama's agency for dope control
E&E	Escape and Evasion	Avoiding capture & then eluding pursuit
ELN	Ejercito de Liberacion Nacional	Marxist guerrilla faction in Colombia
EPR	Popular Revolutionary Army	Marxist guerrilla faction in Mexico
EZLN	Zapatista National Liberation Army	Populist guerrilla movement in Mexico
F-16	U.S. aircraft designator	American fighter jet
FAJIR-3	Iranian military-equipment designator	Chinese-made rocket sent to *Hezbollah*
FAJIR-5	Iranian military designator	Later version of FAJIR rocket
FARC	Fuerzas Armadas Revolucionarias de Colombia	Leftist rebels from Colombia
FARC-EP	Fuerzas Armadas Revolucionarias de Colombia Ejercito del Pueblo	Maoist "people's army" that was once the FARC

FBI	Federal Bureau of Investigation	U.S. criminal monitoring agency
FBIS	Foreign Broadcast Information Service	CIA's other-nation media-monitoring agency
FBP	Frente Brasil Popular	Leftist coalition in Brazil
FC-1	Chinese aircraft designator	PRC jet fighter
FM 3-24	Field manual designator	U.S. Army & Marine Corps' new manual on counterinsurgency
FMLN	Farabundo Marti National Liberation Front	Salvadorian guerrilla faction
14-K	Chinese triad name	Hong Kong syndicate with worldwide reach
4GW	Fourth Generation Warfare	War in four arenas simultaneously— martial, religious, economic, political
FSLN	Frente Sandinista de Liberacion Nacional	Nicaraguan Socialist movement
FTO	Foreign Terrorist Organization	Faction designated by U.S. as terrorists
G15	Group of 15 Nations	Leading economies of the world
GC	Grid Coordinate	Map location with 1,000-meter squares
GDP	Gross domestic product	Market value of all goods & services produced within a country yearly
HQ	Headquarters	Top military echelon

J.F.K.	John F. Kennedy	Airport on outskirts of New York City
JYL-1	Chinese equipment designator	Mobile radar unit for PRC air defense
K-8	Chinese aircraft designator	PRC training plane
KGB	Komityet Gosudarstvyennoy Bezopasnosti	Soviet spy agency
M-4	U.S. weapon designator	Barrel-shortened version of the M-16
M-16	U.S. weapon designator	Assault rifle
M-18	Mara name	Central American youth gang
M-19	Movimiento 19 de Abril	Marxist guerrilla faction in Colombia
MBPD	Million barrels per day	Common measure for oil production
MIG-29	Soviet aircraft designator	Russian fighter jet
MIPT	Memorial Institute for the Prevention of Terrorism	Private think tank
MRTA	Movimiento Revolucionario Tupac Amaru	Tupac Amaru guerrillas from Peru
MS-13	Mara Salvatrucha	Largest Central American youth gang
MSS	Ministry of State Security	One of the PRC's two spy agencies; other is from the PLA
MCWP	Marine Corps Warfighting Publication	Latest series of U.S. Marine manuals
NAFTA	North American Free Trade Agreement	Economic pact between nations

NAM	Non-Aligned Movement	Loose alliance of developing nations
NCO	Noncommissioned Officer	Enlisted leader
9/11	11 September 2001	Attack on America of this date
NPR	National Public Radio	U.S. educational radio network
NVA	North Vietnamese Army	North Vietnam's ground forces
OAS	Organization of American States	Western Hemisphere alliance of nations
OIC	Organization of the Islamic Conference	Saudi-swayed alternative to Arab League (of nations)
PBS	Public Broadcasting System	U.S. educational TV network
PCB	Partido Comunista Brasileiro	Original Brazilian Communist Party
PC do B	Partido Comunista do Brasil	Current Brazilian Communist Party
PCP	Partido Communista del Peru	Same as the SL (Spanish name for Shining Path)
PDPR-EPR	Popular Revolutionary Democratic Party	EPR's illegal political wing
PDVSA	Petroleos de Venezuela	Venezuela's state-owned oil company
PEMEX	Petroleos Mexicanos	Mexico's state-owned oil company
PFC	Private First Class	Second lowest U.S. enlisted rank

PL	Liberal Party	Honduras' rightist political party
PLA	People's Liberation Army	PRC's military arm (covers intell., navy, air, missiles, ground)
PLN	National Liberation Party	Costa Rican political party
PLO	Palestinian Liberation Organization	Coalition of Palestinian groups
PN	National Party	Honduras' center-left political party
PRC	People's Republic of China	Communist Mainland China
PRD	Party of the Democratic Revolution	Left-leaning Mexican political party
PT	Physical Training	Strength building exercises
PTJ	Policia Tecnica Judicial	Panamanian police agency
SAM-7	Surface-to-Air Missile (U.S. designator for Red weapon)	Anti-aircraft missile
SAM-14	Surface-to-Air Missile (U.S designator for Red weapon)	More advanced missile than SAM-7
SAM-16	Surface-to-Air Missile (U.S designator for Red weapon)	More advanced missile than SAM-14
SAW	Squad Automatic Weapon	Light-weight, rapid-fire U.S. machinegun
2GW	Second-Generation Warfare	Based on attacking concentrations of enemy soldiers; U.S. has high-tech variant

SL	Sendero Luminoso	Maoist guerrilla movement from Peru called the Shining Path in English
Su-27 SK	Chinese aircraft designator	PRC fighter-bomber
SWAT	Special Weapons Assault Team	Paramilitary police unit
TAOR	Tactical Area of Responsibility	Zone of U.S. operations
TBA	Tri-Border Area	Corner of Argentina, Paraguay, & Brazil
TFM	Transportacion Ferroviaria Mexicana	Mexican railroad company
3GW	Third-Generation Warfare	Based on bypassing foe's strongpoints to ruin strategic assets instead of killing
TV	Television	Electronic media device
U.N.	United Nations	Alliance of countries
UNE	National Unity for Hope	Guatemalan center-leftist political party
UNICEF	U.N. International Children's Emergency Fund	U.N. monetary receivership for kids
UP	Patriotic Union	One-time political party of the FARC
U.S.	United States	America
USA	United States of America	Same as U.S.
UW	Unconventional Warfare	Loosely structured strife; includes ways of guerrilla and E&E

WWI	World War One	First global conflict
WWII	World War Two	Second global conflict
ZANLA	Zimbabwe African National Liberation Army	ZANU P/F's armed wing
ZANU P/F	Zimbabwe African National Union Patriotic Front	Maoist party that took over Rhodesia
ZIPRA	Zimbabwe's People's Revolutionary Army	Rhodesian resistance movement

Bibliography

U.S. Government Publications and News Releases

"Attorney General's Report to Congress on the Growth of Violent Street Gangs in Suburban Areas." National Drug Intelligence Center, April 2008. From its website, www.usdoj.gov.

"Background Note: Panama." U.S. Dept. of State, November 2007. From from its website, www.state.gov.

"Brazil." *Library of Congress Country Studies,* April 1997.

"Caribbean Region: Issues in U.S. Relations." By Mark P. Sullivan. Congressional Research Service (CRS) Report for Congress, Order Code RL32160. Washington, D.C.: Library of Congress, 25 May 2005.

"China-U.S. Relations: Current Issues and Implications for U.S. Policy." By Kerry Dumbaugh. Congressional Research Service (CRS) Report for Congress, Order Code RL33877. Washington, D.C.: Library of Congress, 1 October 2007.

"China's Growing Interest in Latin America." By Kerry Dumbaugh and Mark P. Sullivan. Congressional Research Service (CRS) Report for Congress, Order Code RS22119. Washington, D.C.: Library of Congress, 20 April 2005.

CIA—The World Factbook. As updated every three months. From its website, www.odci.gov.

Counterinsurgency. FM 3-24. Washington, D.C: Hdqts., Dept. of the Army, December 2006.

Country Reports on Terrorism, 2005. Washington, D.C.: U.S. Dept. of State, April 2006. From its website, www.state.gov.

"Dominican Republic: Political and Economic Conditions and Relations with the United States." By Clare M. Ribando. Congressional Research Service (CRS) Report for Congress, Order Code RS21718. Washington, D.C.: Library of Congress, 8 March 2005.

"Drug Trafficking and North Korea: Issues for U.S. Policy." By Raphael F. Perl. Congressional Research Service (CRS) Report for Congress, Order Code RL32167. Washington, D.C.: Library of Congress. Series of updates: 5 December 2003, 4 March 2005, and 27 November 2006.

El Salvador: A Country Study. DA Pamphlet 550-150. Area
Handbook Series. Washington, D.C.: Dept. of the Army,
1990.

Guatemala: A Country Study. DA Pamphlet 550-78. Area
Handbook Series. Washington, D.C.: Dept. of the Army, 1984.

"Haiti: Developments and U.S. Policy Since 1991 and Current
Congressional Concerns." By Maureen Taft-Morales and Clare M.
Ribando. Congressional Research Service (CRS) Report,
Order Code RL32294. Washington, D.C.: Library of Congress,
21 June 2007.

Honduras: A Country Study. DA Pamphlet 550-151. Area
Handbook Series. Washington, D.C.: Dept. of the Army, 1984.

Iran: A Country Study. DA Pamphlet 550-68. Area Handbook Series.
Washington, D.C.: Dept. of the Army, 1989.

"Latin America: Terrorism Issues." By Mark P. Sullivan. Congressional
Research Service (CRS) Report for Congress, Order Code RS21049.
Washington, D.C.: Library of Congress, 22 January 2007.

"Nations Hospitable to Organized Crime and Terrorism." By LaVerle
Berry, Glenn E. Curtis, John N. Gibbs, Rex A. Hudson, Tara
Karacan, Nina Kollars, and Ramon Miro. Federal Research
Division. Library of Congress, October 2003.

Patterns of Global Terrorism: 1990. Washington, D.C.: U.S. Dept. of
State, 1991. As retrieved from www.fas.org.

Patterns of Global Terrorism, 2003 Report. Washington, D.C.:
U.S. Dept. of State, April 2004. From its website.

Terrorism Chronology. Washington, D.C.: U.S. Dept. of State. From
its url, usinfo.state.gov/is/international_security/terrorism.

"Terrorist and Organized Crime Groups in the Tri-Border Area."
By Rex Hudson. Federal Research Division. Library of Congress,
July 2003.

Terrorist Group Profiles. U.S. Naval Postgraduate School (Dudley Knox
Library), April 2006. From its website, web.nps.navy.mil.

"Transnational Activities of Chinese Crime Organizations." By Glenn
E. Curtis, Seth L. Elan, Rexford A. Hudson, and Nina A. Koll.
Federal Research Division. Library of Congress, April 2003.

Civilian Publications

Analytical Studies and Databases

Atwan, Abdel Bari. *The Secret History of Al-Qa'ida.* London:
Abacus, an imprint of Little, Brown Book Group, 2006.

Bermudez, Joseph S., Jr. *North Korean Special Forces.* Annapolis:
Naval Inst. Press, 1998.

Can, Nguyen Khac and Pham Viet Thuc. *The War 1858 - 1975 in Vietnam*. Hanoi: Nha Xuat Ban Van Hoa Dan Toc, n.d.

Chanda, Nayan. *Brother Enemy: The War after the War*. New York: Collier Books, 1986.

Council on Foreign Relations database (Washington, D.C.). From its website, cfr.org.

Country Profiles. BBC News. From its website, bbc.co.uk.

Evans, Grant and Kelvin Rowley. *Red Brotherhood at War*. London: Verso, 1984.

Fourth Generation War. FMFM 1-A (Draft Copy). By William S. Lind. Washington, D.C., 2005.

The German Squad in Combat. Translated and edited by U.S. Mil. Intell. Service from a German manual. N.p., 1943. Republished as *German Squad Tactics in WWII*, by Matthew Gajkowski. West Chester, OH: Nafziger, 1995.

Gertz, Bill. *The China Threat*. Washington, D.C.: Regnery Publishing, 2002.

GlobalSecurity.org. Alexandria, VA.

Guatemala. N.p.: Lonely Planet Publications, 2007.

Gudmundsson, Bruce I. *Stormtroop Tactics—Innovation in the German Army 1914-1918*. New York: Praeger, 1989.

Gunaratna, Rohan. *Inside al-Qaeda: Global Network of Terror*. Lahore: Vanguard, 2002.

Hammer, Carl. *Tide of Terror*. Boulder, CO: Paladin Press, 2003.

Hutchison Whampoa website, www.hutchison-whampoa.com.

Katzman, Kenneth. *Warriors of Islam: Iran's Revolutionary Guard*. Boulder, CO: Westview Press, 1993.

Knox, Donald. *The Korean War: Pusan to Chosin, An Oral History*. San Diego: Harcourt Brace Jovanovich, 1985.

Llana, Sara Miller and Peter Ford. "Chavez, China Share Oil But Not Goals." *Christian Science Monitor*, 3 January 2008.

Mannes, Aaron. *Profiles in Terror: The Guide to Middle East Terrorist Organizations*. Oxford: Rowman & Littlefield, 2004.

The Memorial Institute for the Prevention of Terrorism (MIPT) Knowledge Base. From its website, www.tkb.org.

Menges, Constantine. *China: The Gathering Threat*. Nashville, TN: Nelson Current, 2005.

Mexico. N.p.: Lonely Planet Publications, 2007.

Mollo, Andrew and Digby Smith. *World Army Uniforms Since 1939*. Part 2. Poole, England: Blandford Press, 1981.

Night Movements. Translated and preface by C. Burnett. Tokyo: Imperial Japanese Army, 1913. Reprint Port Townsend, WA: Loompanics Unlimited, n.d.

Nojumi, Neamatollah. *The Rise of the Taliban in Afghanistan: Mass Mobilization, Civil War, and the Future of the Region.* New York: Palgrave, 2002.

Pakenham, Thomas. *The Boer War.* New York: Avon Books, 1979.

Pintak, Lawrence. *Seeds of Hate: How America's Flawed Middle East Policy Ignited the Jihad.* London: Pluto Press, 2003.

Poole, H. John. *Dragon Days: Time for "Unconventional" Tactics.* Emerald Isle, NC: Posterity Press, 2007.

Poole, H. John. *The Last Hundred Yards: The NCO's Contribution to Warfare.* Emerald Isle, NC: Posterity Press, 1997.

Poole, H. John. *Militant Tricks: Battlefield Ruses of the Islamic Insurgent.* Emerald Isle, NC: Posterity Press, 2005.

Poole, H. John. *One More Bridge to Cross: Lowering the Cost of War.* Emerald Isle, NC: Posterity Press, 1999.

Poole, H. John. *Phantom Soldier: The Enemy's Answer to U.S. Firepower.* Emerald Isle, NC: Posterity Press, 2001.

Poole, H. John. *Tactics of the Crescent Moon: Militant Muslim Combat Methods.* Emerald Isle, NC: Posterity Press, 2004.

Poole, H. John. *Terrorist Trail: Backtracking the Foreign Fighter.* Emerald Isle, NC: Posterity Press, 2006.

Poole, H. John. *The Tiger's Way: A U.S. Private's Best Chance of Survival.* Emerald Isle, NC: Posterity Press, 2003.

Reid-Daly, Lt.Col. R.F. *Pamwe Chete: The Legend of the Selous Scouts.* Weltevreden Park, South Africa: Covos-Day Books, 1999.

Stiff, Peter. *The Silent War: South African Recce Operations, 1969-1994.* Alberton, South Africa: Galago Publishing, 1999.

Taras, A.E. and F.D. Zaruz. *Podgotovka Razvegchika: Sistema Spetsnaza GRU (Training of Agents: Special Forces of the GRU).* Minsk, Belarus: AST Publishing, 2002.

Tehran's War of Terror and Its Nuclear Delivery Capability. By Stephen E. Hughes. Victoria, Canada: Trafford Publishing, 2007.

Thompson, Leroy. *Dirty Wars: Elite Forces vs. the Guerrillas.* Devon, England: David & Charles, 1991.

Unmasking Terror: A Global Review of Terrorist Activities. Volumes I, II, and III. The first two edited by Christopher Heffelfinger, and the third by Jonathan Hutzley. Washington, D.C: Jamestown Foundation, 2005 through 2007.

Unrestricted Warfare. By Qiao Liang and Wang Xiangsui. Beijing: PLA Literature and Arts Publishing House, February 1999. FBIS translation over the internet.

Venezuela. N.p.: Lonely Planet Publications, 2007.

Warfare in Lebanon. Edited by Kenneth J. Alnwick and Thomas A. Fabyanic. Washington, D.C.: Nat. Defense Univ., 1988.

Zabih, Sepehr. *The Iranian Military in Revolution and War.* London: Routledge, 1988.

Photos, Videotapes, Movies, TV Programs, Slide Shows, and Illustrations

"FARC guerrillas in the street in San Vicentedel Caguan, Caqueta." Photograph. By Ariana Cubillos. As extracted from www.colombiajournal.org/farcphotos.htm.
"Guerrilla Wars." *People's Century.* BBC in conjunction with WGBH (Boston). As aired on NC Public TV, 29 June 1999.
"Truth Be Tolled." Written, produced, and directed by William H. Molina. Storm Pictures LLC, 2006. 99 minutes. DVD # 7-44773-0162-6.

Letters, E-Mail, and Verbal Conversations

The author's sister (a long-time resident of, and frequent traveler to, Mexico). In 2007 telephone conversations.
E-5 Marine veteran of the Panama invasion. In conversation with the author around 1990.
E-7 Marine veteran of the Panama invasion. In conversation with the author around 1990.
Former resident of Panama (daughter of Panamanian college professor). In conversation with the author on 9 December 2007.
Infantry school instructor. In conversation with the author in November 2007.
Lind, William S. (writer of adopted 3GW and ignored 4GW handbooks for the U.S. military). In telephone conversation with the author on 7 June 2006.
Molina, William H. (author and producer of "Truth Be Tolled). In a telephone conversation with the author about November 2006.
Mosher, Mark (special-operations-qualified veteran of Iraq War). In e-mail to author on 23 January 2008.
Probable CIA official (McClean address and too much knowledge). In phonecall to author around the middle of October 2006.
Professional military historian. In telephone conversation with the author during January 2008.
Scott-Donelan, David (former member of Selous Scouts and SA Recce). In a telephone conversation with the author in June 2004.
Sexton, Mark (GI formerly deployed to Peru and Afghanistan). In telephone conversation with author between 26 September 2006 and 1 February 2007.
Wife of Marine deployed to Argentina. In conversation with the author in December 2007.

Newspaper, Magazine, Radio, and Website Articles

Aboul-Enein, Lt.Cdr. Youssef H., USN. "The Hezbollah Model:
    Using Terror and Creating a Quasi-State in Lebanon."
    Marine Corps Gazette, June 2003.
"Acting Chief of Mexico's Federal Police Shot Dead." World Briefs
    Wire Reports. *Jacksonville Daily News* (NC), 9 May
    2008.
"Afghan Government Troops Reached the Center of Musa Qala."
    World News in Brief. *Christian Science Monitor,* 11 December
    2007.
"Analysis: Chinese Arms and African Oil." By Andrei Chang.
    United Press International (Hong Kong), 5 November 2007.
    As retrieved from http://www.energy-daily.com/reports/
    Analysis_Chinese_arms_and_African_oil_999.html.
"Analysts Debate al-Qaeda's Strength." By Tom Gjelten. NPR's
    "Morning Edition," 10 March 2008.
Anderson, Mark. "China's Massive Port Grab." *American Free Press*
    (Washington, D.C). Issue 3, 15 January 2007. From its website,
    www.americanfreepress.net.
"Asian Triads," by Wade O. Koromantee. From *Into The Abyss:
    A Personal Journey into the World of Street Gangs,* by Mike Carlie.
    As extracted from faculty.missouristate.edu.
"At Least 31 killed in Guatemala Prison Gang War." MSNBC,
    15 August 2005.
Avila, Jim. "Dream Team of U.S. Bashers Gathers in Cuba."
    New York Times, 11 September 2006.
Baxter, David. "Armed Chinese Soldiers Police Mutare Streets."
    Assoc. of Zimbabwe Journalists, 15 April 2008. From its
    website, zimbabwejournalists.com.
Blanche, Ed. "The Latin American Connection," BNet Business
    Network (a CBS company), May 2003. From its
    website.
Blenford, Adam. "Guatemala's Epidemic of Killing." BBC News,
    9 June 2005.
Boadle, Anthony. "Absent Castro Overshadows
    Non-Aligned Summit." Reuters, 14 September 2006.
Bradsher, Keith. "North Korean Ploy Masks Ships Under Other Flags."
    New York Times, 20 October 2006.
"Brazilian President Party Received Money from FARC, Say
    Documents." *Wikinews.org,* 15 March 2005.
Bridges, Tyler and Casto Ocando. McClatchy Newspapers. "Vote Today
    Decides Chavez's Power." *The News and Observer* (Raleigh, NC),
    2 December 2007.
"A Brief History of Robert Mugabe." *Time,* 7 July 2008.

Brodzinsky, Sibylla. "FARC Acquired Uranium, Says Colombia." *Christian Science Monitor,* 28 March 2008.

Brookes, Peter. "Venezuelan Vagaries." *Armed Forces Journal,* July 2007.

Burns, Robert. Associated Press. "Special Forces Feeling the Strain of War." *Jacksonville Daily News* (NC), 6 May 2006.

"Bushcraft." *Selous Scouts* website.

Cancel, Daniel. "Venezuela's Chavez Presses on Undaunted." *Christian Science Monitor,* 6 December 2007.

"Central America's Street Gangs Are Drawn into the World of Geopolitics." *Power and Interest News Report (PINR),* 26 August 2005. From its website, www.pinr.org.

Chauvin, Lucien. "Peru See Shadowy Hand of Chavez." *Christian Science Monitor,* 3 April 2008.

"Chavez Accepts Defeat in Venezuelan Referendum." By Associated Press. *Jacksonville Daily News* (NC), 4 December 2007.

"Chavez Says No Oil if U.S. Hurts Vote." World Briefs Wire Reports (AP). *Jacksonville Daily News* (NC), 1 December 2007.

"Chavez's Whistlestop World Tour." BBC News, 1 September 2006.

"China and Angola Strengthen Bilateral Relationship." By Loro Horta. *Power and Interest News Report,* 23 June 2006.

"China in Angola: An Emerging Energy Partnership." By Paul Hare. Jamestown Foundation. *China Brief,* volume 6, issue 22, 8 November 2006.

"China's Influence on Africa." By Ernest J. Wilson III. International Development and Conflict Management. Univ. of Maryland. In testimony before Congress on 28 July 2005.

"China Winning Resources and Loyalties of Africa." *The Financial Times* (UK), 28 February 2006.

"Chinese Military to Make Billions through Capitalism." *Geostrategy Direct,* 16 January 2008.

"Chinese Regime Eyes Texas Port Facilities." *American Free Press* (Washington, D.C.), Issue 33, 14 August 2006. From its website, www.americanfreepress.net.

"Chinese Triads." As extracted from www.geocities.com.

"Chinese, Venezuelan Oil Majors Start Joint Venture." From China National News and Indo-Asian News Service (IANS), 6 April 2008.

Cody, Edward and Molly Moore. "Analysts Attribute Hezbollah's Resilience to Zeal, Secrecy and Iranian Funding." *Washington Post,* 14 August 2006.

"Colombia Says FARC Rebels Operating in Bolivia, Paraguay." Xinhua. *People's Daily on Line* (Beijing), 23 June 2006.

"Colombian Leader Ends FARC Talks." BBC News, 20 October 2006.

"Colombia's Civil War." PBS's Online News Hour, 2003. As retrieved from www.cocaine.org.

"Colombia's Most Powerful Rebels." BBC News, 19 September 2003.

"Concession Brings Honduras Result." BBC News, 8 December 2005.

Dagher, Sam. "Anger Follows Fight with Sadr Army." *Christian Science Monitor,* 1 April 2008.

Dagher, Sam. "Baghdad Safer, But It's a Life behind Walls." *Christian Science Monitor,* 10 December 2007.

Dagher, Sam. "Baghdad Strategy: 'Preserve Gains'." *Christian Science Monitor,* 30 January 2008.

Dagher, Sam. "Sadr Sends Mixed Signals." *Christian Science Monitor,* 31 March 2008.

Dagher, Sam. "The Shiite Militia Front Reopens." *Christian Science Monitor,* 26 March 2008.

Daremblum, Jaime. "Bolivia on the Brink." *New York Sun,* 8 April 2008.

"DEA Boosts Its Role in Paraguay." By Jack Sweeney. *Washington Times,* 21 August 2001.

"Defying Silence in Honduras." BBC News, 4 July 2007.

Downie, Andrew. "Is Latin America Heading for an Arms Race?" *Christian Science Monitor,* 16 January 2008.

"Ecuador Offers Concession Of Manta Air Base To China, Declines To Renew Contract With U.S." By Vittorio Hernandez. AHN News (Ecuador), 26 November 2007. As retrieved through ACCESS@g2-forward.org and MILINET.

Eshel, Lt.Col. (Ret., IDF) David. "Counterguerrilla Warfare in South Lebanon." *Marine Corps Gazette,* July 1997.

"FARC Weapons Supplies Revealed." *Santa Fe de Bogota Semana* (on-line edition), 6 September 1999. FBIS translation. As retrieved from www.fas.org.

"Former Roman Catholic Bishop Fernando Lugo Won the Presidency . . . ," World News in Brief, *Christian Science Monitor,* 22 April 2008.

"Four Spies for the U.S. Have Been Caught by Venezuelan Security." World News in Brief. *Christian Science Monitor,* 21 August 2006.

Gamel, Kim. Associated Press. "Iraqi Cleric Orders His Forces off the Streets." *Jacksonville Daily News* (NC), 31 March 2008.

"Gang-Related Gun Battle Kills Three in Southern Mexico." From Associated Press, 23 September 2004.

Garcia-Navarro, Lourdes. "Calderon Fights Mexico's Gangs with Little Success." NPR's *All Things Considered,* 16 May 2007.

Garcia-Navarro, Lourdes. "Drug Violence Rampant in Mexico." NPR's *Morning Edition,* 18 May 2007.

Garrastazu, Antonio and Jerry Haar. "International Terrorism: The Western Hemisphere Connection." Organization of American States. *America's Forum North-South Center Update,* 2001.

Gearan, Anne. Associated Press. "Drugs Grim Side of Afghanistan."
 Jacksonville Daily News (NC), 1 March 2008.
Gentile, Lt.Col. Gian P. "Eating Soup with a Spoon." *Armed Forces
 Journal,* September 2007.
Gertz, Bill. "China-Made Artillery Seized in Afghanistan." *Washington
 Times,* 12 April 2002.
Gertz, Bill. "Chinese Military Trains in West." *Washington
 Times,* 15 March 2006.
Gertz, Bill and Rowan Scarborough. "China-Trained Taliban." Inside
 the Ring. *Washington Times,* 21 June 2002. Unedited version
 from www.gertzfile.com.
Gibb, Tom. "El Salvador Buries Revolutionary." BBC News,
 30 January 2006.
"The Gift of Ourselves." Knights of Columbus. *Columbia Magazine,*
 October 2007.
Gutierrez-Boronat, Orlando. "The Emergence of the Terrorist
 International." United Press International, 14 September 2001.
"Hizbullah Infiltrates Israeli Military." By Geostrategy-Direct.
 Middle East Report, 9 April 2008.
"Hizbullah Suspected of Joining Sunni Insurgents." *Iraqi
 News,* 17 February 2005, from www.iraqinews.com.
Hoffman, Lisa. Scripps Howard. "Cocaine Use Is on the Rise in the U.S."
 Jacksonville Daily News (NC), 11 November 2007.
"Honduras Acts over Child Killings." BBC News, 14 March 2003.
"A 'Huge' New Discovery of Natural Gas." World News in Brief.
 Christian Science Monitor, 23 January 2008.
Hurt, Charles. "Senate Denies Funds for New Border Fence."
 Washington Times, 14 July 2006.
"In Another Blow to Colombia's Largest Left-Wing Rebel Force." World
 News in Brief. *Christian Science Monitor,* 28 March 2008.
"Intel. Report: Venezuela Training Ecuador Rebels." *World Tribune,*
 25 October 2005.
"Iran's Improved Fajr-5 Rockets Can Be Fired Remotely."
 Geostrategy-Direct, 31 May 2006.
"Iraqi Wahabbi Factions Affiliated with Abu Musaab al Zarqawi." By
 Deanna Linder, Rachael Levy, and Yael Shahar. Internat. Policy
 Inst. for Counter-Terrorism, November 2004.
Keane, Fergal. "Honduras's Child Killings." BBC News, 5 October
 2002.
Kirk, Alejandro and Dalia Acosta. "Non-Aligned Summit Opens amidst
 Suspense over Castro." Inter-Press-Service News Agency,
 21 September 2006.
Kouri, Jim. "Threat from Violent MS-13 Gang Continues to Escalate."
 Family Security Matters, 19 January 2008. From its website,
 http://familysecuritymatters.org.

Lafranchi, Howard. "Anti-Iran Sentiment Hardening Fast." *Christian Science Monitor,* 22 July 2002.

Lafranchi, Howard. "Free Trade Accords Face Rocky Road." *Christian Science Monitor,* 7 February 2008.

"Left Claims El Salvador Victory." BBC News, 17 March 2003.

Levinson, Charles. "Ballot-Box Win Boosts Iraqi Radical." *Christian Science Monitor,* 30 January 2006.

Lind, William S. "More on Gangs and Guerrillas vs. the State." Anti-war.com, 29 April 2005.

Llana, Sara Miller. "Chavez Plan Stirs a Rising Backlash." *Christian Science Monitor,* 28 November 2007.

Llana, Sara Miller. "Mexico, U.S. Step Up Drug Cooperation." *Christian Science Monitor,* 23 January 2008.

Llana, Sara Miller. "Nicaragua Plans a Big Dig to Rival Panama Canal." *Christian Science Monitor,* 1 December 2006.

Lubold, Gordon. "In Iraq, More Detainees Released." *Christian Science Monitor,* 22 February 2008.

Machain, Andrea. "This Is Oviedo's Third Coup Attempt in Seven Years." BBC News, 19 May 2000.

MacLeod, Scott. "A Date with a Dangerous Mind." *Time,* 25 September 2006.

"The Maras: A Menace to the Americas." By Frederico Breve (former Minister of Defense of Honduras). *Military Review,* July/August 2007.

Marks, Thomas A. "A Model Counterinsurgency: Uribe's Colombia (2002-2006)." *Military Review,* March-April 2007.

Marshall, Claire. "Combatting El Salvador's Gangs." BBC News, 20 March 2004.

McClam, Erin. Associated Press. "Americans See No End to Iraq War." *Jacksonville Daily News* (NC), 16 September 2007.

Melia, Michael. "Fourth JFK Terror Suspect Surrenders." *Jacksonville Daily News* (NC), 6 June 2007.

"Mexico's Internal Drug War." By Sam Logan. *Power and Interest News Report (PINR),* 14 August 2006.

Miller, Leslie. "Cross-Border Trucking Plan Draws Criticism." Associated Press, 24 February 2007.

Miller, S.A. and Stephen Dinan. "Spending Bill Shrinks Border Fence." *Washington Times,* 18 December 2007.

Montlake, Simon. "Pro-Muslim Tilt in Malaysia's Courts," *Christian Science Monitor,* 29 January 2008.

Montlake, Simon. "Tension Grows between Thai Security Forces and Muslim Locals." *Christian Science Monitor,* 12 July 2005.

Murphy, Dan. "A Militia Tightens Grip on Healthcare." *Christian Science Monitor,* 25 May 2006.

Myers, Lt.Col. Patrick and Patrick Poole. "Hezbollah, Illegal Immigration, and the Next 9/11." *Front Page Magazine,* 28 April 2006.

"NATO and Afghan Troops Searched for Remaining Taliban." World News in Brief. *Christian Science Monitor,* 12 December 2007.

"Nicaragua Corredor de Armas." By Elizabeth Romero. *La Prensa,* 17 April 2005.

"1945: Marine Corps Fights Its Most 'Savage' Battle Ever." *Mission: History.* Vol. 3, no. 2. San Francisco: Naval Order of the United States, 5 February 2001.

Nordland, Rod. "Al-Sadr Strikes." *Newsweek,* 10 April 2006.

"North Koreans Assisted Hezbollah with Tunnel Construction." Jamestown Foundation. *Terrorism Focus,* vol. III, issue 30, August 2006.

Ommani, Ardeshir. "The Non-Aligned Movement Has Been an Organization of, More or Less, Deprived Nations of the Planet." *Iran Heritage,* 18 September 2006.

Painter, James. "Crime Dominates Guatemala Campaign." BBC News, 10 May 2007.

"Partners in Crime." Parts I and II. By Fredric Dannen. *The New Republic,* 14 and 27 July 1997. From www.copi.com/articles/triads.

Perry, Tony. "U.S. 'Micro-Loan' Effort Yields Big Results In Iraqi Province." *Los Angeles Times,* 22 February 2008. 28 October 2003.

Plushnick-Masti, Ramit. Associated Press. "Militant Groups Join Forces, Get Hezbollah Help." *Jacksonville Daily News* (NC), 28 October 2003.

"Police Chief from Mexican Border Town Seeks Asylum." World Briefs Wire Reports (AP). *Jacksonville Daily News* (NC), 23 March 2008.

Pollack, Ricardo. "Gang Life Tempts Salvador Teens." BBC News, 24 January 2005.

Powell, Bill and Adam Zagorin. "The Sopranos State." *Time,* 23 July 2007.

"Profile: Oscar Arias." BBC News, 3 February 2006.

Reid, Robert H. Associated Press. "U.S. Jets Targeting Rebel Force." *Jacksonville Daily News* (NC), 30 March 2008.

Reid, Robert H. Associated Press. "U.S. Steps Deeper into Iraqi Fights." *Jacksonville Daily News* (NC), 29 March 2008.

Reid, Robert H. and Qassim Abdul-Zahra. Associated Press. "Iraq's Prime Minister Orders Freeze in Raids Versus Militants." *Jacksonville Daily News* (NC), 5 April 2008.

Rohter, Larry. "Fighting in Panama: Panama's Military; Changing an Army Poses a Challenge." *New York Times,* 23 December 1989.

Romero, Simon. "Files Released by Colombia Point to Venezuelan Bid to Arm Rebels." *New York Times,* 30 March 2008.

Romero, Simon and Juan Forero. "Bolivia's Energy Takeover: Populism Rules the Andes." *New York Times,* 3 May 2006.

Rotella, Sebastian. "Jungle Hub for World's Outlaws." *Los Angles Times,* 24 August 1998.

Rubin, Michael. "Ansar al-Sunna: Iraq's New Terrorist Threat." *Middle East Intelligence Bulletin,* vol. 6, no. 5, May 2004.

"Saints of Service." Knights of Columbus. *Columbia Magazine,* November 2007.

Santoli, Al. "The Panama Canal in Transition: Threats to U.S. Security and China's Growing Role in Latin America." American Foreign Policy Council Investigative Report, 23 June 1999. From its website, www.afpc.org.

Scales, Maj.Gen. Robert H., U.S. Army (Ret.). "Infantry and National Priorities." *Armed Forces Journal,* December 2007.

Schearf, Daniel. "China-North Korea Relations Tested as Reports Say Kim Jong Il to Visit Beijing." *VOA,* 24 August 2006.

Servin, Pedro. "Kidnapped Daughter of Ex-President Killed." *The Independent* (London), 18 February 2005.

Simpson, Jim. "Scouts to the Rescue." *Defense Watch,* 17 September 2003.

"Smuggled Chinese Travel Circuitously." By Irene Jay Liu. NPR's "Morning Edition" News, 20 November 2007.

"Soldiers and Police Began a Manhunt along the Border." World News in Brief. *Christian Science Monitor,* 20 February 2008.

"South African Union Refuses to Unload Chinese Arms Destined for Zimbabwe." Reuters, 18 April 2008.

Stewart, Rory. "How to Save Afghanistan." *Time,* 28 July 2008.

"Strong Chinese-Hamas Intelligence Connection." *DEBKAfile* (Israel), 19 June 2006.

"[The] 3 members of China's Politburo visited Mexico in 2005." East-Asia-Intel.com. *World Tribune,* 10 March 2006. From its website, worldtribune.com.

"U.S. Hires Foreign Firm to Help Detect Nuclear Materials at Bahamas Port." Associated Press, 24 March 2006. As extracted from the FOX News website.

"U.S. Hopes China Will Help Moderate Havana Meeting." *China Confidential,* 11 September 2006.

"U.S. Nun Killed In Brazil." Associated Press, 12 February 2005. As retrieved from CBS's website, www.cbsnews.com.

"Venezuela's Chavez Planning Arms-for-Oil Trip to N. Korea." East-Asia-Intel.com. *World Tribune,* 5 July 2006. From its website, worldtribune.com.

Vermaak, Chris. "Rhodesia's Selous Scouts." *Armed Forces Journal,*
    May 1977.
"The Virgin of the Massacres." By Lynn F. Monahan. *Maryknoll*
    Magazine, April 2007.
Warrick, Joby and Carrie Johnson. "Chinese Spy 'Slept' in U.S.
    for 2 Decades: Espionage Network Said to Be Growing."
    Washington Post, 3 April 2008.
Watts, Simon. "Guatemala Secret Files Uncovered." BBC News,
    5 December 2005.
Webb-Vidal, Andy. "Farc Guerrillas Kill 29 Colombian
    Soldiers." *Financial Times* (London), 28 December
    2005.
"Who Needs the Panama Canal." By Robert Morton. *Washington*
    Times, National Weekly Edition, 1 -8 March 1999.
    As reprinted in *World Tribune,* 4 March 1999. From its website,
    worldtribune.com.
Wood, Daniel B. "Where the Border Fence Is Tall, It Works."
    Christian Science Monitor, 1 April 2008.
Wood, William (ambassador to Afghanistan). In interview on
    NPR's "Morning Edition" News, 31 December
    2007.
Wright, Robin and Peter Baker. "Iraq, Jordan, See Threat to
    Election from Iran." *Washington Post,* 8 December
    2004.
"Zimbabwe: No Money to Print Currency." From IRIN (Harare). As
    reprinted in *Khartoum Monitor,* 31 May 2006.

About the Author

After 28 years of commissioned and noncommissioned infantry service, John Poole retired from the United States Marine Corps in April 1993. While on active duty, he studied small-unit tactics for nine years: (1) six months at the Basic School in Quantico (1966); (2) seven months as a rifle platoon commander in Vietnam (1966-67); (3) three months as a rifle company commander at Camp Pendleton (1967); (4) five months as a regimental headquarters company (and camp) commander in Vietnam (1968); (5) eight months as a rifle company commander in Vietnam (1968-69); (6) five and a half years as an instructor with the Advanced Infantry Training Company (AITC) at Camp Lejeune (1986-92); and (7) one year as the Staff Noncommissioned Officer in Charge of the 3rd Marine Division Combat Squad Leaders Course (CSLC) on Okinawa (1992-93).

While at AITC, he developed, taught, and refined courses on maneuver warfare, land navigation, fire support coordination, call for fire, adjust fire, close air support, M203 grenade launcher, movement to contact, daylight attack, night attack, infiltration, defense, offensive Military Operations in Urban Terrain (MOUT), defensive MOUT, Nuclear/Biological/Chemical (NBC) defense, and leadership. While at CSLC, he further refined the same periods of instruction and developed others on patrolling.

He has completed all of the correspondence school requirements for the Marine Corps Command and Staff College, Naval War College (1,000-hour curriculum), and Marine Corps Warfighting Skills Program. He is a graduate of the Camp Lejeune Instructional Management Course, the 2nd Marine Division Skill Leaders in Advanced Marksmanship (SLAM) Course, and the East-Coast School of Infantry Platoon Sergeants' Course.

In the 15 years since retirement, John Poole has researched the small-unit tactics of other nations and written eight previous books: (1) *The Last Hundred Yards: The NCO's Contribution to Warfare,* a squad combat study based on the consensus opinions of 1,200 NCOs and casualty statistics of AITC and CSLC field trials; (2) *One More Bridge to Cross: Lowering the Cost of War,* a treatise on enemy proficiency at short range and how to match it; (3) *Phantom Soldier: The Enemy's Answer to U.S. Firepower,* an in-depth look at the highly deceptive Asian style of war; (4) *The Tiger's Way: A U.S. Private's Best Chance of Survival,* a study of how Eastern fire teams and individual soldiers fight; (5) *Tactics of the Crescent Moon: Militant Muslim*

Combat Methods, a comprehensive analysis of the insurgents' battlefield procedures in Palestine, Chechnya, Afghanistan, and Iraq; (6) *Militant Tricks: Battlefield Ruses of the Islamic Insurgent,* an honest appraisal of the so-far-undefeated *jihadist* method; (7) *Terrorist Trail: Backtracking the Foreign Fighter,* how many of the *jihadists* in Iraq can be traced back to Africa; and (8) *Dragon Days: Time for "Unconventional" Tactics,* an unconventional warfare technique manual that also reveals the extent to which China may have hidden its own strategic agenda behind Muslim insurgency.

As of September 2008, he had conducted multiday training sessions (on 4GW squad tactics) at 39 (mostly Marine) battalions, nine Marine schools, and seven special-operations units from all four U.S. service branches. Since 2000, he has gone to Mainland China (twice), its hermit neighbor, Vietnam, Cambodia, Thailand, Russia, India, Pakistan, Iran, Lebanon, Turkey, Egypt, Sudan, and Tanzania. Over the course of his lifetime, he has been to the following Caribbean nations: Bahamas, Turks & Cacos, Caymans, Haiti, Puerto Rico, St. Thomas, St. Martin, Antigua, Guadaloupe, Martinique, St. Lucia, Barbados, Trinidad, and Aruba. He has lived in Mexico and Panama and revisited both places on several occasions. He has also been through every other Central American country except Belize. As for South America, he has traveled within the last year to Venezuela, and previously throughout Brazil, Chile, Bolivia, Peru, Ecuador, and Colombia.

Between early tours in the Marine Corps (from 1969 to 1971), John Poole worked as a criminal investigator for the Illinois Bureau of Investigation (IBI). After attending the State Police Academy for several months in Springfield, he was assigned to the IBI's Chicago office.

Name Index